Working with
Written Discourse

SAGE has been part of the global academic community since 1965, supporting high quality research and learning that transforms society and our understanding of individuals, groups, and cultures. SAGE is the independent, innovative, natural home for authors, editors and societies who share our commitment and passion for the social sciences.

Find out more at: **www.sagepublications.com**

Working with Written Discourse

Deborah Cameron and Ivan Panović

Los Angeles | London | New Delhi
Singapore | Washington DC

Los Angeles | London | New Delhi
Singapore | Washington DC

SAGE Publications Ltd
1 Oliver's Yard
55 City Road
London EC1Y 1SP

SAGE Publications Inc.
2455 Teller Road
Thousand Oaks, California 91320

SAGE Publications India Pvt Ltd
B 1/I 1 Mohan Cooperative Industrial Area
Mathura Road
New Delhi 110 044

SAGE Publications Asia-Pacific Pte Ltd
3 Church Street
#10-04 Samsung Hub
Singapore 049483

Editor: Mila Steele
Editorial assistant: James Piper
Production editor: Imogen Roome
Marketing manager: Michael Ainsley
Cover design: Jen Crisp
Typeset by: C&M Digitals (P) Ltd, Chennai, India
Printed in Great Britain by Henry Ling Limited
at The Dorset Press, Dorchester, DT1 1HD

Library of Congress Control Number: 2013948119

British Library Cataloguing in Publication data

A catalogue record for this book is available from
the British Library

MIX
Paper from
responsible sources
FSC™ C013985

ISBN 978-1-4462-6722-6
ISBN 978-1-4462-6723-3 (pbk)

Contents

About the Authors

Deborah Cameron teaches at Oxford University, where she is Professor of Language and Communication in the English Faculty. Her main research interests are in sociolinguistics, discourse analysis and the study of gender and sexuality; her previous publications include *Working with Spoken Discourse* (2001), *On Language and Sexual Politics* (2006) and *Verbal Hygiene* (1995/2012).

Ivan Panović received his doctorate from Oxford University, where he went on to spend two years as a postdoctoral research fellow in Arabic sociolinguistics. He is now Assistant Professor of sociolinguistics at Nanyang Technological University in Singapore. His book *Literacies in Contemporary Egypt* will be published in 2014.

Acknowledgements

Anyone who writes a book for students will owe a debt of gratitude to their own students, and we are no exception. We are particularly indebted to those former students who have generously allowed us to make use of their work: Ksenija Bogetić, Henry Hawthorne, Tamar Holoshitz and Beth McCarthy. We are also very grateful to Meryl Altman for her comments on drafts of the book. For various other kinds of assistance, support and inspiration, our thanks go to Philipp Sebastian Angermeyer, Winnie Chan, Zoe Ilić Duhandžija, Camilo Gómez-Rivas, Domenico Ingenito, Nour Ismail, Matt Melvin-Koushki and Adam Talib. Last but not least, we thank each other: we learnt a lot from working together, and we also had a lot of fun.

Deborah Cameron

Иван Пановић

The authors and publisher are grateful to the following for permission to reproduce photographic and other images:

Figure 8.3: 'Cartoon Theories of Linguistics—Phonetics vs. Phonology', copyright H. Parenchyma, 2007, reprinted by permission of *Speculative Grammarian*.

Figure 10.8: photograph by Camilo Gómez-Rivas, used by permission of the photographer.

Figures 2.1, 10.1–10.7 and 10.9: photographs by Ivan Panović, used by permission of the photographer.

Introduction

Working with Written Discourse is a mixture of 'theory' and 'practice'. It deals with discourse analysis both as a subject readers want to know about, and as a method (or a set of methods) which they want to know how to use. The uses of discourse analysis are many and varied: it is relevant not only to people studying language and linguistics, but also to people working in a range of other disciplines, including anthropology, cultural studies, education, history, law, literature, media studies, philosophy, sociology and social psychology. Wherever researchers are dealing with linguistic or textual materials, they may find they have something to gain by applying the insights or the methods of discourse analysis.

In this book we focus on *written* discourse, and that requires some comment. Many textbooks on discourse analysis include both the spoken and the written varieties, and not infrequently their emphasis falls more on the former than the latter. One reason for that is the long-established view in linguistics, that speech—ancient, universal in human cultures and naturally acquired—should be the primary object of any 'scientific' inquiry into human language. When this idea was articulated by some of the great pioneers of linguistic theory (notably Ferdinand de Saussure in Europe at the beginning of the twentieth century and Leonard Bloomfield in the USA in the 1930s), it was a reaction against the earlier tendency to treat written or literary language as the only kind worthy of being studied. As Theresa Lillis comments, though, developments in linguistics since the early twentieth century have 'turned the worthiness argument on its head' (2013: 6). Modern sociolinguistics, the study of language 'in society', accords most value not just to spoken rather than written language, but more specifically to 'vernacular' speech, meaning the casual, spontaneous utterances of ordinary people in everyday situations. The effect, Lillis suggests, has been to marginalize not only the most prestigious forms of writing, such as literature, but all kinds of written discourse. In her view, this relegation of writing to a peripheral place in linguists' thinking is unwarranted, since in contemporary literate societies, writing is just as much an everyday practice as speaking. Florian Coulmas concurs: over time, he points out, and particularly in the course of the last century, 'writing has evolved from a specialized skill into a mass mode of communication', and 'humanity has moved steadily towards relying on written communication in ever more domains of life' (2013: ix). Our own view is similar: in this book we place writing at the centre, considering its uses in 'ever more domains of life', and highlighting the distinctive resources it provides for language-users.

But although we have just used the singular pronoun *it*, we will not be approaching written discourse as a single, simple category. On the contrary, we will emphasize that it is complex and diverse, taking many different forms and serving many different purposes. One issue we will need to consider in that connection is the influence of technology, and of technological change, on the ways in which people use writing and thus the kinds of written discourse they produce. Writing, in all its forms, depends on technology: it is therefore relevant to ask, when analysing any kind of written discourse, how far and in what ways it has been shaped by the use of particular technologies.

It is evident, for instance, that many people today routinely use writing to communicate in ways that were not possible before the advent of digital technology. Earlier technological developments, such as the introduction of the printing press in early modern Europe, also made possible new uses and forms of writing: as a technology which allowed large numbers of identical copies of a text to be produced in a relatively short time, printing facilitated the emergence of genres addressing a large or 'mass' audience at regular intervals, like newspapers and other periodicals. And it should not be forgotten how dramatically the original invention of writing—that is, of a system for representing language visually—extended the scope of linguistic communication beyond what was possible in a purely oral/aural medium.

The relationship between discourse, technology and medium will be an important theme of this book, and a number of chapters will consider, in particular, the discourse of the 'new' or digital media. This is a subject we know many readers will be interested in: computer-mediated communication (CMC) is an expanding area of linguistic research, and it is also of interest to the many social researchers who are now using the web as a source of data, or interacting with research subjects through online social media. But in line with our earlier point about the complexity and diversity of written discourse, we will be attentive to the complexity and diversity of its digital incarnations. Generic labels like 'new media discourse' and 'computer-mediated discourse' can encourage over-generalization: in reality, these categories encompass a considerable range of different practices and text-types. For the purposes of discourse analysis it is necessary to consider not only what these may have in common, but also what distinguishes them from one another.

Consider, for example, the much-repeated claim that writing in new digital media is closer to speech than it is to more traditional forms of written discourse. In some cases that may be a useful starting-point for analysis, but how useful it is depends on what kinds of speech and writing you are comparing. An exchange conducted via social media may be more 'speech-like' than a newspaper editorial, but many blog-posts have more in common with the editorial. Conversely, the handwritten postcard someone sends to their colleagues while on holiday may be more 'speech-like' than the emails s/he sends to the same people while at work. At the same time, it can be argued that the comparison is always to some degree inexact: even when they are serving similar communicative purposes, spoken and written language are necessarily organized and processed in different ways. Some important characteristics of digital communication are related to its reliance (at least, so far) on the visual medium of writing rather than the oral/aural medium of speech. How 'speech-like' new media discourse is, and in what ways it is speech-like, is a question best addressed by examining the evidence in specific cases.

We will also be wary of overstating the 'newness' of new media. One of the topics we discuss in this book is *multimodality*, the use of different semiotic systems in a single text, which requires analysts to pay attention not merely to the language of the text, but to the way language interacts with, for instance, images, graphic devices and music. This kind of analysis is often applied to the products of digital technology, which has made it easier to produce complex multimodal texts (the average website, for example, is highly multimodal). But multimodal communication in itself is not a new phenomenon. A (far from exhaustive) list of pre-digital discourse genres where written language is combined with other semiotic systems might include illuminated manuscripts, choral scores integrating words with musical notation, treatises on anatomy and natural history illustrated with drawings and diagrams, picture books, printed advertisements, cartoons, comic books, newspaper reports containing photographs, silent movies with written captions and any film or TV programme to which subtitles have been added. Conversely, multimodality does not have to be a feature of the discourse produced in and for new media. Among the digital social media which have emerged in the last decade, one of the newest and most popular—Twitter—limits single messages ('tweets') to 140 written characters.

While it is understandable that so many researchers are interested in studying the most recent developments in written discourse, this enthusiasm for the new should not obscure the continuing currency of more traditional forms of writing. Not everyone has participated in the digital revolution: one survey conducted in Britain in 2012 found 15% of respondents (half of whom were under the age of 70) reporting that they had never been online.[1] In parts of the world less affluent than Britain, that percentage would be much higher. And even if they do spend significant time online, most people also continue to engage in other reading and writing practices. Schoolchildren still learn to write with pencils and paper; university students still read textbooks and write essays. On trains and buses, in coffee shops and at kitchen tables, people can still be seen reading books, newspapers and magazines. And all of us still move through offline linguistic landscapes where print, and even some kinds of handwriting, remain pervasive—think of street signs, notices, posters, flyers and graffiti. In this book we will try to reflect the diversity of written discourse, and to pay attention to all those forms of it that play a significant part in people's lives.

We will also pay attention to the fact that both the online discourse world and many of the offline linguistic landscapes mentioned above are multilingual rather than monolingual spaces. Though this book is written in English, and we cannot assume that all its readers have any other language in common, we can and do assume that for many readers, English will not be the only language they know or the only one they use to read and write. Such readers may want to analyse written texts which are themselves multilingual, combining different languages and/or scripts. Like the multimodal texts already mentioned, multilingual written texts are not a new phenomenon, but digital technology and other social developments of the current, 'global' era have increased their public visibility. We have chosen to discuss them because we think they will be relevant to an increasing number of researchers working with written discourse in future.

HOW THIS BOOK IS ORGANIZED

Working with Written Discourse is divided into three parts, 'Preliminaries', 'Approaches' and 'Applications'. 'Preliminaries' (Part I) deals with a number of theoretical questions which it is helpful to consider in advance of any particular project. Chapter 1 discusses definitions of *discourse* and the general goals of discourse analysis. Chapter 2 considers the nature of writing itself: after offering a brief account of its history, we review the long-running debate on how writing differs from speech and look at some recent research on the linguistic characteristics of spoken and written discourse. Chapter 3 turns to the question of how written discourse is affected by the use of different technologies for producing and consuming it, and by the characteristics of the media through which it circulates, while Chapter 4 examines the various scripts and spelling systems that are used to write human languages, and the ways in which these may be exploited as a source of meaning.

'Approaches' (Part II) introduces a series of different approaches to discourse analysis, and gives examples illustrating their application to written discourse in particular (though many of them are applicable to spoken discourse as well) (Chapter 5). The approaches we have chosen to consider are defined in a number of different ways. The first one, critical discourse analysis or CDA (Chapter 6), is defined primarily by its analytic *stance*: the starting assumption for analysts using this approach is that no representation of the world is ideologically neutral, and the goal is to uncover the assumptions and presuppositions that are embedded in a text by looking closely at the linguistic choices made by the text's producer(s). In contrast to this, the second approach we consider, corpus-based discourse analysis (Chapter 7), is defined primarily by its use of particular analytic *methods*: at the most general level, these are methods for identifying statistical patterns in (usually quite large) samples of text. The other approaches presented in Part II, multimodal discourse analysis (Chapter 8), computer-mediated discourse analysis (Chapter 9) and multilingual discourse analysis (Chapter 10) are not primarily defined either by stance or by the use of particular methods, but rather by their focus on particular *categories* or *characteristics* of discourse. In multimodal discourse analysis what is highlighted is the interaction of multiple semiotic systems or 'modes': rather than focusing exclusively on the language used in texts, this approach examines the interplay between language and other communicative resources, such as visual images or music. Computer-mediated discourse analysis is concerned with the effects of digital technology and culture on discourse. Multilingual discourse analysis looks at the way different languages and scripts are combined in texts. These approaches are not mutually exclusive, but can be used in combination if that is appropriate to the analyst's goals and the data s/he has chosen to work with. Critical discourse analysis, for instance, can be done on texts which are multimodal or multilingual (or both); it can also be combined with the use of corpus methods. Multimodal analysis is often applied to texts which are also examples of computer-mediated discourse. In Part II we use examples that illustrate not only how each of the approaches works, but also how different approaches can be made to work together.

Part III, 'Applications', addresses some of the practicalities of working with written discourse. Chapter 11 considers how written discourse analysis can be used by those who are not linguists, and whose research questions are not primarily about language, focusing on a topic which is of interest to researchers across disciplines, sex. Chapter 12 offers some more general advice to researchers who want to work with written discourse, and discusses some examples of projects designed and carried out by students. One topic this chapter deals with—potentially an important one for readers who are planning their own projects—is the ethical issues that may be raised by working with written discourse, especially those forms of it which are private rather than public (e.g. personal letters, emails and text messages, unpublished student writing, and contributions to sites like Facebook where users control who has access).

All chapters end with a brief summary and a short section headed 'Further reading' (there is also a full bibliography at the end of the book). In addition, most chapters include one or more practical activities for readers to do (many of these can be done either by individuals working on their own, or by a small group working collaboratively—the second option is probably most relevant for those readers who are using the book as a course text). Some activities ask readers to reflect on their own experience or to find and comment on their own data, while others invite them to carry out some kind of analysis using data we provide. At the end of the book there is a glossary of selected technical terms. In most cases these terms are also explained elsewhere in the book (the relevant parts can be located by using the index), but readers, especially those who are not linguists, may find it helpful to have brief definitions/explanations in one place. Terms included in the glossary appear in bold type the first time they are used in the main text.

A single book cannot cover every kind of written discourse or every possible approach to analysing it. Though we have tried to cast our net widely, there are some areas we do not venture into, or that we touch on only briefly and in passing. We do not, for instance, discuss the forensic applications of written discourse analysis—its use in criminal or other legal proceedings for purposes such as establishing the authorship of a text. Nor do we consider the approaches to written discourse that have been developed specifically to analyse literary texts (though some of the approaches included in Part II have been applied to literature, and we do give some examples of their application to works of fiction). Even in the areas we cover in detail, the examples we have chosen will inevitably reflect our own interests, which not all our readers can be expected to share. Nevertheless, we hope this book will equip readers with tools—both conceptual and practical—that they can use to frame their own questions about written discourse, and to analyse the texts that interest them.

NOTE

1   Source: UK Office for National Statistics, Internet Access Quarterly Update, Q3 2012. www.ons.gov.uk/ons/rel/rdit2/internet-access-quarterly-update/2012-q3/stb-iaqu.html, accessed 24 November 2012.

Preliminaries

1 Discourse and discourse analysis

One important preliminary to the study of anything is defining your object, the phenomenon you are studying. In this first chapter we will consider some definitions of *discourse*, and how they are related to different analytic approaches.

If you look up the word *discourse* in a general-purpose dictionary, you will probably find something like the following (taken from the *Concise Oxford Dictionary (COD)*):

> **Discourse**, n[oun] & v[erb]: a. conversation, talk; b. a dissertation or treatise on an academic subject; c. a lecture or sermon.

This entry tells us that the word *discourse* is used in ordinary English to talk about language—both speech, as in sense (a), and writing, as in (b). (Sense (c) names two 'mixed' genres, 'lecture' and 'sermon', which are delivered orally but are usually composed at least partly in writing.) However, none of these senses is exactly what *discourse* means when it is used as a technical term. Acknowledging this point, the entry continues by listing another sense of the word, which it identifies as belonging to the specialist vocabulary of linguistics: 'a connected series of utterances, a text'.

But *discourse* is not only a technical term in linguistics. As Sara Mills observes (1997: 1), it 'has become common currency in a variety of disciplines: critical theory, sociology, linguistics, philosophy, social psychology and many other fields'. This, she suggests, can be a source of confusion, because although they are all using the same word, people in different academic disciplines or theoretical traditions do not all define it in exactly the same way. That might not matter if the disciplines and traditions in question were completely separate enterprises, each carried on in isolation from all the others. But as we noted in the Introduction, discourse analysis is an interdisciplinary enterprise, influenced by ideas from more than one tradition. Consequently, anyone who wants to understand the field or contribute to its discussions must be aware of the various ways in which its terms may be defined and used.

THREE DEFINITIONS OF DISCOURSE

Definitions of discourse are many and varied, but most are variations on the following three themes:

1. Discourse is language 'above the sentence'.
2. Discourse is language 'in use'.
3. Discourse is a form of social practice in which language plays a central role.

The first definition, 'language above the sentence', comes from linguistics, and is closer than the others to the dictionary definition quoted above, 'a connected series of utterances, a text'. To understand what it means, it is useful to bear in mind that the traditional aim of linguistics is to describe and explain the way language works as a system: what its basic units are and what the rules are for combining them. In that connection, one fundamental insight is that language has different kinds and levels of structure which articulate with one another. Smaller units of linguistic structure combine to form larger ones: for instance, speech-sounds are combined into syllables, syllables into words, words into phrases and phrases into sentences. Importantly, however, the units and the rules for combining them are not the same ones at every level. We need different kinds of units and rules for phonology (the sound system of a language) and syntax (its sentence structure). This principle explains what is meant by *above* in 'language above the sentence'. As your units get larger (e.g. words are larger than sounds and sentences are larger than words), you metaphorically move 'up' from one level to the next. If discourse analysis deals with 'language *above* the sentence', that means it looks for structural patterns in units which are larger, more extended, than one sentence—the 'connected series of utterances' or 'text' of the dictionary definition.

One of the earliest discourse analysts, the linguist Zellig Harris (1952), posed the question: how do we tell whether a sequence of sentences is, in fact, a **text**—that the sentences relate to one another and collectively form some larger whole—rather than a random collection of unrelated bits? The answer to that question, Harris thought, would make clear what kind of structure exists 'above the sentence'. Texts would have this structure, whereas random collections of sentences would not. As an illustration of the kind of structure he had in mind, consider the following two sentences taken from the first page of *The Handbook of Discourse Analysis* (Schiffrin et al. 2003: 1):

> (1) Discourse analysis is a rapidly growing and evolving field. (2) Current research in this field now flows from numerous academic disciplines that are very different from one another.

Intuitively, it seems clear that these two sentences belong to a single text: they are not just separate statements that have been randomly juxtaposed. In this they contrast with the following (invented) sequence:

> (1) Discourse analysis is a rapidly growing and evolving field. (2) Many millennia ago, the earth was inhabited by dinosaurs.

In the invented example there is no obvious link between the two sentences, but in the textbook example the two sentences can easily be understood as discussing a single topic, discourse analysis, with the second sentence building on the proposition put forward in the first.

Our intuitions about this are not just prompted by the *content* of the two sentences in the textbook example; they also have to do with their *form*. One aspect of their form is the order in which they appear. Imagine that the order of the two sentences were reversed: 'Current research in this field now flows from numerous academic disciplines that are very different from one another. Discourse analysis is a rapidly growing and evolving field'. We might still be able to connect them topically—they would not seem as randomly juxtaposed as the 'dinosaurs' example— but the sequence would strike us as disjointed in a way the original version is not.

In the textbook, connections between the two sentences are made not only by ordering them in a certain way, but also through the use of *cohesive* devices which tie the second one back to the first: an example is the expression *this field*, which occurs in the second sentence but refers to something mentioned (and described as 'a field') in the first: 'discourse analysis'. Confronted with the reference to 'this field', a reader does not wonder, 'which field can the writer mean?' Since 'a field' has already been mentioned—and named—in sentence (1), it makes sense to assume that '*this* field' in sentence (2) refers to the same field, not some entirely different and previously unmentioned field. This kind of structural **cohesion** is one of the formal clues that we are dealing with a text rather than with two separate and unconnected sentences—and it is this which may be lost, or at least obscured, when the order of the sentences is reversed.

But it might still be asked whether we can distinguish texts from random collections of sentences using purely formal/structural criteria. As readers, we are predisposed to treat adjacent chunks of language *as if* they were connected, and to make connections even when none were intended. This is what produces the humour in examples like the radio programme announcement quoted in Stubbs (1983: 93): 'later, an item on vasectomy, and the results of the do-it-yourself competition'. Connecting the parts on either side of the conjunction *and* generates an interpretation of 'the do-it-yourself competition' as a reference to a 'do-it-yourself vasectomy competition'. Yet while we recognize this as a possible reading, we also recognize that it cannot be the intended one, because we know no one would organize a competition where men performed vasectomies on themselves. When we approach a text with a view to making sense of it, we do not just consider its structural linguistic properties, we also refer to two other considerations: our background knowledge about the world outside the text, and what we think the producer of the text might have intended to communicate. If an interpretation based on the structure of the text is implausible on these other criteria, we will normally discard it. This makes discourse a somewhat different case from phonology or syntax. You do not need to know anything about the world to decide that /krin/ is a possible word in English whereas /rkin/ is not, or that *stood boy the on up a chair* is not a well-formed English sentence. Our intuitions in these cases are entirely based on what we know about language structure. But once we get 'above the sentence', our ability to make sense of sequences and decide whether/how they are connected involves more than just applying a set of quasi-grammatical rules.

Another objection to the 'language above the sentence' definition of discourse has been put forward by Henry Widdowson (1995), who argues that a text does not have to be larger than one sentence; indeed, it can be much smaller. The legend LADIES on the door of a public lavatory could be described as a text, for example, as could the letter P which is used in Britain to indicate a space for parking cars. Clearly, a single word or letter cannot have 'structure above the sentence'. But in Widdowson's view it can nevertheless be a text, if in context it communicates a complete message. Once again, though, the recognition of something like LADIES as a text, and the interpretation of what it means, relies on real-world knowledge that is not contained in the text itself. Looking up the word *ladies* in a dictionary would not, on its own, make clear what message it conveys when written on a door. A great deal of general knowledge and contextual information has to be brought to bear on even the most banal texts we encounter if those texts are to serve their communicative purpose. And an interest in what and how language communicates is an essential feature of discourse analysis.

From that perspective, a better definition of *discourse* than 'language above the sentence' might be the second one listed above, 'language in use'. 'Language in use' is the broadest of the three definitions; it is also implicitly a more 'social' definition than 'language above the sentence'. The latter definition suggests that discourse analysis, like syntax, will be concerned primarily with formal patterns in language itself. 'Language in *use*', by contrast, need not imply any lack of interest in linguistic form, but it does suggest that attention will be given to other questions, such as who is using language and what purposes it is serving for its users in a particular **context**.

Most discourse analysts who locate themselves within linguistics are concerned with both form and function, and with the relationship between the two. But not all discourse analysts are linguists: many are social scientists, for whom the analysis of discourse is not an end in itself, but a way of gaining insight into various aspects of social life. That does not mean they are *un*interested in language and how it is used. All discourse analysis has both a social and a linguistic dimension. But when the emphasis falls on the social, the general notion of discourse as 'language in use' is often combined with the third definition listed above, in which discourse is approached as a form of social practice. This definition comes from critical social theory rather than linguistics (though it has influenced many discourse analysts who are linguists), and it requires some additional explanation. In the following section we examine it in more detail.

POWER, KNOWLEDGE AND PRACTICE: DISCOURSE(S) AND THE CONSTRUCTION OF SOCIAL REALITY

Social scientists have always treated discourse—in the 'language in use' sense—as a source of information about people's attitudes, beliefs, experiences and practices. Some commonly-used methods in social research, such as face-to-face interviewing, involve spoken discourse; others, such as asking people to fill in questionnaires, keep diaries or, more recently, interact with researchers using online social media, rely on written language. Most researchers who use these methods are not interested in discourse primarily for its linguistic qualities, but rather for what it can tell them about some other social phenomenon—for instance, about their subjects' experiences of childbirth, their feelings about getting older or their beliefs about climate change. The experiences, feelings and beliefs are taken to exist independently of the discourse which expresses them: language is simply a vehicle for transmitting the relevant information from the subject to the researcher.

One social scientific approach to analysing data is known as *content analysis*: as that label suggests, its aim is to extract and then analyse the information which is 'contained' in questionnaires or interview transcripts or whatever other texts are being examined for research purposes. Analysts go through a sample of data identifying items which are relevant for their purposes, using a set of categories selected in advance to 'code' them. This approach is used in media studies, for instance, to investigate questions like how frequently a particular issue is covered in news reports, whether the coverage has increased or decreased over time, and what items of information or range of opinions are presented in reports.

But although this approach is applied to discourse *data*, it differs from discourse *analysis* as we define the latter in this book. To give a clearer idea of what the difference is, we will consider some examples of media discourse relating to body size and weight. The examples below are all taken from the website of *Bliss* magazine, a UK-based publication for pre-adolescent and early adolescent girls (mybliss.co.uk). Specifically, they are from the electronic version of the magazine's 'problem page', which features letters and emails from readers expressing their anxieties and asking for advice. On the website, there is a large archive of these communications: it includes a section on body problems, where size and weight are among the most frequently-aired concerns.

1. I hate my body, I'm so overweight! I hardly go out because I think people are laughing at me.
2. I am overweight for my age and height and really want to lose a healthy amount of weight.
3. I'm thinking of losing weight, not just to be super skinny, but because I want to be healthy.
4. I am trying to lose weight because I am a bit chubby.
5. Help! I'm 12 years old (nearly 13) and I've tried and tried to lose weight but I can't! I always think I look fat.
6. My Mum and Dad say I'm getting big and need to lose weight.
7. I hate being the weight I am. My friends are all really skinny and I hate being the odd one out.

Someone carrying out a content analysis of these letters would probably be most interested in the nature and range of the concerns writers express about their weight. The correspondents whose words are reproduced above give several reasons for needing or wanting to lose weight: some mention not liking the way their bodies look (e.g. 1, 4, 5), some allude to other people's negative reactions to their size (1, 6, 7), and some assert that they want to lose weight for health reasons (2, 3). A coding system could be devised to tag every instance of each of these concerns: the analyst could then extract all the examples of each type, and on that basis draw conclusions about how prevalent particular concerns were in the sample.

A discourse analyst, by contrast, would want to look not only at the content of the letters, but also at the way the writers have chosen to formulate their accounts linguistically. Their concerns, attitudes and feelings are not only evidenced by *what* they have written, but also, a discourse analyst would argue, by *how* it is written. To illustrate what we mean, we will focus on examples (2) and (3) above. Both contain a proposition that could be rendered as 'the writer wants to lose weight to be healthy'; but a closer look at the writers' linguistic strategies suggests that something more complicated may also be going on.

The writer of (3) frames her own motivation for losing weight by contrast with a different motivation which she mentions in order to make clear that it is not her main or only concern: she is 'thinking of losing weight, *not just to be super skinny*, but because I want to be healthy'. A content analysis which coded this as 'wants to lose weight for health reasons' would not be 'wrong', since that is indeed the main proposition asserted by the writer. But such an analysis would be leaving aside the question of why she mentions, but downplays, an alternative motivation, the desire 'to be super skinny'. When people downplay or disclaim a motive in discourse (which is quite a common move: a clichéd example is the prefatory formula 'I'm not a racist/sexist/feminist, but…'), it is usually because they anticipate that others are likely to ascribe that motive to them, and judge them negatively for it. They are staking a claim to legitimacy by contrasting themselves with some other group who do, by implication, deserve the criticism. In this case, the writer may be anticipating and trying to pre-empt a common negative judgment of young girls who want to lose weight, that their concerns are driven more by a preoccupation with the way they look (and with the impossible ideal represented by the supermodels and celebrities they see in the media) than by any understanding of what would be a healthy weight. This girl is at pains to present herself as a responsible individual who has thought about this and come to sensible conclusions. The writer of (2) uses a different strategy to serve a similar purpose. She stakes her claim to legitimacy by adopting the kind of authoritative voice we might associate with an expert like a scientist or a doctor. 'I am overweight for my age and height' is a bald assertion of fact—no hedging with 'I think' or 'my mum and dad say'; the formal/medical word *overweight* is preferred to the softer, vaguer and more colloquial terms used by other writers (e.g. *big, chubby, fat*); the reference to 'age and height' displays a knowledge of how experts judge whether someone is 'overweight'.

ACTIVITY

The writers of examples 1, 5 and 7 seem to be presenting themselves and their desire to lose weight in a different way from the writers of 2 and 3. What kinds of personae are these writers constructing in their letters to *Bliss,* and what details of the language they use can be related to that construction?

The discussion above suggests some reasons why 'content', in the sense of recurring themes and propositions, might not be the only thing a social researcher might want to look at in discourse data, and why it might also be revealing to consider the details of language-use. But our analysis of the *Bliss* letters also raises a more 'theoretical' question about the use of discourse data in social research—one that would apply not only to texts like the ones we have just analysed, which were not originally written for the purposes of research, but also to texts which were produced specifically for a research project, such as questionnaire responses. Can it ever be assumed that the discourse people produce is simply a report of experiences, feelings, attitudes and concerns which exist independently of the discourse itself, and of the context in and for which that discourse was produced?

Discourse analysts, and many other social researchers today, would argue that the answer is no: there is no single, objective 'truth' about people's experiences or feelings which their discourse simply 'puts into words'. Rather, people design their discourse for a particular audience, in a particular context; whatever else they may be discoursing about, they are always also making choices and calculations about how to present *themselves.* Above we argued that the two writers who chose to foreground health concerns in their letters to *Bliss* were presenting their desire to lose weight as 'legitimate', and themselves as rational and knowledgeable, in contrast to the stereotype of girls who diet as foolish, insecure creatures led astray by peer pressure and celebrity culture. It is possible that this self-presentation is partial in both senses of the word: it could be that the writer of (3) is entirely motivated by the desire to be 'super skinny', and is denying it only because she thinks she will be judged more positively if she emphasizes 'being healthy'. But it would be hard to establish that with certainty: we can't know what is in people's heads; we can only try to interpret their verbal representations. For that purpose, it is important to consider the linguistic choices they have made. There is always more than one way of representing any given state of affairs linguistically: in producing one representation rather than another, a language-user is also constructing a particular version of reality.

This is one part of what is meant by the claim some theorists make that social reality is not a set of fixed truths which we will discover if we ask the right questions, but is rather a *discursive construct,* made and remade as people talk or write about things. In some kinds of social theory, the idea of reality as a discursive construct is taken a step further, by observing that while individuals make choices about how to represent their reality, their choices are inevitably shaped by larger social forces. As the discourse analyst Jay Lemke puts this point (1995: 24–5):

> We speak with the voices of our communities, and to the extent that we have individual voices, we fashion them out of the social voices already available to us, appropriating the words of others to speak a word of our own.

Lemke is not suggesting that individuals never dissent from their communities, or that they do not have their own ideas. He is, however, suggesting that their contributions have to be framed in relation to the understandings of the larger community. This is partly a matter of some ways of speaking being more socially acceptable than others (for instance, the *Bliss* writers discussed above have evidently understood that the adult community regards 'being healthy' as a more legitimate reason to want to lose weight than 'being super skinny'). But it is also a more fundamental matter of what will be found intelligible. Language-using is an *intersubjective* rather than purely subjective process: a 'voice' that is wholly individual runs the risk of being incomprehensible.

Analysts who follow this line of argument view discourse analysis less as a method for finding out what particular individuals 'really think', and more as a method for investigating the range of 'social voices' in a community. This can be related to the third, 'social practice' definition of the term *discourse*. The idea that speakers and writers 'appropriat[e] the words of others', drawing on resources 'already available' is expressed by other theorists by saying that individuals' understandings and accounts of the world are constructed out of the 'discourses' in circulation. Evidently, the word *discourse* in this formulation is not being used in the way linguists typically use it, to mean 'language above the sentence' or 'language in use'. An obvious difference is that the linguist's 'discourse' has no plural, whereas social theorists often talk about *discourses*. This plural usage reflects the influence of the philosopher and cultural historian Michel Foucault, who defined *discourses* as 'practices which systematically form the objects of which they speak' (Foucault 1972: 49). To see what Foucault meant, let us consider another example relating to the issue of body size and weight: current discourse about 'obesity'.

The term *obesity* belongs to the vocabulary of science and medicine, where it has a precise scientific definition: a person is 'obese' if they have a body mass index (BMI) equal to or greater than 30. BMI is calculated from an individual's height and weight: a value of 18.5–24 is considered 'normal', below 18.5 is 'underweight' and 25–30 is 'overweight'. Since height and weight are physical realities, you might think that nothing could be more 'objective' and less 'discursively constructed'. But a follower of Foucault would point out that there is nothing inevitable about the existence of a formula for calculating 'body mass index'. Measuring people's height and weight, working out their BMI, and on that basis categorizing them as 'underweight', 'normal', 'overweight' or 'obese' are examples of the kinds of 'practices' Foucault refers to in his definition of discourse: their invention and subsequent adoption in clinical practice have brought into being a state of affairs whereby people can be classified, evaluated and treated (e.g. exhorted to lose weight, prescribed drugs or even surgery) according to where they are on the BMI scale. Without this set of practices there would still be people of objectively varying size, but there could be no such thing as 'obesity'. In that sense, obesity is very much a discursive construct.

Foucault's formulation says that discourses are 'practices that systematically form the objects *of which they speak*', which suggests that the practices in question are linguistic practices, or at least have a significant connection to language (and thus to discourse in the linguist's sense). So far, our explanation of the idea that 'obesity' is an object constructed in discourse has placed more emphasis on non-linguistic practices like weighing, measuring and classifying people: the main linguistic phenomenon we have mentioned is the labelling of the categories this set of practices produces, using terms like *normal*, *overweight* and *obese*. That is not, of course, unimportant, but it is not the only way in which we can connect the discursive construction of obesity to language. The non-linguistic practices just listed are embedded in a larger context where language—spoken and written—plays a very significant role: it is used to explain what obesity is and why it matters, to argue about how it should be defined and measured, to debate its causes and remedies, etc.

Until recently, most utterances and texts dealing with obesity belonged to the domain of science and medicine. Though body weight, fat and dieting were topics of everyday discussion, the term *obesity* itself was not much used outside medical contexts. But recently that has changed: the term is now in common use, and the subject generates large quantities of discourse. This development illustrates another important aspect of Foucault's thinking about discourse, his concept of 'power/knowledge'. In modern societies, he points out, a great deal of power and control is exercised not by brute physical force or economic coercion, but by the activities of 'experts' who are licensed to define, describe and classify things and people. These practices are carried out in large part by means of language-use. Words can be powerful: the institutional authority to describe, categorize and label people is frequently inseparable from the authority to judge them and to do things to them. This is what is going on in current discourse about obesity. It was always defined as an individual medical problem, but today it has also acquired the status of a collective social problem. Attempts to define and control it have intensified, and many new kinds of experts and other commentators have been drawn into the ongoing discussion. With so many institutions and interest-groups involved, not surprisingly there are multiple 'discourses' on obesity. They may be concerned with the same subject, but they do not represent it in only one way.

To illustrate this, below we reproduce five extracts from news reports on the subject published in the UK and the USA. We found these reports by conducting an online (Google) search in January 2013, using the search-term 'obesity news': the examples we selected are a subset of the items that came up on the first page of results. We chose them because they represent a number of current discourses on the 'problem' or 'crisis' of obesity: in particular, they illustrate that there are varying definitions of the problem (of why it is a problem and what kind of problem it is), and competing accounts of where the responsibility for it lies. (Before you read our analysis of the 'discourses' that are present in these extracts, you might find it interesting to try to make your own, and see how closely it resembles the one we offer later on.)

1. Obese adults are costing the N[ational] H[ealth] S[ervice] in London £883.6 million each year. Childhood obesity is costing a further £7.1 million. But the bill to treat youngsters if they remain obese into adulthood, could rise to a staggering £111 million each year, in the capital alone. ('Obesity crisis solved: eat less, says health secretary', *London Evening Standard*, 13 October 2011).
2. Societal changes in recent decades have helped spur growing waistlines, and now a third of U.S. children and teens and two-thirds of adults are either overweight or obese. Today, restaurants dot more street corners and malls, regular-sized portions are larger, and a fast-food meal can be cheaper than healthier fare. Not to mention electronic distractions that slightly more people surveyed blamed for obesity than fast food. ('Poll: fight obesity crisis but keep the junk food', *Associated Press/Guardian*, 7 January 2013).
3. Poor families are more likely to be obese, a health minister has said. Anna Soubry said children were suffering because of 'an abundance of bad food' in their homes. ('Anna Soubry says parents should ensure children have proper meals', *Daily Mail*, 23 January 2013).
4. Matt Goold, of Meadow Lane, Beeston said the comments were 'ridiculous'. The 39-year-old added: 'How does she know this? It's just a stereotypical assumption. It's absolute rubbish. She says people don't sit around the table – a lot of people can't afford a table for a start.' Richard Oldham, 40, of Field Lane, Beeston said the comments were 'nonsensical', adding: 'It is difficult to eat well on low money'. ('Outrage at Broxtowe MP's comments about the poor', *thisisnottingham*, 24 January 2013).
5. Unhappy with the slow pace of public health efforts to curb America's stubborn obesity epidemic, a prominent bioethicist is proposing a new push for what he says is an 'edgier strategy' to promote weight loss: ginning up social stigma. Daniel Callahan, a senior research scholar and president emeritus of The Hastings

Center, put out a new paper this week calling for a renewed emphasis on social pressure against heavy people—what some may call fat-shaming—including public posters that would pose questions like this: 'If you are overweight or obese, are you pleased with the way that you look?' (...) 'For him to argue that we need more stigma, I don't know what world he's living in,' said Deb Burgard, a California psychologist specializing in eating disorders and a member of the advisory board for the National Association to Advance Fat Acceptance. (NBC news website, 24 January 2013).

In these extracts there is evidence of several different 'discourses' on 'the problem of obesity'. In the first place, there are references to it as a *medical* problem: these are overt in (1) and (5), which use terms like 'health service', 'treat', 'public health', 'epidemic', but the idea is also present as a background assumption in (2) and (3). It can remain in the background because the idea that obesity causes illness and premature death is now a well-established proposition that readers are assumed to be familiar with. In most of the extracts what is foregrounded is a newer proposition, or set of propositions, about why and for whom obesity is a problem. In (1), for instance, the obesity of an increasing number of individuals is presented as an *economic* problem for the society they live in, putting more and more pressure on its publicly funded healthcare system. In (2) and (3), by contrast, the emphasis is on obesity as a *social* problem, connected either with 'societal changes' which mean we are all eating more while being less physically active, or else with the unhealthy choices made by a particular section of society. Finally, on the fringes of mainstream media reporting—so marginal that it is almost completely hidden in our sample of news reports, though it is hinted at in the quote from Deb Burgard in (5)—there is an 'oppositional' discourse which challenges the view that obesity in itself is a problem, and instead defines the problem as the stigma and discrimination obese people face.

Another thing we see in this set of extracts is a division between accounts which attribute the problem of obesity (whether it is seen as medical, social or both) to the shortcomings of obese people themselves—for instance, the ignorance or irresponsibility of the 'poor families' whose diet consists of 'an abundance of bad food' in (3), and the lack of self-control which the bioethicist in (5) proposes to 'shame' fat people out of—and accounts which cast obese people as victims of external forces, such as poverty, inequality and the easy availability of cheap junk-food (2, 4). This division dramatizes Foucault's argument that discourses are not 'just words', but have material consequences for people in the real world. Once it has been defined as a problem, obesity also becomes an object of social policymaking, and competing accounts of what causes the problem go along with competing proposals for what to do about it. In the version of the 'social' discourse which emphasizes personal responsibility, the solutions proposed are punitive: scolding and publicly shaming obese people. The version that emphasizes factors outside the control of individuals is more likely to produce proposals for interventionist social policies, like taxing junk food, placing restrictions on the advertising of unhealthy foods, or forcing the food industry to reduce levels of fat, salt and sugar in its products. 'Radical' versions of this discourse may also call for a broader policy of reducing poverty and inequality. 'Fringe' versions which entirely reject the postulate 'obesity is a problem' are associated with campaigns for 'fat acceptance'.

The one thing no one proposes, however, is ceasing to concern ourselves with 'obesity' in any way at all. Discourse has formed this object and brought it into sharp focus, making it impossible to ignore. Even those who dispute the scientific validity of what is said about 'obesity' must acknowledge it as part of our social reality. And in that reality, the various 'discourses' we have identified in our discussion of the extracts above form what a critical theorist might call the 'discursive field', a network of assumptions and propositions in relation to which we will interpret and evaluate all new statements on this subject. It is impossible to say anything intelligible about obesity which does not in some way refer to, and thus recycle, these already-established discourses, even if the speaker's purpose is to challenge them. As Lemke says, 'we appropriate the words of others to speak a word of our own'.

At this point, though, alert readers may be thinking that we have not had much to say about the words, and wondering whether our discussion should be put in the category of discourse analysis, or whether it is more akin to content analysis. That would be a fair question: we cannot claim that the account we have just presented of competing discourses on obesity was based on a close analysis of the *language* used in media reports. But that kind of analysis could be done, and in fact it is often done by linguistically-oriented discourse analysts who have been influenced by Foucault's ideas. Many practitioners of critical discourse analysis, for example, are interested in exploring how certain patterns of linguistic choice may contribute to the production of competing discourses as more or less important, reasonable, authoritative or persuasive. Though we will defer detailed discussion of this approach until Chapter 6, it is worth giving a brief indication of the kinds of choices that might be examined in a critical discourse analysis of the media reports on obesity quoted above.

Such an analysis might consider, for example, the way *numbers* are used to lend an air of authority and certainty to claims like the ones made in (1)—though there are competing figures, and all such figures depend on assumptions that could be disputed, and projections which experts do not regard as 100% certain. Another point of interest is the recurrent use of particular *metaphors* in relation to obesity. An example in our own set of texts is 'obesity *epidemic*' (5). This now-commonplace expression likens obesity to an infectious disease, and so tends to imply that it requires the same drastic measures as an outbreak of cholera or plague. And there are also some observations to be made about the non-parallel ways in which sources representing different views are identified. In the extracts reproduced above, the people who are quoted most frequently and (arguably) given most credibility are those who voice the discourses in which obese people are blamed. Experts who take that view are described in ways that tend to boost their perceived credibility (e.g. 'a health minister', 'a prominent bioethicist'). By contrast, the 'oppositional' voices in the sample are described in ways that suggest either that they have no claim to expertise (as in (4), which identifies the speakers only as local residents), or else that their view is partisan rather than objective. Extract (5) explicitly links the psychologist Deb Burgard to a pressure group that campaigns for 'fat acceptance', for instance, while describing the other expert quoted, bioethicist Daniel Callahan, as 'a senior research scholar'.

We have explained the sense of *discourse* that comes from the work of Foucault in some detail, because it is currently influential across the range of disciplines where discourse analysis goes on. However, not all social researchers who adopt discourse analysis as a method are committed to the ideas of Foucault, or those of any other theorist. There are also varying views on the more general question of whether and to what extent social reality is 'discursively constructed'. Whatever position is taken on that question, though, it remains the case that a researcher who sets out to investigate some aspect of reality by eliciting discourse from a group of research subjects, or by sampling a subset of the discourse that circulates in society, will end up with data in the form of language. And if we recognize that language is not just a transparent medium, a window through which we can see into the language-user's mind—that it is shaped by its context and by the way verbal communication works—we might also conclude that paying attention to the form as well as the content is not only important for analysts who are linguists, but for any researcher who works with discourse data.

DISCOURSE, UTTERANCE, TEXT

This book's subject is specifically *written* discourse, and in that context the reference made above to 'the way verbal communication works' must raise the question of what difference it makes whether 'verbal communication' takes the form of speech or writing. The definitions of *discourse* discussed in this chapter are in principle applicable to either, but some attempts to define the term do seem to lean towards one as the prototypical case. For instance, the *COD* entry we quoted earlier places 'talk, conversation' first in its list of senses, and when it offers a more technical linguistic definition, that also begins with a sense that seems to relate to the spoken word ('a connected series of *utterances*'). It is not entirely clear whether what follows this ('a text') is intended to mark a distinction (utterances are spoken, texts are written) or just to provide further information about what *discourse* means as a general term ('a text is a concrete example of discourse').

Text is another term whose meaning can vary with the user's disciplinary and theoretical allegiances. Outside linguistics it is most often used to refer to written discourse (e.g. a work of literature is 'a text'); within linguistics it is commonly used to refer to any specific piece of discourse, whether spoken, written or multimodal (we will use it in this way ourselves, though that may not be obvious, since most of the examples we describe as 'texts' will, in fact, be written). But some linguists do make a more theoretical distinction between *discourse* and *text*. For Henry Widdowson (1995), for instance, the term *text* denotes a linguistic object (e.g. the words on a page in a book, or the transcript of a conversation), whereas *discourse* is the process of interaction with/interpretation of the object that produces its meaning in context. It follows that Widdowson makes a distinction between speech and writing. In speech, discourse precedes text—there is no textual representation of talk that comes before the negotiation of meaning in interaction—whereas in writing it is the text that comes first, and discourse is produced by the reader in the process of interpreting its meaning.

In this book we focus more on the practice of discourse analysis—the 'working with' part of our title—than on theoretical debates about terms and definitions. However, our subject, written discourse, means we do have to consider the much-debated question of differences between writing and speech. We have already indicated in the Introduction what our general position will be: in our view, it is not helpful analytically to discuss either speech or writing in generic, homogenizing terms, because of the diversity of forms each can take. We do not think there is an absolute dividing line between all spoken and all written discourse; but at the same time we do not want to present speech and writing as interchangeable modes of communication with no distinctive features at all. So, how should we understand the relationship between these modes, and what are the implications for discourse analysis? Those are the questions we will address in Chapter 2.

SUMMARY

This chapter has been concerned with the meaning of the term *discourse* and the goals or purposes of analysing it. The view of discourse analysis taken here and throughout this book is a 'holistic' one, which acknowledges that discourse analysis is several things at once. It is a method for doing social research; it is a body of empirical knowledge about how talk and text are organized; it is the home of various theories about the nature and workings of human communication, and also of theories about the construction and reproduction of social reality. It is both about language and about life.

FURTHER READING

A book whose purpose is to 'unpack' the complex term *discourse* is Sara Mills's *Discourse* (1997). A shorter survey of various tendencies in contemporary discourse analysis is provided by the introduction to *The Discourse Reader* (Jaworski and Coupland 2006). This volume also includes an edited extract from Michel Foucault's *The History of Sexuality*, 'The incitement to discourse', which gives a sense of what Foucault and his followers mean by the term. A more traditionally 'linguistic' perspective is taken by the editors in their general introduction to *The Handbook of Discourse Analysis* (Schiffrin, Tannen and Hamilton 2003), which also contains more than 40 chapters giving overviews of key topics in the field.

2 Speech and writing: the debate on difference

'Written discourse' encompasses many kinds of writing, and its diversity will be one theme of this book. But in a section devoted to 'Preliminaries', it is also necessary to consider what, if anything, distinguishes written discourse as a general category from the contrasting category of *spoken* discourse. 'How is written language different from the spoken variety?' has been a frequently asked question in linguistics. A related question—'how do reading and writing make a person, or a culture, different?'—has been hotly debated by scholars across disciplines. In this chapter we discuss the varying, and sometimes opposing, views that have been advanced in this debate. We also ask how the form of written language is affected by the purposes it serves and the conditions in which it is produced.

WRITING, FROM ANCIENT TO MODERN TIMES

Unlike spoken or signed language, written language is not acquired 'naturally'. Individuals need to be taught to read and write, and many societies have managed perfectly well without any knowledge of the written word. For thousands of years, indeed, the whole of humanity managed without writing. Making visual representations is a very ancient cultural practice—some cave-paintings are over 30,000 years old—but the first evidence we have of visual symbols being used specifically to represent language dates from less than 6,000 years ago. The people responsible for this innovation were the Sumerians of ancient Mesopotamia (modern Iraq), who devised a **script** known as 'cuneiform' around 3500 BCE. The system of hieroglyphs used by the ancient Egyptians is almost as old (dating from around 3000 BCE), and the logographic writing used in China goes back to around 1500 BCE. Alphabetic writing also emerged in the second millennium BCE: the earliest known alphabet, Phoenician, is the ancestor of many of the alphabets in use today, including Arabic, Cyrillic, Greek, Hebrew and Roman.

Writing developed to serve the needs of urban civilizations whose relatively complex economic and administrative systems gave rise to a need for systematic record-keeping. Sumerian cuneiform writing, for instance, seems to have evolved from an earlier system of tokens used to represent commodities like oil and grain for accounting purposes. If we consider that the most immediate advantage of written over spoken language is that it allows information to be preserved without the need to memorize it, it is not surprising that the earliest uses of writing focused on recording information of a kind that was not intrinsically very memorable, like details of the movement of goods or the ownership of property. It was not until later that writing came to be used for what we would now call 'literary' purposes, such as poetry and storytelling.

Non-literate cultures had developed high levels of verbal artistry; skilled artists were (and in parts of the world still are) able to sustain lengthy oral performances using a combination of memory and improvisation.

We have just noted the utility of writing as an alternative to memorizing information and transmitting it orally, but that is a 'modern' view which the earliest writers might not have shared. When societies first adopt writing, it is generally as an adjunct rather than an alternative to speech: written records are not necessarily accorded greater authority or reliability than the spoken word. In Anglo-Saxon England (the society that produced the earliest writing in English, between approximately the eighth and the eleventh centuries CE), legal transactions might be recorded in writing, but what was legally binding was the speech the parties uttered in front of witnesses. In any subsequent dispute, more weight was given to the recollections of witnesses than to the written record, in part because oral testimony could be interrogated whereas a written document could not. Other early English texts, such as poems, charms and riddles, are thought to have been written down initially not so that individuals could read them in private, but as an aid to oral performance. The individual, private and silent reading which modern literate people think of as the norm was a much later development than literacy itself.

'Mass' literacy, the ability of most people in a society to read and write, is a very recent historical phenomenon, and is still not found in all parts of the world. As we noted above, written language has to be taught: in most societies for most of history, most people had no access to the necessary instruction. It has been estimated that in 1500, only about 10% of English men and 1% of women possessed what is called 'signature literacy', the ability to sign their names on a document as opposed to just making a mark like a cross.[1] These figures probably overestimate the number of people who were 'literate' in the modern sense of the word. Signature-literate individuals would have been able to read (in sixteenth-century England it was standard practice for writing instruction to be deferred until after the basics of reading had been taught), but their ability to write much more than their names may well have been very limited. By 1800, however, according to Eliot (2007), the proportion of the English population that could read and write had risen to around 60% of men and 45% of women, and by the end of the nineteenth century—after the introduction of compulsory elementary schooling—the figure was over 90% for both sexes.

The statistics just given for literacy in England since 1500 refer to the ability to read and write in English, or in other words what is termed **vernacular** literacy, literacy in a language which is also used in everyday speech. But in many societies past and present, becoming literate may mean learning to read and write in a language which you do not speak, and possibly one which is not spoken natively by anyone. In mediaeval and early modern Europe, many texts were written or printed in Latin, which was no longer a spoken first language, but remained the pre-eminent language of (western Christian) religion and learning. Vernacular literacy in English was established very early (though research on the texts printed in England before 1500 has found that more than a quarter of those that survive are in Latin); but many European vernacular languages, some of them—like German—spoken by large numbers of people, only began to be used extensively in printed texts between 1500 and 1800.[2]

Vernacular literacy is the norm for most people in present-day Europe, but elsewhere in the world it is still the case that many local vernacular languages are not written, and their speakers become literate in some other language. Today this is less likely to be a 'dead' language like Latin, and more likely to be a living 'language of wider communication', like English, French or Swahili in Africa, or Spanish in South America. But sizeable numbers of people continue to acquire literacy in a non-vernacular language for religious reasons. Observant Jews and Muslims, for instance, accord high value to the ability to read the Torah in Hebrew or the Qur'an in Arabic. In both cases this means learning to read a 'classical' variety which diverges significantly from modern spoken vernaculars.

SPEECH VERSUS WRITING: A 'GREAT DIVIDE'?

The emergence of writing after thousands of years when humans had relied exclusively on the spoken word is often described as an event of unprecedented and incalculable significance for the history of humankind. In his influential book *Orality and Literacy*, Walter J. Ong declares (1982: 78): 'More than any other single invention, writing has transformed human consciousness'. An earlier commentator who argued along similar lines, Marshall McLuhan, wrote in *The Gutenberg Galaxy* (a book about the transformative effect of printing) that 'the interiorization of the technology of the phonetic alphabet translates man from the magical world of the ear to the neutral visual world' (1962: 18). These writers belong to a current of thought which holds that literacy profoundly alters the way humans understand themselves and relate to the world around them. They posit what might be described as a 'great divide' between the spoken and the written word, between oral and literate cultures, and by extension, perhaps, between literate and non-literate individuals.

On the question of how reading and writing affect thinking, Ong cites the pioneering research done in the 1930s by the psychologist A. R. Luria, who worked with non-literate and minimally literate adults in remote areas of what was then the Soviet Union. Luria had found that literacy made a difference to the way his subjects reasoned: for instance, when he showed people pictures of four objects—a hammer, a saw, a hatchet and a log—and asked them to say which ones belonged together, the classification task was more likely to be understood by those who had some knowledge of reading and writing. They would identify the log as the 'odd one out' because all the others were tools. Non-literate subjects, by contrast, often insisted that all four objects belonged together, since any practical activity involving the tools would also require wood. They also struggled to make sense of tasks that required syllogistic reasoning. One of Luria's questions was, 'In the far north, where there is snow, all bears are white. Novaya Zembla is in the far north and there is always snow there. What colour are the bears?' One of the responses this elicited (quoted by Ong 1982: 53) was: 'I don't know. I've seen a black bear. I've never seen any others ... each locality has its own animals'.

For Ong, Luria's research supports the argument that speech and thought in oral cultures are concrete rather than abstract, rooted in people's embodied experience of performing specific actions in specific situations. Writing detaches the language from the person who produced it and from the situation in which it was produced, and so enables, or indeed requires, a more abstract, analytic engagement with it. This makes possible the kind of context-free logic that is involved in deducing the colour of the bears in a place you have never been to.

Other scholars, however, have made criticisms of this 'literatist' view. One objection is that it treats literacy as 'autonomous', capable of producing certain effects in and of itself. This over-looks the possibility that the effects observed by Luria were not produced specifically by literacy, but were more general consequences of exposure to formal schooling. The two things are dif-ficult to disentangle because most people acquire literacy through formal schooling. However, familiarity with the written word is not the only thing you learn at school which might have a bearing on your performance on the kinds of tasks psychologists use to test cognitive skills. Another of Luria's subjects responded to the instruction 'try to explain to me what a tree is' by saying, 'Why should I? Everyone knows what a tree is.' Was he displaying a non-literate tendency to favour concrete over abstract ways of thinking, or was he just showing a lack of acquaintance (and a degree of understandable impatience) with the pedagogic practice of asking questions like 'what is a tree?' Fifty years after Luria, the psychologists Scribner and Cole (1981) studied one group, the Vai people of Liberia, whose indigenous writing system was learnt and used outside the context of formal education. They reported that literacy did not have the predicted effect on individuals' ability to classify or reason abstractly.

Alternatives to 'great divide' thinking have been elaborated by researchers like Brian Street (1984) and David Barton (2007) who study literacy using ethnographic methods. **Ethnography** is an approach developed in anthropology for studying the workings of culture through 'participant observation': ethnographers immerse themselves in the life of the group they are studying, observing its activities and interacting with its members. Ethnographers of literacy ask what place reading and writing have in the life of a particular community by looking at the range of things people actually do with the written word. They do not just examine texts, but pay attention to the whole social context in which those texts are embedded. Proponents of this approach (sometimes labelled the 'new literacy studies') are wary of the generic, universalizing term 'literacy': they prefer to talk about 'literacies' or '**literacy practices**', underlining the point that reading and writing are activities with a wide range of different uses and meanings. They are critical of global claims about the consequences of becoming literate, either for individuals or for society as a whole.[3] If there is no single decontextualized 'literacy', but only local and contextually situated 'literacy practices', then it is not helpful to generalize about the effects of reading and writing: different practices will have different effects.

The abstract, analytical writing which is implicitly treated as prototypical in 'great divide' accounts—the kind of writing we find in official documents, newspaper reports and academic books—is a product of the formal literacy practices which are taught in educational and professional institutions. But many ethnographers are more interested in informal or 'everyday' literacy practices, which are not regulated by official rules or judged by institutional standards, and which people engage in outside the context of education or work (examples include writing cards to friends and family members, making shopping lists, keeping appointments diaries, texting, or posting on social media websites). Like all social and communicative practices, these informal writing practices depend on shared or conventionalized ways of doing things: it would not be true to say that they have no rules or procedures at all. Rather than being taught explicitly, however, the rules and procedures are acquired through active participation in a practice and interaction with others who engage in it.

Some interesting recent studies have focused on cases where new media have generated new literacy practices, like bilingual text messaging in South Africa (Deumert and Masinyana 2008), and writing on the photo-sharing website Flikr (Barton and Lee 2013). But it should not be thought that everyday informal writing is a new phenomenon, a product of today's digital technology. Below we reproduce a much older example: the text of a handwritten postcard sent in 1907 by a father to his young daughter (for ease of reading we have transcribed the text shown in the photograph, retaining the original spelling and punctuation).[4]

> Dear Wee Peggy I hope you are keeping well. I am feeling a bit better but the weather is very wet. tell your Ma. to send me all the wooden pipes that is on the shelf and a pipe cover at a 1[d.] to fit any pipe hoping you are well Your Loving <u>Father</u>

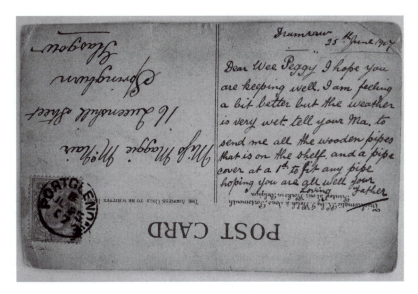

Figure 2.1

Postcards like this one are the subject of an article about ordinary writing in the Edwardian period by Julia Gillen and Nigel Hall (2010). Gillen and Hall chose to study postcards because of their extraordinary popularity at this time: almost six billion were posted in Britain between 1901 and 1910. This statistic reflects, among other things, the rise in literacy rates that occurred following the introduction of compulsory basic education in 1870. By 1901, most adults in Britain had some competence in reading and writing. Though many less educated writers would have struggled to produce extended formal texts, the picture postcard, designed for short, informal messages, was an accessible form of written communication. Postcards are therefore a rich source of evidence about the characteristics of everyday written discourse.

One way in which everyday writing very often diverges from the model of literate discourse presented in 'great divide' accounts is in serving communicative purposes which are not 'abstract and analytic', but more practical and personal. The text reproduced above is a case in point. The writer devotes part of it to making a concrete, practical request: he asks his daughter to pass on a message to his wife, telling her to send him some pipes he has left at home, and an additional item which she will need to buy (he gives the specification, 'a pipe cover to fit any pipe' and the price, one penny). The rest of the text has the function which is most typical of postcards as a genre: maintaining contact with significant others, in this case the writer's family, during a period of absence from home. Even though the writer has little new information to communicate, the important point—that he is thinking about the addressee(s)—is communicated by the act of writing itself. The interpersonal orientation of the text is underlined by the frequency with which it refers to the sender and addressee, using the personal pronouns *I* and *you/your* and affectionate appellations like 'Dear Wee Peggy' and 'Your Loving Father', as well as by the repeated good wishes for the recipient's health ('I hope you are keeping well/hoping you are well'). The salutations and stock expressions just quoted exemplify another characteristic of many everyday literacy practices, their reliance on generic formulas—one more thing they share with oral discourse as described by Ong.

This written text fits Ong's description of **orality** in other ways too. For instance, it is clearly anchored in what the writer assumes to be shared contextual knowledge. His statement 'I am feeling a bit better' implies that the reader is aware of the previous state of his health, and the reference to 'all the pipes that is on the shelf' presupposes that she can identify the shelf he means. The text also displays the 'additive' quality often attributed to orally-composed discourse: it moves from one topic to another (from health to the weather to pipes and then back to health) without making explicit connections or following any obvious logical progression. Gillen and Hall, studying a much larger sample of Edwardian postcards, found this loose, additive structure to be typical.

Everyday writing may also diverge from the rules of formal literacy in its vocabulary, grammar, spelling, punctuation and arrangement on the page or other writing surface. In some cases this is a deliberate choice made by the writer, exploiting the fact that everyday writing does not have to conform to the rules imposed on more formal written texts by gatekeepers like teachers, publishers and editors. In other cases, divergence from the institutionalized rules of writing may reflect the writer's incomplete or imperfect acquisition of them. The writer of the postcard text above, for instance, was a working-class man from Glasgow who had received only minimal education. This is reflected in his occasional non-standard grammar (e.g. 'all the pipes that is on the shelf') and his inconsistent use of full stops and capital letters to mark sentence divisions. The written sentence, structured by its syntax (whereas informal spoken language is organized by devices like rhythm, stress and pitch) is evidently not a completely transparent and 'natural' unit of discourse for him. At the same time, it would not be true to say that this text exhibits no characteristics of formal writing. The opening and closing salutations, though affectionately worded, and the formulaic 'I hope you are keeping well', follow the institutional rules for letter-writing, and the abbreviated forms (like *Ma.* for 'mother' and *a 1^d.* for 'one penny') are 'correctly' marked with full stops. These features suggest careful rather than casual composition, and they give the text a slightly stilted feel.

These observations underline that learning to write entails more than just learning a set of correspondences between written symbols and the sounds, syllables or words they represent. Written language is distinctive in other ways as well. That might raise another 'great divide' question: whether it is possible to generalize about the formal linguistic differences between spoken and written discourse.

THE LANGUAGE OF SPEECH AND WRITING

The short answer to that question is 'yes and no'. On one hand, the 'great divide' approach invites the same objections when applied to language as it does when applied to cultures, or ways of thinking: binary oppositions like speech/writing, or oral/literate, do not capture the complexity and variability that exists on either side of the supposed dividing line. The language of the postcard just discussed, for instance, is a mixture of different elements, some quite 'speech-like' and others very 'writing-like'. On the other hand, the argument that written language is nothing more than a **transcription** of speech is not satisfactory either. If you have ever made, or looked at, a full and faithful transcription of casual speech, you will know that in some respects it is quite different from anything originally produced in writing. If you have ever compared the official written transcript of the proceedings of a law court or a legislative assembly with a recording of the original spoken discourse, you will know how much is routinely edited out when speech is transcribed for purposes other than linguistic research.

If we are looking for a more nuanced approach to the relationship between spoken and written language, we could start with an observation made by the linguists Douglas Biber and Susan Conrad: 'the spoken and written modes provide strikingly different *potentials*' (2001: 190, emphasis added). This formulation suggests that speakers and writers can in principle do very different things with language, but it leaves open the question of what they actually do with it in practice. Not all forms of speech and writing exploit the potential offered by their mode in the same way or to the same extent. Later on we will look more closely at some of the evidence which supports this point. First, though, what are the characteristics that give speech and writing such 'strikingly different potentials'? The table below summarizes some key differences which we will expand on in the following discussion.

Spoken	Written
aural and transient	visual and more permanent
produced/processed in real time with limited opportunity to plan	can be extensively planned and edited, and processed in different ways
usually permits interaction and feedback	generally does not permit interaction or feedback
speaker and hearer typically share a spatiotemporal context	writer and reader need not be in the same time and place

Figure 2.2

The most basic difference between speech and writing is that speech is *aural*—its raw material is sound—whereas writing is *visual*, communicating by way of visible marks on surfaces (or occasionally, as with the Braille writing system designed for blind people, through marks on surfaces which are read by touch). This difference has consequences for the production and processing of spoken and written messages. Sound waves travelling through the air are inherently transient: speech has to be processed as it is heard, in 'real time'. This is true even when technology is used to preserve it. It is possible to listen to the same piece of recorded speech repeatedly, but on each occasion it will have to be processed in real time. If, for instance, you are listening to someone saying 'hello, Kitty', you will always hear 'hello' before 'Kitty' and 'hello' will always be gone before you get to 'Kitty'.

Writing, as a visual representation of language, makes other kinds of processing possible. When you read 'hello Kitty', both words will be present in your field of vision simultaneously. And when you read a longer and more complicated text, like this chapter, you can do various things with it that you cannot do with an orally-delivered lecture covering the same material. For instance, you can read it at your own pace, whereas in a lecture you would be obliged to try to process the information at the speaker's pace. You would also have to process the points made in a lecture in the order the lecturer presented them in; when reading, by contrast, you have various other options. You can skim to get a sense of the whole text before you read any of it in detail, you can skip parts you decide are irrelevant or boring, and you can go back and read part or all of it again whenever you feel the need. Whether you do this in an hour's time, a week's time or a year's time, the text will still be there on the page or the screen, exactly as it was before.

Then again, there are some things you cannot do with this chapter which you would be able to do with an orally-delivered lecture or in a conversation on the topic. In a lecture or a conversation you would be able to ask for clarification or additional information. In some lectures and most conversations you would be able to contribute your own opinions. As readers, you cannot do these things because you do not have direct access to the producers of the text. This has implications for us as writers. Since we are writing for readers we do not know personally, who cannot ask us questions, and who do not share our location in space and time, we must provide all the information they need explicitly in the text itself.

In speech, the production and reception of utterances are more or less simultaneous processes, whereas in writing the two are normally separated: it is rare for the composition and the reading of a written text to occur simultaneously in real time. Even in **synchronous** forms of digital communication involving rapid exchanges between people who are both online at the same time, like instant messaging, contributions are typed in their entirety first, and only then sent to be read by the intended recipient; they cannot be read by that person while they are still in the process of being composed (though in other media this is not impossible: for instance, in an exchange of handwritten notes with the person next to you in a lecture you might read each note as the writer produced it, word by word, rather than waiting for the whole thing to be completed). This separation between production and reception has consequences for the way writers can write as well as for the way readers can read. Just as our readers do not have to process this text at a fixed pace and in a fixed order, so we did not have to produce it in that way. We could plan what we were going to write extensively in advance, we could draft the various sections of the book in any order (possibly a completely different order from the one they actually appear in), and we could edit what we had written after the initial composition of the text. The way in which writers can edit their texts is a significant difference between writing and speech. Speakers can correct errors and clarify obscurities in what they have already said, but they cannot unsay it: whatever has been uttered has also been heard. Writers, by contrast, can remove all traces of their factual errors, conceptual confusions, inelegant sentences and poorly structured paragraphs before a text is read by anyone else.

There are some features of unplanned, spontaneous speech that will rarely appear in a finished written text. No one, for instance, not even a novelist trying to write realistic dialogue, would present a reader with the following sequence, taken from a transcript of a conversation among friends (each line represents a different speaker's contribution, and the brackets show where they are speaking simultaneously):

```
and she didn't she didn't like Katy she didn't ge[t on with Katy at all]
                                                 [no she didn't get on with] Katy
```

The reformulation of essentially the same point in (slightly) different words here ('she didn't like Katy'/'she didn't get on with Katy') is probably done for emphasis, and in the case of the second speaker, to align herself with her interlocutor, but the initial repetition of 'she didn't' has more to do with the fact that the speaker is composing the utterance in real time. Inevitably that process will produce false starts and slips of the tongue, as well as hesitations, pauses and repetitions which 'buy time' to formulate the next chunk of speech. This redundancy can be helpful to hearers as well as speakers, compensating for the transience of the spoken word. In writing, however, it is unnecessary and distracting. Readers can cope with a higher density of information, while writers can compose more carefully: as well as avoiding or removing errors and repetitions, they can use more varied vocabulary than we see in the 'Katy' example (which repeats many of the same words as well as the same information), and they can structure their texts in different ways.

The 'Katy' conversation exemplifies the 'additive' structure we have already mentioned in relation to Ong's account of oral discourse: points are either placed one after the other with no explicit connection ('she didn't like Katy/she didn't get on with Katy') or else conjoined with *and* ('and she didn't like Katy'). This kind of structure is described as **paratactic**: it is 'flat', presenting each piece of information as equally important. The alternative is a **hypotactic** structure in which information is hierarchically organized: there are main clauses and dependent or **subordinate clauses**, linked by words which make the logic of the connection more explicit (e.g. *because, although, while*). In his discussion of this difference (1982: 37), Ong reproduces two English translations of the opening of the Book of Genesis, one from the 1610 Douay Bible and the other from the 1970 New American Bible:

1. In the beginning God created heaven and earth. And the earth was void and empty, and darkness was upon the face of the deep; and the spirit of God moved over the waters.
2. In the beginning, when God created the heavens and the earth, the earth was a formless wasteland, and darkness covered the abyss, while a mighty wind swept over the waters.

There are a number of differences between the two versions, but one striking difference is that the earlier translation is more consistently paratactic, a series of assertions conjoined by *and*. The later one uses the subordinating conjunctions *when* and *while* to set the clauses they introduce apart from the main thread of the sentence (the main clause is 'in the beginning the earth was a formless wasteland', with God's creation of heaven and earth relegated to a subordinate clause). Ong's point is that the earlier translation preserves the grammatical patterning of its more ancient original, which was strongly marked by oral tradition, whereas the later one has moved towards what he calls 'the analytic, reasoned subordination that characterizes writing ... and appears more natural in twentieth-century texts' (1982: 37). Arguably, however, it is not the spoken mode as such that favours parataxis, but rather the constraints of real-time production, which do not allow for elaborate planning: where writing is composed under similar conditions, as it is for instance in online chat, it may have a similar additive structure (and where speech is prepared in advance, as in lectures for instance, it may have a more hypotactic structure).

Other linguistic consequences flow from the fact that speech is more likely to be embedded in a context shared by the participants, whereas writing often has to function independently of any particular context. In face-to-face interaction we rely on shared context to interpret what are called **deictic** terms—items like *this, that, here, there, then, now, tomorrow, last year*, and pronouns referring to people and objects (e.g. *you, them*), whose precise meaning depends on the situation. In writing, however, the relevant information needs to be made explicit. It is no use writing 'meet me here in a month's time' if the recipient of the message does not share your space-time coordinates, or referring to a 'she' whose identity has never been established.

Writing also has to function without feedback from the recipient (like the minimal responses—*mm, yeah, OK*, and so on—that signal attention or understanding in spoken interaction), and without recourse to the **prosodic** and **paralinguistic** cues (e.g. stress, pitch variation, tone of voice, laughter, facial expressions) which make a significant contribution to meaning in face-to-face communication. Spoken language is organized, divided up into units or chunks of information, primarily by the rise, fall and rhythm of the speaking voice. The written sentence, on the other hand, is defined by its syntactic structure. Writing is more reliant than speech on grammatical resources because the resources of prosody and paralanguage are not available.

You may have noticed that many of the statements made in this section refer to what is 'often' or 'usually' the case, and what writers and readers 'can do' or 'might do', rather than what they *must* do or will invariably do. This is because, in the spirit of the observation we quoted from Biber and Conrad, the differences we have been describing are differences in the *potentials* of speech and writing, which may or may not be fully realized in any given case. Not every example of written language has the characteristics outlined in Figure 2.2 on p. 21; some kinds may have the characteristics prototypically associated with speech, such as being interactive, minimally planned and unedited, and addressed to a reader in close proximity rather than one who is distant in time and space (a handwritten note passed between students in a lecture has all of these characteristics). If writing shares both a communicative purpose and some of its conditions of production with speech, it may also have formal similarities to speech. But as Biber and Conrad point out (2001: 190), the range of possibilities offered by writing is greater: 'writers can produce dense expository texts as well as texts that are extremely colloquial, but speakers do not normally produce texts that are similar to written expository registers'.

This statement is not just based on intuition or common sense, but is also supported by the evidence of extensive research carried out by Biber and his collaborators, using statistical methods to analyse a range of different kinds of spoken and written language. This work has played an important part in shifting recent discussions of the formal characteristics of spoken and written language away from the older, dichotomizing approach. Essentially, what it suggests is that there is no set of linguistic properties which divide writing-in-general from speech-in-general (or to put it another way, there is no such thing as writing or speech 'in general'), but it is possible to distinguish different **registers**, both spoken and written, on various formal linguistic criteria.[5] Because this register-based approach has been so influential in linguistics, it is worth examining in a little more detail.

ANALYSING SPOKEN AND WRITTEN REGISTERS

The approach developed by Biber involves compiling a **corpus** (see Chapter 7 for more discussion)—a sample of real language that includes a wide range of different genres or text types (Biber's included face-to-face and telephone conversation, spontaneous and pre-planned speeches, broadcasts, personal and business letters, various types of fiction, academic writing, print journalism and official documents). This corpus is then analysed to determine the frequencies of certain lexical and grammatical variables. The variables examined by Biber are too numerous to catalogue in full, but they included items such as first- and second-person pronouns, different kinds of questions, contracted versus full forms, active versus **passive** verbs, uncommon words and complex **nominal** constructions. Statistical methods are used to see which of the variables tend to cluster together, and how clusters of variables are distributed across categories of texts. This allows the analyst to identify what Biber calls 'dimensions of variation'. In his work on English, described in *Variation across Speech and Writing* (1988), Biber identified six dimensions of variation[6] which are important for distinguishing different registers:

1. Involved versus informational production
2. Narrative versus non-narrative concerns
3. Explicit versus situation-dependent reference

4. Overt expression of persuasion
5. Abstract versus non-abstract information
6. Online versus informational elaboration

To illustrate what is meant by a 'dimension of variation', we will concentrate here on just one of these six, the 'involved—informational' dimension (the others are briefly explained in note 6).

What Biber calls 'involved' discourse foregrounds the speaker or writer's opinions, attitudes and feelings, and the relationship between addressor and addressee: the linguistic features that occur frequently in it include 'private' verbs, such as *think* and *know*, first- and second-person pronouns (*I*, *we*, *you* and their variants), WH-questions (beginning with words like *who*, *what*, *where*), contracted forms (e.g. *I'm*, *don't*), **hedges** (e.g. *a bit*, *maybe*), and emphatics (e.g. *really*). 'Informational' discourse, by contrast, focuses primarily on referential content. It 'convey[s] information about non-immediate (often abstract) referents with little overt acknowledgement of the thoughts or feelings of the addressor or addressee' (Biber and Conrad 2001: 191). The linguistic features which are associated with this kind of discourse include long and uncommon words, a high 'type–token ratio' (i.e. many different words each used once, rather than the opposite, illustrated by the 'Katy' conversation quoted above, where the same few words are used repeatedly), and complex nominal constructions containing **prepositional phrases** and/or **relative clauses** (an example appears at the beginning of this sentence: '*the linguistic features which are associated with this kind of discourse* include...'[7]). 'Involved—informational' is treated as a single dimension because there is a statistical relationship between the frequencies of the two sets of features: high involvement scores tend to go along with low informational scores, and vice versa. The 'dimension' is like a line running between two poles, from 'most involved and least informational' to 'most informational and least involved': different text-types can be arranged along the line according to their scores for features of each type.

When this analytic procedure was applied to Biber's sample of different text-types, the ones with the highest frequency of involved features and the lowest frequency of informational features turned out, unsurprisingly, to be telephone and face-to-face conversation. At the opposite pole, also unsurprisingly, were texts belonging to the 'written expository registers' mentioned earlier, such as scientific research articles, official documents and press reports. But any generalization to the effect that 'speech is involved and writing is informational' breaks down in relation to the text-types that fall between the two extremes. For instance, the personal letters in the sample not only scored higher on markers of involvement than any other written genre, they also scored higher than any spoken genre other than private conversation.[8] They contained more involved features than public conversations or spontaneous speeches, and many more than prepared speeches or broadcasts. If you go back to the text of the 1907 postcard, which is similar to a personal letter, you will notice that it contains many of the involvement features listed in the last paragraph, such as first and second person pronouns, 'private' verbs like *feel* and *hope*, hedges ('a *bit* better') and emphatics ('*very* wet'), and conversely that it has few informational features like uncommon words or a high ratio of word types to tokens—in a text that is only about 50 words long, many items, including 'content' words like *hope* and *pipe* as well as 'function' words like *the* and *to*, are repeated two or three times.

Analysis also revealed differences between text-types belonging to the same general category of writing. Within the 'fiction' category, for instance, romance fiction was more involved/less informational than mystery or adventure fiction; science fiction was less involved and more informational than any other kind of fiction. In newspapers, the most informationally-focused texts were reports, whereas reviews and editorials had somewhat higher levels of involvement.

It is not difficult to think of reasons for these differences (e.g. romance fiction deals with relationships and feelings whereas science fiction has science and technology among its themes; reviews and editorials express opinions, whereas news reports are primarily factual). But even if these findings are not particularly startling, they are nevertheless important in relation to the issues discussed in this chapter. They underline the need to be wary of broad generalizations about spoken and written discourse, and even of not-so-broad generalizations about, say, 'the discourse of fiction' or 'newspaper discourse'.

Research on register variation suggests that there is a particularly significant distinction to be made between 'expository' writing, as exemplified in genres like scientific articles, academic essays, official documents and news reports, and writing of other kinds (including some which are highly planned and edited, like published fiction, as well as many that are not, like personal letters and other forms of 'everyday writing'). Expository writing is the register which most fully exploits the potential of writing to do different things from speech, and which is furthest, linguistically speaking, from unplanned casual conversation. Perhaps for that reason, it is often the kind of writing 'great divide' theorists implicitly take as their reference point when they make general observations about written language, literacy or literate cultures. But while expository writing is an important category of written discourse, it is not the only kind, and should not be treated as the norm from which other varieties deviate.

ACTIVITY

Choose an extract from a written text which is intended to represent or simulate speech: for instance, an extended piece of dialogue from a novel, short story or comic book, or part of the script of a play, film or TV programme (i.e. a written text intended for oral performance). Read your chosen example carefully, and then consider the following questions, bearing in mind the points discussed in this chapter.

1 What kind(s) of speech are being represented in the text, and how has the writer used the resources of written language to represent the characteristics of the relevant varieties of spoken discourse? For instance, has s/he deviated from the rules of formal written discourse, or used particular devices to convey or suggest the features of speech that writing does not fully represent? Are there aspects of speech which the writer seems not to have tried to simulate?
2 How would you explain your observations? You might consider, for instance, how the linguistic features of the text relate to the purpose for which it was produced, the context and medium in which it will be received, and the genre or text-type it belongs to (e.g. novel, play, comic book).

SUMMARY

In this chapter we have examined debates on the nature and significance of writing, contrasting the argument that 'literacy', in the singular, has universal consequences for human communication, thought and culture, with an approach that treats reading and writing as local, variable and context-dependent practices. We also considered the question of how spoken and written discourse differ in linguistic terms, using work done by linguists on register variation to illustrate that the two modes of linguistic communication have different potentials, but how different they are in practice (and in what ways they differ) will depend on a number of factors, such as what the purpose of communication is, what conditions it is being produced and received in, and what relationship the speaker or writer has to the addressee(s). A point our discussion hinted at, but did not pursue in detail, was that the production and reception of discourse, as well as the social relationships associated with it, are affected by the workings of particular communication technologies and media. That is the subject to which we turn in the next chapter.

FURTHER READING

A short introduction to the history and social functions of writing is Florian Coulmas's *Writing and Society* (2013), while Theresa Lillis's *The Sociolinguistics of Writing* (2013) offers an overview of different approaches to writing as a social and linguistic practice. Walter Ong's *Orality and Literacy* (1982) is an accessible presentation of the 'great divide' argument; a fuller discussion of the same issues can be found in David Olson's *The World on Paper* (1994). A classic discussion of the ethnographic perspective on literacy is Brian Street's *Literacy in Theory and Practice* (1984), while David Barton's *Literacy* (2007) is a more recent text representing this approach. *The Anthropology of Writing* (2010), a collection Barton edited with Uta Papen, contains a selection of specific case studies, including Gillen and Hall's study of Edwardian postcards. Douglas Biber's book *Variation across Speech and Writing* (1988) gives a more detailed account of the register-based approach discussed in this chapter.

NOTES

1   These figures are taken from Brewer (1997), but estimates of signature literacy are quite variable, and their value as indicators of the ability to read has also been questioned: some scholars have argued that many more people in early modern England could read than ever demonstrated it by signing their names. More generally, historical statistics relating to literacy and text-production are inevitably subject to dispute about both their accuracy and their meaning, since historians can only consider the evidence of surviving records, and we know that many records have not survived.

2   See Hellinga (2007) on the languages of print texts in England before 1500, and Fishman (2010) on the history of vernacular literacy in Europe.

3   This position, adopted by adherents of the new literacy studies, is sometimes described as 'culturalist' to distinguish it from the 'literatist' view of 'great divide' theorists.

4   This postcard belongs to one of the authors of this book (DC): it was written by her great-grandfather to her paternal grandmother.

5   The term *register* is generally used in linguistics to denote a variety of language associated with a particular context of use: registers are differentiated from one another by things like topic, genre and institutional setting (one can talk about, for instance, the register of science, tabloid journalism or courtroom discourse). However, Biber takes a different approach. Instead of defining registers by contextual criteria (e.g. purpose, topic) and then asking questions about their formal linguistic characteristics (e.g. vocabulary and grammar), Biber defines registers on the basis of their shared linguistic characteristics (identified by statistical analysis) and then asks how those characteristics can be related to their communicative purposes and contexts of use.

6   We do not have space to discuss more than one of these dimensions, 'involved—informational', in detail, but we will briefly summarize the key features of the other five. 'Narrative versus non-narrative concerns' means what you would expect: an important linguistic marker of 'narrative concerns' is the use of past-tense verbs, and the text-types which get high scores on this dimension include, not surprisingly, the various fictional genres in the sample. The dimensions labelled 'overt persuasive content' and 'abstract versus non-abstract information' are also fairly self-explanatory. 'Explicit versus situational reference' relates to the issue of how far communication relies on shared context (linguistic markers for situational reference include adverbials specifying time and place: these were found to be very frequent in broadcast talk and quite frequent in personal letters and fiction, but rare in official documents). 'Online versus informational elaboration' relates to the issue of production/processing conditions, and how the constraints of composing 'online' (i.e. in real time with little planning or revision) affect the presentation of information in different kinds of discourse. Minimally planned conversation may contain fragmentary sentences and vague expressions or 'fillers', where highly-planned expository texts are precise and densely packed with information.

7   The italicized part is a 'complex nominal construction': the whole thing is a noun phrase (the subject of the verb *include*), and it contains a relative clause ('which are associated with this kind of discourse').

8   One anthropological study of writing, conducted among the Nukulaelae people of Polynesia (Besnier 1995), found that personal letters showed a higher degree of involvement and emotional expressiveness than most conversational speech.

3 Writing, technologies and media

The word *technology* probably conjures up a mental picture of tools, machines and gadgets. But when writing is described as 'the first linguistic technology', this is not usually a reference to the invention of the mechanical tools needed to write (in the case of the ancient Sumerians, sharpened reeds which were pressed into wet clay); rather it means the invention of a system using visual symbols to stand for units of language. However, technology in the 'tools and machines' sense is also part of the history of written discourse, and part of what gives writing its potential as a mode of linguistic communication.

All writing has the potential unleashed by giving language an enduring material form. This is what allows messages to be preserved exactly as they were composed, and transmitted to recipients remote from the writer in time and space. But the precise ways in which that potential can be used are affected by the ways in which written texts are produced and disseminated. Clearly, it will make a difference to the purposes writing can serve whether it involves carving marks into stone, drawing brushstrokes in ink on parchment, printing on paper using moveable type, or touching virtual keys on the screen of a smartphone. It will also make a difference whether texts have to be copied by hand or whether they can be mechanically reproduced, and what means are available to disseminate them to an audience (for instance, messengers on horseback, postal services, circulating libraries, the internet).

That said, we do not want to endorse 'technological determinism'—the idea that the characteristics of a technology determine the purposes for which it will be used, and that technological change is the most important factor driving social and cultural change. Technology does not exist in a social vacuum: technological and social change are interconnected processes, reciprocally influencing and interacting with each other. In this chapter we will look at a number of examples, both historical and contemporary, which illustrate that interdependence. We will also ask how the technological and social aspects of communications media contribute to shaping the forms of written discourse that circulate through them.

WRITING, TECHNOLOGY AND SOCIETY

We noted in Chapter 2 that writing in ancient Mesopotamia is thought to have evolved from a pre-existing system of tokens used in accounting. It was not, in other words, a sudden, isolated innovation, but was bound up with a larger process of economic and social development. The same is true of later communication technologies. As Daniel Allington (2011) points out, people do not generally invent things with no practical purpose in mind.

Technological innovation is usually a response to already apparent needs, often ones that have arisen from, or been intensified by, changes in the wider society.

Allington makes this observation in a discussion of the introduction of printing in western Europe in the mid-fifteenth century.[1] This was a time when demand for written texts was growing, along with the class of people who could read and afford them. This increasing demand could not easily be met when written texts had to be copied by hand. The printing press, a mechanical device designed to make large numbers of identical copies, was taken up by entrepreneurs like William Caxton, who opened the first press in England around 1475, as a more efficient way of supplying the expanding market: quicker, more reliable, and if you could sell a sufficient number of copies, cheaper. The effects of printing, however, would ultimately go beyond just addressing the limitations of older production methods. The technology also helped to create conditions in which new communicative possibilities could emerge—the possibility, for instance, of *mass* communication, the dissemination of a single message to a large and diverse group of recipients. In the centuries that followed the introduction of printing, the new text-types that emerged included political pamphlets and newspapers, both ephemeral genres in which individual texts have a short shelf-life. The invention of printing did not make it inevitable that these genres would come into existence, but it is hard to imagine that they could have done so before it became possible to produce large numbers of copies quickly.

The last 30 years have seen further dramatic advances in the speed with which texts can be produced, thanks to the introduction of digital technology. Once again, though, the effects have gone beyond just making it easier to do what was already being done using other methods. Digital technology has enabled 'ordinary' writers, people who do not own cumbersome machinery, or have a specialized craft-skill like typesetting, to produce their own texts and disseminate them through global networks to potentially very large audiences. Consequently, digital mass communication is no longer just 'one to many' but 'many to many'. This has led to the creation of new forms of communication and new textual genres. As we will see later on, it has also opened up some new linguistic freedoms.

Initially, it is common for a new communication technology to be conceived as just a more efficient version of an older one. It is only over time that its potential to do different things from its precursor becomes apparent, and new uses develop, on occasion eclipsing the original ones. As their name suggests, for instance, computers were originally designed to perform mathematical calculations: early computer designers and manufacturers did not predict the range of other purposes their products would come to serve. Mobile phones were imagined as just portable versions of the traditional telephone: no one foresaw that they would be used to play games and watch TV; nor was it clear in advance that SMS ('short message service'), originally designed so that telecommunications engineers could exchange brief technical updates, would be one of their most popular applications.

The internet is another recent innovation whose uses have diversified over time, in ways that illustrate the interdependence of the social and the technological. When it first became accessible to ordinary computer users, the internet was dubbed 'the information superhighway': it was thought of as an enormous, universally accessible reference library. But today's 'Web 2.0' reflects the realization (both imaginative and technical) of the internet's even greater potential as an *interactive* medium, where users are not just passive recipients of content but are able to respond, modify and add to that content. The web still functions as a repository of information, but it is also used extensively for interactive purposes, such as social networking and commerce. For some users it is an arena for public performance: they do not just download the commercially-produced output of the entertainment industry, they also upload self-produced materials to entertain themselves and one another. One popular site, YouTube, sums up its purpose in the slogan 'broadcast yourself'; other forms of online self-expression include blogging, tweeting, and writing and sharing 'fan fiction' based on commercially-produced books, movies or TV series. Meanwhile, the 'information superhighway' has become more of a two-way street. Some widely-used resources are produced collaboratively by web-users interacting with one another (we discuss one well-known example, Wikipedia, in Chapter 9). Many online news sources now carry 'user-generated content', ranging from brief comments left by readers at the end of a report, to so-called 'citizen journalism', comprising verbal accounts, photographs and/or film segments recorded at the scene of a news event and then uploaded to a news outlet's website.

Though these new uses of the internet have become possible because of advances in technology, technology did not make it inevitable that particular practices would be widely taken up, or even that they would come into being at all. People do not generally invent or adopt a new practice just because it has become technically possible. They embrace the practices that, for social reasons, they find relevant, useful and/or pleasurable. The following activity asks you to reflect on your own day-to-day communicative practices, the purposes they serve for you and the role technology plays in them.

ACTIVITY

1   For a period of one day, keep a record of your own activity as a producer and a receiver of messages. Include all episodes of as many of the following as apply: face-to-face speaking and/or listening (or among Deaf readers, their sign-language equivalents); telephone talk; making/listening to broadcast speech; making/viewing television broadcasts; making/viewing movies or video clips; making/listening to music; handwriting/reading handwritten text; producing/reading printed text; sending/receiving text messages; producing/reading email; producing/reading/downloading texts on websites; playing games online; shopping online; online chatting or IM; other online social networking (e.g. posting/reading/commenting/sharing on Facebook); anything else not on this list. (Note that some episodes of communicative activity might involve more than one of the categories on this list at the same time—for instance, you might be involved in an exchange of text messages while also having a face-to-face conversation, or you might read a magazine while also listening to music; a single period spent social networking might involve instant messaging a specific person as well as posting to or reading posts from a larger group. If so, make a note, since this is interesting in itself.) For each item you record, briefly note what device you used, if any (e.g. pen and paper, TV set, computer, phone, electronic reading/listening device), approximately how much time the communication occupied, who else (if anyone) was a participant in communication and what the communication was about or for (e.g. was it academic, work-related, social, practical?)

2   Now consider what part different communication technologies and media play in your communicative life by analysing the record you have compiled and reflecting on the following questions. What range of technologies do you use, and which do you use most? What purposes do you use them for—do you use more than one to do the same thing? In terms of the time you spend with them and their importance for you (which may or may not be

(Continued)

(Continued)

closely related), what is the balance between 'old' and 'new' (i.e. digital) technologies in your communicative life? What is the balance between spoken and written communication? Between linguistic and non-linguistic (e.g. visual or musical) communication?

3   Compare your conclusions with those of others who did this activity. Are there big individual differences? Are there differences that might be related to social factors, like a person's age or their occupation?

TRICKY TERMS AND DIFFICULT DEFINITIONS: TECHNOLOGIES, MODES AND MEDIA ('OLD' AND 'NEW')

By now, readers may have questions about the way we (and other writers whose work we discuss) are using, and defining, certain terms. For instance, at the beginning of this chapter we said that writing was a *technology*; in the last chapter we referred (following writers such as Biber) to spoken and written *modes*; elsewhere speech and writing may be described as different *media*. How are these terms different from one another, and what exactly do they mean?

Let's begin with '**mode**' and '**medium**'. For those scholars who make a consistent distinction between the two, 'modes' are the various *semiotic resources* that can be used, separately or together, to create a message (e.g. spoken, signed and written language, still and moving images, music and sound effects), whereas 'media' are the *communication channels* used to transmit a message to a recipient (e.g. print, radio, TV, film, the internet). 'Technology' refers to the tools—both conceptual and physical—which enable particular communication channels to function as such (e.g. communication via the internet is made possible by digital computing technology). Using this definitional framework we could say that the printing press is a technology, print is a medium and written language is the mode predominantly used in that medium. We could also make the useful observation that written language as a semiotic mode is not tied to the single medium of print (written texts may also be disseminated via hand-copying or through the internet); conversely, print as a medium can be used to transmit messages using modes other than written language (e.g. visual images).

But even when it is used consistently, this set of definitions and distinctions does not solve every problem of terminology. 'Medium' and 'media' are particularly tricky terms because of the range of uses they have acquired in both everyday and academic discourse. 'Media' appears frequently in the generic phrase 'the [mass] media', where it means something like 'institutions which publish or broadcast messages for a mass audience'; it also appears in more specific expressions like 'the print/broadcast/digital media', which distinguish different categories of media on the basis of the technology used to produce and disseminate their messages. To complicate matters even further, some writers apply the term 'medium' to, for instance, advertising: this might fit with the institution-based definition of a medium but it is at odds with the technology-based one, in that messages which everyone would recognize as instances of advertising may be disseminated via the print, broadcast or digital media. (We would prefer to call something like advertising a **genre**, defined as a culturally recognized text-type; where the status of something as 'culturally recognized' is less clear, we might call it just a text-type or a textual category.)

One reason why terminology varies is that communication is studied within a number of different academic disciplines and traditions, which have developed slightly different ways of defining and labelling things. This is a characteristic of inter- or multidisciplinary areas of inquiry which just has to be acknowledged and negotiated. But in addition, labels and definitions can be fuzzy because the real-world phenomena they relate to are complex, and it is genuinely difficult to make the relevant distinctions. In this case, the difficulty is compounded by the fact that the communicative and technological landscape is continually changing.

Many writers, for instance, make a distinction between the 'new' or 'digital' media that emerged at the end of the twentieth century along with the digital technology they rely on, and the 'old' media that existed before digital technology (print, audio-recording, telephony, film, photography, radio, television, etc.). But the logic of this division into 'new/digital' and 'old/non-digital' categories has become increasingly unclear. We still have the various types of output associated with the 'old' media, like books and films and photographs and recorded music, but they are now generally produced using the same digital technology that underpins the 'new' media. Printing as Caxton and his successors knew it is virtually extinct; non-digital photographs, films and musical recordings have become specialist niche products. Increasingly, too, digital technology is used to disseminate all kinds of media output. You may be reading these words in the traditional way, from the pages of a printed volume that you have bought from a bookshop or borrowed from a library, but equally you may be reading them from the screen of a computer or an electronic reading device. You may have some photographs in frames or albums in your home, but you probably have far more which you store and look at on a computer or a mobile phone, or which you have shared on a website like Facebook or Flikr. It is no longer necessary to have specific equipment to receive the output of each different medium: multi-purpose devices like smartphones can be used to make calls, send and receive text messages and email, watch TV, surf the web or read the newspaper. Habitual users of these devices may not have the same sense people had in the past of distinct and separate media, each relaying particular kinds of content.

The questions raised by recent changes in the way media output is produced and consumed are not just questions about terminology. We might ask whether these changes have altered the nature of the media themselves, and of the discourse that circulates through them. For instance, we pointed out earlier that online editions of newspapers use the interactivity of the web to offer readers a more active role in shaping what gets reported and what range of opinions are expressed about it. They also enable readers to engage with the text in different ways: instead of leafing through the pages of today's edition, scanning the headlines and pausing to read whatever looks interesting, the online newspaper reader might work through a series of links that connect thematically related items, including items from earlier editions; or s/he might access the newspaper from a social networking site which offers links to items already read or 'liked' by friends. Are these just minor modifications to the content or format of a newspaper, or do they redefine what 'a newspaper' is? Should online newspapers be categorized as part of the 'old'/'print media', or should they be reassigned to the 'new'/'digital' category? Alternatively, might they be a mixture of both—'new' insofar as they exploit the characteristics of digital media, but 'old' insofar as they retain many features from their earlier history as non-digital, printed texts? Questions like these are potentially relevant for the analysis of discourse from genres and media that have both a pre- and a post-digital history. In the previous chapter, we warned against conflating all types of spoken and written discourse with the most iconic or stereotypical cases (e.g. casual conversation and formal expository writing); similarly, it cannot be assumed that all written texts are going to fit neatly into boxes marked 'print' and 'digital' or 'old media' and 'new media'.

In this book, the terms 'new' or 'digital' media will be applied mainly to those forms of computer-mediated communication (CMC) that did not exist before digital technology. For our purposes, these are especially interesting because of their reliance on *written* language. Though the discourse produced in and for them is often **multimodal**, combining language with non-linguistic resources like images and music, the language of CMC is in most cases written rather than spoken. Advances in computerized speech recognition and synthesis might change this in future, making spoken language the default option for many kinds of CMC (it is already becoming an option for users of some smartphone apps, but until recently it was a 'marked' choice, exercised most often by people with disabilities that made it difficult for them to read or to type). For the moment, however, the predominance of written language is a significant characteristic of CMC. It is also one that has prompted new uncertainties about labelling and definition. To conclude this section we will present an example (and an activity relating to it) from a sphere in which definitions can be highly consequential: the law.

In the English legal system (which has influenced many other jurisdictions around the world because of Britain's history as a colonial power), *defamation*—the making of statements which are damaging to a person's reputation—is a possible cause for legal action: a person who believes s/he has been unjustly defamed can sue the defamer for damages in the civil courts. However, English law distinguishes between a defamatory statement made in writing, which is called *libel*, and defamatory speech, which is called *slander*. The two are not treated in completely parallel ways: libel is considered more serious than slander, and the sums of money that can be awarded in damages are higher for libel than slander. However, new communication technologies and the practices associated with them have called this distinction into question. In some cases, courts have considered defamatory statements made on websites or in email to be libel: analogies have often been made between circulating material via the internet and publishing it in a newspaper or a book. But in a case heard by the English High Court in 2008,[2] a defamatory statement made in a comment posted to an online bulletin board was judged to constitute slander, in spite of the fact that it appeared in writing.

Below we reproduce an extract from the judgment on this case[3] in which the judge, Justice Eady, explains his reasoning:

> … Particular characteristics [of online bulletin boards] which I should have in mind are that they are read by relatively few people, most of whom will share an interest in the subject-matter; they are rather like contributions to a casual conversation (the analogy sometimes being drawn with people chatting in a bar) which people simply note before moving on; they are often uninhibited, casual and ill thought out; those who participate know this and expect a certain amount of repartee or 'give and take'.

> The participants in these exchanges were mostly using pseudonyms (or 'avatars'), so that their identities will often not be known to others. This is no doubt a disinhibiting factor affecting what people are prepared to say in this special environment.

> When considered in the context of defamation law, therefore, communications of this kind are much more akin to slanders … than to the usual, more permanent kind of communications found in libel actions. People do not often take a 'thread' and go through it as a whole like a newspaper article. They tend to read the remarks, make their own contributions if they feel inclined, and think no more about it.

This judgment contrasts with the view taken by an English court in a more recent case involving the microblogging site Twitter. In 2012, a senior member of the British Conservative Party was accused on a BBC TV programme of having committed a serious crime in the past. It subsequently became clear that this was a case of mistaken identity: the accuser had confused the man he named with someone else. Both he and the BBC acknowledged this and apologized for the error. But in the meantime, many people had already recirculated or alluded to the accusation on Twitter. The wrongly-accused man's lawyer announced that he was considering whether to sue the authors of these tweets for libel. He suggested that everyone who used online social media was effectively a publisher, and like other (commercial) publishers, they would have to learn to avoid repeating defamatory statements. Ultimately, he did sue one of the people who had repeated the accusation on Twitter—a high-profile user with a very large number of followers. The court decided that the tweet had been libellous, and awarded damages against its author.

ACTIVITY

Read the extract from the judgment on the bulletin board case, and then consider/discuss the following questions (you may find it helpful to return to some of the points made in Chapter 2):

1 The judgment effectively treats a written comment as if it had been spoken. What ideas about speech, writing and the differences between them appear to have influenced the decision to treat the comment in this way?
2 How do you think defamatory comments made in forums like the ones in these cases should be treated? Should all online forums (e.g. bulletin boards and Twitter) be treated in the same way? In the age of digital communication, is it possible or desirable to maintain a distinction between spoken and written defamation—or any distinction based on the mode, medium or technology used to communicate a message?

AFFORDANCES: RELATING THE MEDIUM TO THE MESSAGE

The cultural critic Marshall McLuhan once memorably announced that 'the medium is the message'. Exactly what he meant has been a much-debated question, but he was evidently challenging the common-sense assumption that the 'message' of a text is equivalent to its content, while the 'medium' is simply a neutral vehicle for transmitting that content. Most discourse analysts would agree that the medium is not just a neutral vehicle that has no effect on the message. If that were the case, different media or modes of communication would be interchangeable vehicles for any kind of content, and in practice they are not completely interchangeable. Each of them has its own **affordances**, characteristics which both *enable* its users to do certain things and *constrain* what they can do. Consequently, the medium and mode will play a part in shaping the message.

We can begin by considering this point in relation to writing as a general linguistic mode. Although there is a high degree of overlap in the kinds of messages that can be communicated using written and spoken language, the differing affordances of speech and writing mean that each of them is easier to use for some purposes than for others. Speech, especially face-to-face speech, offers rich prosodic and paralinguistic resources for communicating feelings, attitudes and **stances**. In writing, these resources are absent, and when writing is used for purposes which make feelings and attitudes relevant, writers have to find ways around this constraint. One strategy online writers have developed is the use of emoticons or 'smileys', which can signal both feelings (e.g. that the writer is happy or sad) and the status of the proposition they are attached to (e.g. that it is meant to be taken as ironic or humorous). However, this does not have the same potential as speech does to convey fine emotional nuances.

Writing, on the other hand, offers the affordances of a visual medium, one of which is the potential for meaningful information to be communicated through the spatial layout of a text. The headings and paragraph breaks in the text you are reading now are not just decorative features, but ways of conveying how the content of the text is organized: headings signal major shifts in topic, for instance, and paragraph divisions offer clues to what items of information go together. Other written text-types depend more heavily on spatial layout. Bus timetables use a grid structure with destinations along one axis and times along the other: if you understand this convention you do not have to read the whole text, but can immediately zoom in on the relevant area of the page or screen. Speech, organized temporally rather than spatially, does not offer this possibility. It is far easier and quicker to find out when the last bus leaves by looking at the timetable than by listening to a recorded message in which the same information is recited orally.

But while some of the possibilities and constraints of writing arise directly from its being a visual representation of language, and as such are relevant to written discourse in general, others arise from the specific characteristics of particular technologies and media. As we pointed out at the beginning of this chapter, the purposes served by writing are affected by the way in which it is produced and disseminated. It is obvious, for instance, that if writing involves physically carving a message onto a hard surface like a rock, it does not have much potential as a medium for rapid interactive exchange. Rapid interactive forms of written communication, like instant messaging (IM) and texting (SMS), depend not only on the technology that allows messages to be transmitted almost instantly, but also on the speed with which written messages can be produced when the mechanism involved is simply pressing keys on a keyboard (or in the case of newer devices, touching virtual keys laid out on a screen). These features are among the affordances of the new digital media which make them different from, and in some ways more flexible than, the written media which preceded them.

Of course, as anyone will know who ever passed notes during a boring lesson at school, it was possible to exchange written messages quite rapidly using the ancient technology of handwriting. But IM and SMS are not just hi-tech versions of handwriting. Their possibilities and constraints are not identical. One difference is that handwriting only permits rapid real-time interactions if participants are in close proximity, whereas IM and SMS allow interaction over much greater distances. This is a technologically-based difference, and it is reflected in certain features of the messages people exchange. A handwritten note passed from one person to another during a lecture or a meeting is unlikely to state the writer's current location, since the reader, by definition, knows exactly where s/he is. In text messages, on the other hand, it is common for information on a writer's current location to be requested or provided.

But the affordances of a medium are not all about the capabilities of the technology that supports it: as usual, these interact with social and cultural factors. Consider, for instance, the fact that handwriting is particularly valued, and often preferred to the alternatives, when people are writing messages of a 'personal' nature, such as letters or cards marking important life events (births, marriages, deaths, anniversaries, etc.). The perception of handwriting as more appropriate than printed, typed or word-processed forms of writing for the most personal kinds of messages is not completely arbitrary: it reflects the fact that a handwritten text bears the visible trace of the individual writer, whereas machine-produced texts do not. However, the significance we accord to that difference is historically and culturally specific: when few people had access to any other way of producing written messages, as was the case until relatively recently, there was nothing especially personal about a handwritten text. It has acquired its current meaning from the contrast with other writing technologies, or put another way, from the fact that it is now a choice. The value we attach to that choice is context-dependent, based on judgments of what would be the most socially appropriate way for a particular kind of text to be produced. A handwritten letter of condolence will probably be judged positively (the writer has 'made the effort' to get out a pen, paper, an envelope and a stamp rather than just touching a few keys and clicking 'send'), but a handwritten job application is more likely to be judged negatively, as evidence that the writer is either too lazy or too incompetent to use the appropriate technology.

Notions of social appropriateness may also be applied to the choice between one transmission medium and another. People often react with disapproval when they read that, say, a company has sacked some of its employees by email, or when a friend tells them that s/he has been 'dumped' by a lover in a text message. The issue here is not whether email or SMS is capable of serving these communicative purposes, but whether the medium is too casual, or too remote, for the message it is being used to send. In your discussion of the bulletin board defamation case, you probably noticed that the idea of online communication as 'casual and ill thought out' was part of the judge's justification for treating the defamatory comment as slander rather than libel. His judgment also mentions another of the affordances of digital media, one which has turned out to have some unwelcome social consequences: the combination of anonymity—in many kinds of online interaction users do not have to reveal their offline identities—and remoteness from one's interlocutors. As the judge observes, this is a 'disinhibiting factor affecting what people are prepared to say'. A medium whose users do not have to witness the distress or anger their casual comments might cause another person, or fear reprisals in the non-virtual world, creates conditions in which the practices variously labelled 'flaming', 'online bullying' and 'trolling' can thrive.

The affordances of a medium can be related not only to the communicative purposes it is typically employed to serve, but also to the forms of language that are typical of the messages circulated through it. We have already mentioned one example, the use of emoticons in some kinds of writing as markers of stance or attitude: this is a strategy used to compensate for one of the constraints of the written mode, its inability to make use of prosodic or para-linguistic cues. Another constraint of some media or genres which is associated with particular linguistic features is *brevity*. Telegrams, newspaper headlines, the breaking news 'ribbons' scrolling across the screen on TV 24-hour news channels, text messages and tweets are all cases where short messages are favoured for reasons of space, cost, the recipient's limited attention span, or in the case of Twitter because the 140-character limit on tweets is a defining generic convention. The language used in messages can therefore be expected to contain features related to the limited space, word length or number of characters permitted. These *economy features* include abbreviations, contracted forms, **ellipsis** (the omission of contextually predictable words/grammatical constituents), and a preference for shorter over longer words and expressions.

If you examine actual examples, however, it becomes evident that the relationship between the medium and the message is not fully explained by generic constraints on message-length. There are differences in the way economy features are used (and in the extent to which they are used) which reflect social considerations, such as the relationship between the producer and the recipient, and what is considered an appropriate level of formality. To illustrate the point, here are two examples from the same medium (SMS), sent to the same recipient; the first is a text message from a friend, while the second is a reminder of a forthcoming dental appointment.

1. safely back 2 my colourful rooftop in [city]. thank you 4 a gr8 time & delicious dinner yesterday. pls say hi to [first name of recipient's partner]. will email u tmrw
2. [title + last name], don't forget your appointment at 11/12/12 at 14.30 at the Oxford Dental Centre with [name of dentist] Please call [phone number] if you can't attend.

Each of these two text messages contains the same number of words (28), but in other respects they differ strikingly. The first one uses a number of the abbreviations which have become iconic of the SMS medium (the prepositions *to* and *for* written with the numerals 2 and 4, gr8 for *great*, & rather than *and*, u for *you*, commonly occurring words like *please* and *tomorrow* written without vowels). The writer uses full stops to mark the end of a sentence, but does not bother marking the beginning of a new sentence with a capital letter. He also uses ellipsis: where the subject of a sentence is the first person pronoun *I* (as in the first and last sentences) it is omitted. In the second text, by contrast, none of these 'typical' SMS features appear. There are some features which might be related to the need for brevity: for instance, the opening salutation dispenses with the 'Dear' that would be conventional in a letter, and just uses the recipient's name; the message also contains the contracted forms 'don't' and 'can't'. However, the inclusion of the apostrophes in these contractions suggests careful rather than casual composition, and the choice of 'title + last name' as an opening salutation also suggests that considerations of formality and politeness have taken precedence over considerations of economy. Other markers of greater formality in the second text include the spelling out in full of *please* and *you*, the preference for the formal word *attend* over the more informal (and shorter) *come*, and the marking of sentence divisions with both initial capital letters and final full stops.

Both these texts deviate from the hypothetical objective of maximizing economy, in that both contain what might be considered unnecessary or redundant information. Once again, though, the nature of and reasons for the deviations are different in the two cases. In the second text, the most obviously redundant item is the opening salutation: in this medium, the identity of the recipient (and often the sender as well) is fully specified in the transmission process, and therefore does not need to be restated in the message itself. When salutations are included, it is more for reasons of politeness than because the information is needed, and that kind of politeness is more likely to be considered relevant when the sender and recipient are communicating in the context of a business relationship rather than a personal one. In the first text, sent to a friend, there is no salutation. On the other hand, the second text is more economical than the first in the sense that the information relevant to its purpose (reminding the recipient of an appointment with a certain dentist at a certain date, time and place, and giving a number to call if the appointment will not be kept) is provided without elaboration. In the first text, the writer's basic purposes are to tell the recipient he has arrived home safely and to thank her for her hospitality. But the writer has chosen to elaborate on these points by using longer and more detailed formulations. Since the recipient knows where he lives, he could have just said 'safely home', but instead he uses the phrase 'my colourful rooftop in [city]'. He also describes the dinner he is thanking the recipient for as 'delicious'.

Though in both cases the message is prompted by a need to tell the recipient something which is relevant at that moment ('I arrived home safely'; 'don't forget your appointment tomorrow'), the form of each message is also strongly influenced by its interpersonal function. Where the second writer is 'doing business'—focusing on the informational basics while also observing the niceties of polite address and 'correct' standard English—the first writer is 'doing friendship'. The inclusion of embellishments like 'colourful rooftop' and 'delicious' make the message more expressive both of the writer's personality and of his positive feelings towards the recipient, while the use of abbreviations and ellipsis is not just motivated by the need to save space, money or keystrokes, but also gives the message the relaxed, informal tone that is felt to be appropriate in communications between friends.

We may conclude that the technological affordances of a medium, its possibilities and constraints, do not operate in isolation from the social relations and cultural meanings which are part of the context for its use. When we investigate the discourse that is typically found in a particular medium, or in a textual genre associated with that medium, we will need to pay attention to the ways in which technological and social influences interact.

TECHNOLOGY, STANDARDS AND VARIATION

Our discussion of text messages raises a subject that will also come up elsewhere in this book: the relationship between technologies/media and the process of language **standardization**— codifying norms that restrict the variability of language in a particular domain of usage, by establishing what linguistic forms (e.g. words, spellings, grammatical variants) will be considered the 'standard' or 'correct' ones. Although standards may be codified for spoken as well as written language (there may be norms of 'correct' pronunciation, for example), in most cases it is the written language that is standardized first, and the written standard that often serves (however ineffectively in practice) as a model for standardizing speech. For instance, the idea that it is 'incorrect' for speakers of English to 'drop' word-initial /h/ in words like *have* or word-final /t/ in words like *what* depends on the knowledge that the words in question are spelled in writing with the letters h and t. To talk about speakers 'dropping' these letters is to give the written word priority: this is not a rule anyone would make for a language that had no written form. More generally, many linguists would argue that the development of writing was an essential precondition for any kind of language standardization: it is only when language is given a fixed and static representation through the use of visual symbols that people become able to focus on it as a system with regular patterns that can be captured by rules.

However, the process of standardization may be affected by the development of specific technologies for producing written texts. In English, the earliest surviving written texts, those produced in the Middle Ages by hand copying, are very variable linguistically. There was no variety of the language that had currency across the whole of England (in the early mediaeval period England was not even a united country), and surviving texts from different parts of the country are written in different regional dialects. Even when they come from the same region, their spelling is not uniform, but reflects the varying practices of different scriptoria (the institutions where manuscripts were copied) and different individual scribes. As England became more unified for administrative purposes, however, moves were made towards a more standard or uniform way of writing, and the dialect of the region around London, where wealth and power were concentrated, acquired more currency outside its own immediate area. This development was already underway before the introduction of printing in the late fifteenth century, and according to some histories, the immediate effect of printing was to increase rather than reduce variability. Printing in England was an imported technology, and the earliest presses also imported labour from elsewhere in Europe, which meant that many early typesetters were unfamiliar with the existing conventions of written English.

Ultimately, though, printing did advance the shift towards a uniform written standard. In his preface to one of the first works he published, *Eneydos*, Caxton explicitly remarked that the existence of multiple and linguistically divergent dialects was an obstacle to the success of his business. He wanted to be able to print texts in a single dialect for the entire English-language market, and he concurred with previous standardizers in seeing the dialect used by the higher social classes in and around London as the obvious choice. He was also using a production technology which eliminated one major source of variability, the lack of consistency among copies of the same text which had been made by different scribes/scriptoria. Over time, rules for writing in English were elaborated and codified in dictionaries, grammars and publishers' style-guides; printed texts became more and more uniform in their grammar and especially their spelling. Though even today there is still some variation, it is no longer the case that every writer or printer makes their own decisions about how to spell. The only dialects which are acceptable in every kind of writing are dialects with national currency, like American, British and Indian English, rather than local ones like Northumbrian and Kentish.

It is important to point out, though, that what we have just given is an account of the standardization of *printed* English rather than all forms of written English. Ordinary/everyday writing, as exemplified by the postcard discussed in Chapter 2, has never been as uniform as printed text, nor as fully compliant with the norms of standard English. As James and Lesley Milroy (2012) point out, the most significant effect of standardization is not actually to eliminate variation in language-use, but to make people believe it could and should be eliminated. The Milroys call this 'the ideology of standardization', and although it is at odds with the reality of variable usage, it is reinforced as a belief by literate people's exposure to published, printed text which has been *made* 'standard' by the labour of professional editors, typesetters and proofreaders. In a professionally-edited text, any trace of the original author's lack of conformity to the rules will have vanished, leaving the (inaccurate) impression that everyone with enough education to write a book can also spell, punctuate and construct sentences without any deviation from the norms of the standard language.

Today, the question is often asked whether the uniformity of written standard English (and other standard languages) is breaking down because of recent technological developments. There is evidence that language is being used more variably, not only in 'everyday' or private writing, but also in texts which are intended to be public and can be accessed by a global audience (ranging from tweets and blog-posts to electronically self-published novels). Writers in new media are freer to ignore established convention, or to experiment deliberately with linguistic form, than those who are subject to the editorial gatekeeping practices of traditional mainstream publishers. However, the effects of new media on language are still a matter of debate: though many commentators emphasize their 'diversifying and de-standardizing' effect, some suggest that this is not the whole story. The language historians Thomas Kohnen and Christian Mair (2012) argue that the influence of new technologies and media is pushing languages—especially English, because of its status as a global **lingua franca**—in two directions simultaneously. On one hand, by making it easier for people to produce and disseminate their own content, the new media promotes diversification, bringing a greater range of languages and language varieties, including unconventional and non-standard forms of writing, to the attention of a global audience. On the other hand, by making it easier for people around the world to access the products of the global media and entertainment industry, the new media are also contributing to the wider dissemination of globally dominant, standardized language varieties like US and British English.

Whatever is happening to written language, though, we should be wary of attributing it entirely to the effects of technological change. Some current developments are clearly not recent innovations driven by digital technology: historical research on register variation shows that the trend towards more informal and colloquial writing began long before the computer age, while the literary use of non-standard dialects goes back centuries. Digital technology has undoubtedly made it possible for more people to use writing for public self-expression, but the invention of the technology did not make its current uses inevitable. As we have emphasized throughout this chapter, the ways in which communication technologies are taken up, and the purposes they serve, reflect the needs and desires of the social beings who use them.

SUMMARY

In this chapter we have discussed the relationship between linguistic technologies, media and socially-situated communicative practices. Beginning with the observation that writing itself is a technology, we went on to discuss the historical development of technologies such as printing, pointing out that these both responded to prior social changes and contributed to subsequent ones. We also argued that the forms and functions of written discourse cannot be explained simply by considering the characteristics of the technologies used to produce and disseminate writing; they are equally affected by social and cultural factors, such as the nature of users' relationships and what is seen as appropriate for specific kinds of communication.

FURTHER READING

Two accessible historical discussions of the impact of technology on language, written from somewhat different perspectives, are Naomi Baron's *Alphabet to Email* (2000), which focuses specifically on writing, and Dennis Baron's *A Better Pencil* (2009). Daniel Allington's 'Material English' (2011) is a concise but informative discussion of the issues raised by printing technology in particular. Readers who are interested in the relationship between writing, prescription and language standardization will find useful material in James and Lesley Milroy's *Authority in Language* (2012).

NOTES

1   We are referring here to the introduction to Europe in the fifteenth century of 'letterpress' printing. A small block of metal is cut to leave the raised imprint of a single letter of the alphabet, and these pieces of 'moveable type' are lined up in the sequence needed to print the words of a text; ink is applied to the blocks, which are pressed against the printing surface. Europeans did not invent this technique, which had been used in China from the eighth century onwards to print images, and later whole pages of text. But Chinese is not written alphabetically (see Chapter 4): to print Chinese texts character by character would have required so many different characters to be cut, the innovation would not have been economically worthwhile (it was not in fact adopted in China until the nineteenth century). In early modern Europe, printing benefited both from economic and political conditions which were not present in China at the time, and from the fact that the technology was well suited to alphabetically-written languages.

2   The case, 'Smith v. ADVFN', stemmed from a conflict between the members of a shareholders' action group and Nigel Smith, who had run the group. Believing that Smith had defrauded them, the group members used a bulletin board run by a financial website, ADVFN, to air their grievances anonymously. Smith regarded their comments as defamatory, and sued ADVFN. We thank former student Henry Hawthorne for giving us this example.

3   *Smith v ADVFN Plc & Ors* [2008] All ER (D) 335 (Jul).

4 Scripts and spelling

As a visual/graphic representation of language, writing makes use of graphic resources that do not exist in speech. In this chapter, we look more closely at what those resources are, how they can be used, and what meanings are communicated by the choices writers make about them. Our discussion will emphasize that how words are written is not a purely technical question, but may also have social and political implications.

FROM *ÇAPULCU* TO *CHAPULLING*: SPELLINGS, SCRIPTS AND GLOBAL PROTEST

In May 2013 the Turkish police forcibly dispersed a group of environmentalists who had been occupying Gezi Park near Taksim Square in central Istanbul, protesting against a planned urban development project which would have bulldozed the park to make way for a shopping mall and luxury housing. As dramatic images of these events circulated via the internet, the protests gained momentum: they spread from Istanbul to other parts of Turkey, and the movement attracted international support.

On 2 June, the Turkish Prime Minister Recep Tayyip Erdoğan gave a speech in which he announced his intention to proceed with the development project, and referred to the protestors as *çapulcu* (pronounced /tʃapuldʒu/). Variously translated into English as 'looter', 'vandal', 'marauder', or 'riff-raff', the term was obviously meant as an insult. Its targets, however, quickly reappropriated it, giving it the meaning 'a person who fights for their rights using democratic means'. The word started appearing on signs, banners, T-shirts and graffiti. It was also taken up by supporters of the movement outside Turkey. On 4 June, a video called 'Everyday I'm Çapuling' was uploaded on YouTube[1] (the title alluded to the line 'Every day I'm shuffling' from the 2011 hit 'Party Rock Anthem' by the American electronic dance music duo LMFAO). A day later another video appeared, featuring the linguist and social critic Noam Chomsky. After expressing support for the protests, he went on to pronounce in Turkish: 'Her yer Taksim, her yer direniş' ('Taksim everywhere, resistance everywhere'). Behind him stood a handwritten sign on a whiteboard saying 'I'm also a "çapulcu" in solidarity. Resistanbul'.[2] On the same day, two related entries were introduced to Wikipedia—'çapuling' in Turkish and 'chapulling' in English. By 6 June, Urban Dictionary, a popular online forum for defining new terms, featured six entries for 'chapulling'. By 9 June, photos were circulating via social media of protestors in Kreuzberg (a district of Berlin with a sizeable Turkish community), carrying signs with slogans in German like 'Auch Berlin tschapuliert' ('Berlin is also chapulling') and 'Heute tschapulieren wir auch in Berlin für Gezi' ('Today we are also chapulling in Berlin for Gezi'). In this way, a

Turkish word became a powerful symbol of political resistance, often among people who could not speak a word of Turkish.

Popular culture, online social networking and the internationalization of protest movements all contributed to the global journey of *çapulcu*, but that journey also has something to do with the form of the written word. As it travelled, *çapulcu* (along with the Anglo-Turkish hybrid verb-form *çapuling*) got adapted to fit the spelling conventions of other languages, yielding forms like *chapule* in French, *chapulo* in Spanish, English *chapulling* and German *tschapulieren*. These adaptations not only reflected the growing currency of *çapulcu* outside Turkey, they also facilitated the word's continued spread, by making it easier for non-Turkish speakers to decode. And what makes this a particularly interesting case is that written Turkish was not always so adaptable.

Critics of the current Turkish prime minister have often likened his authoritarian grip on power to that of the Ottoman sultans who ruled Turkey until the early twentieth century. But at the time of the real Ottoman sultans, the word Erdoğan used to decry the protestors as 'vandals' and 'riff-raff' would have been written not as *çapulcu*, but as چاپولجو or perhaps چاپولجى. We say 'perhaps' because there was variation in the way Ottoman Turkish was written: this arose mainly from the fact that there was no one-to-one mapping between the sound system of the Turkish language and the script used to represent it graphically—Arabic script with some modifications introduced by the Persians (because of these, the script is often referred to as 'Perso-Arabic'). The spelling of vowels was particularly variable since Turkish has eight vowels and the Arabic script offered only three letters to write them with. In modern Turkish, which is written in Roman script, this problem no longer exists. But had it not been for the script and language reform launched in 1928 by Mustafa Kemal Atatürk (1881–1938), the founder and first president of the Republic of Turkey, Turks writing today would still be using Arabic script. And if that were the case, we doubt whether the word چاپولجو would have had the same trajectory as *çapulcu*. The other European languages to which *çapulcu* migrated so quickly are all written in Roman script; to the vast majority of their users, our hypothetical Ottoman Turkish version of the word, written cursively from right to left in Perso-Arabic (as shown at the top of Figure 4.1), would have been impenetrable. In Chapter 10 we look at some of the written discourse produced during the Egyptian revolution of 2011: this was also a

Figure 4.1   1ˢᵗ row: a way of writing *çapulcu* in Perso-Arabic script, right-to-left cursive

2ⁿᵈ row: the letters that make up the word in their isolated form

3ʳᵈ row: their contemporary Turkish counterparts

4ᵗʰ row: *çapulcu* in modern Turkish

linguistically creative protest movement, but because most texts were written in Arabic script (which has currency beyond Egypt but not the global reach of the Roman alphabet), it did not produce anything comparable to the 'çapuling phenomenon'.

SOUNDS TO SIGNS: DEFINING OUR TERMS

One of the observations we made above, that the Perso-Arabic script used in Ottoman times was not a good fit with the sound system of Turkish, raises the question of how writing systems work, and how they relate to the spoken forms of the languages they represent. Before we can analyse the use made of scripts and spelling in particular textual examples, it is necessary to address that more general question. In this section, therefore, we will introduce some of the key concepts and terms that are used to discuss it.

Since one of the central questions about writing systems concerns the relationship of written characters to sounds in the spoken language, we will begin by explaining a convention we will be using to distinguish between the two. In linguistics, the individual sounds in a spoken language system are called **phonemes**. They are represented in writing using symbols from the International Phonetic Alphabet (IPA), and their status as phonemes is marked by enclosing them between slashes. The signs which function as units in the written form of the language are called **graphemes**. They are represented by the characters used to write the language in question (in English these would be letters of the Roman alphabet) and they are conventionally enclosed between angled brackets. Using these conventions, we might write: 'In English, /k/ corresponds to <k> or <c>'. The brackets are a kind of shorthand, telling you that /k/ refers to a phoneme, while <k> and <c> refer to the graphemes which represent that phoneme in written English (for instance, in the words *kettle* and *cattle*).[3]

More than once in the last two paragraphs we have used the term **writing system** to mean the system used for writing a particular language. As Florian Coulmas points out, though, the term can also be used in a second, more 'abstract' way, to mean a general category or type of system for representing languages graphically. 'In the first sense', Coulmas says (2003: 35), 'there are as many writing systems as there are written languages, but in the second sense the number is limited to a few types'. Like most commentators, Coulmas divides writing systems into three major types, which are 'distinguished by their basic operational units' (2013: 17): *logographic*, *syllabic* and *alphabetic*.

A logographic writing system, such as Chinese, operates with *logograms*—written characters that represent entire words or morphemes (e.g. 女 [nǚ] – 'woman; female'). Other examples of logograms include numerals (1, 2, 3,...) and other conventionalized signs whose meaning we understand even when they are embedded in unfamiliar scripts and languages (e.g. %, $, @, &,...).

A syllabic writing system or *syllabary* is a set of written signs that represent syllables (which may be either consonant–vowel combinations or isolated vowels). The main characteristic of most 'true' syllabaries (distinguishing them from alphasyllabaries, which we define below), is that phonetically related syllables (like /ba/, /be/, /bu/, etc., which all begin with the same consonant) are not represented with similar written characters. The Japanese scripts known as *kana* (e.g. *hiragana* and *katakana*) are examples of 'true' syllabaries. (Japanese is a good example of how complex an individual language's writing system can be: it includes not only *hiragana* and *katakana*, but also *kanji* (Chinese logograms), and occasionally *romaji* (Japanese written in Roman script)).

An alphabet is a set of *letters* that represent the individual phonemes of a language. There is a further distinction between full alphabets, which have letters for all the phonemes of a language, and *abjads* and *abugidas*, whose letters represent only some phonemes. An *abjad*, thought to be the oldest type of alphabet, has letters representing consonants, but may not have any vowel signs at all. The Arabic writing system is an example, though it does represent some vowels: short vowels are not marked, but long ones always are (e.g. كتاب, <ktab>, pronounced /kita:b/, 'book'[4]). An *abugida*, also called an *alphasyllabary*, is a system in which a symbol represents a consonant plus a so-called 'inherent vowel' (it might mean, say, /pa/). If the same consonant occurs with a different vowel (as in, say, /pu/) that is shown not by using a completely different symbol, but by modifying the symbol with a **diacritic** (a mark attached to a written character which indicates that it has a different phonetic value from the same character without a mark—like the <ç> and the <c> in *çapulcu*). This means that unlike true syllabaries, abugidas/alphasyllabaries represent phonetically related syllables (those containing the same consonant) in a graphically similar way. An example is Devanagari (also known as Nagari), an alphasyllabary used for writing Sanskrit and its modern descendant Hindi (e.g. महिला – 'woman' in Hindi).

A *script* is the inventory of graphic units that are used to write a language. Some authors, when discussing a single language, make no distinction between its *script* and its *writing system*, but in principle there is a difference. Coulmas (2013: 18) gives the example of Chinese in China, Hong Kong and Taiwan. The writing system is the same in all three, but there are differences in the script: simplified characters are used in mainland China, while traditional ones are used in Hong Kong and Taiwan.

Representing one script in a different script is called **transliteration**. For instance, the Russian name of the city English-speakers call 'Moscow' is written in Russian—using the Cyrillic alphabet—as Москва. Transliterated into Roman script, the same word would read 'Moskva'. The word has retained its Russian form, but each Cyrillic letter has been replaced with its Roman equivalent. A transliteration can also be distinguished from a *transcription*, a representation in writing of spoken language. Whereas transcription takes something that was originally speech and makes it into a written text, transliteration begins with a written text and rewrites it using a different set of signs.

Another term that is frequently encountered in discussions of this subject is **orthography**. From the Greek for 'right writing', this word refers to the set of rules or conventions for writing a particular language. Though orthography in principle covers all aspects of how to write, including the use of punctuation and capitalization, its central concern is spelling, and the relationship between phonemes and graphemes. That relationship differs across languages, and is more straightforward in some than in others.

An orthography is called *phonemic* if the relationship between sound and spelling is transparent, following the principle 'one letter, one sound'. In an 'ideal' phonemic orthography, each phoneme of the spoken language would be represented in writing by one grapheme—only one, and always the same one. Conversely, each grapheme would represent only one phoneme. Languages whose orthographies exemplify this principle to a high degree include Turkish, Finnish and the language formerly known as Serbo-Croatian (now Serbian, Croatian, Bosnian and Montenegrin).

English's orthography, on the other hand, is remote from the phonemic ideal. Some graphemes can represent more than one phoneme: for instance, <c> can stand for either /k/ or /s/; some phonemes can be represented by more than one grapheme (/f/ can be written <f> or <ph> or even <gh>, as in *enough*), and the sound a grapheme represents may depend on its position in a word (<gh> at the beginning of a word stands for /g/, as in *ghost, ghoul*; in other positions, however, <gh> represents /f/ (*enough*) or is 'silent' (*though, thought*)). There are many cases where a letter in the written form of the word does not correspond to any sound in the spoken form: the <k> in *knight* and the <b> in *debt* are examples.

Unlike phonemic orthographies, which are sometimes referred to as *shallow*, the orthography of English is *deep* or *etymological*. Many features of English spelling reflect not the current pronunciation of the language but the way it was pronounced in earlier historical periods (the 'silent' <k> in *knight* was once pronounced as /k/; the differing spellings of what is now the same vowel in words like *meet* and *meat* go back to a time when the two vowels were distinct). Other spellings reflect the fact that terms were borrowed into English from, or constructed using elements of, another language (e.g. the <ph> spelling of the sound /f/ in *phoneme* indicates its origins in Greek). As Mark Sebba comments (2007: 16), 'in many cases the phonetic forms of [English] words are virtually irrecoverable from the spelling, so the system is logographic at least to some extent'. Its lack of orthographic transparency makes English a difficult language to learn to read and write. Research has found that children acquiring literacy in English take longer to develop decoding skills than their counterparts learning to read in other European languages, and this appears to have more to do with the orthographic characteristics of the languages than with differences in the education systems or the teaching methods used in different countries (Hanley 2010).[5]

Though orthography is often treated as synonymous with spelling, Mark Sebba suggests a reason why we might want to distinguish between them: 'the former may be seen as the set of conventions for writing words of the language, while the latter is the application of those conventions to write actual words' (2007: 10–11). Orthography tells you how to spell, and spelling is orthography in action. In practice, spelling may deviate from the standard conventions of orthography, and this potential for deviance or 'non-standardness' is an expressive resource: used creatively, it may contribute to the meaning of a text.

CREATIVE WRITING: STANDARD AND NON-STANDARD ORTHOGRAPHY

The story we told earlier about the global uptake of Turkish *çapulcu* is a story about linguistic creativity, but in this case the creativity involved did not take the form of deviance from standard orthographic conventions. When the word was first reappropriated by Turkish-speaking protestors, who turned it from an insult into a positive term of self-reference, the spelling was not affected. Even when it was incorporated into a new Anglo-Turkish hybrid, the verb form *çapuling*, the Turkish part of the word continued to be spelled in the Turkish way. Its spelling began to vary when non-Turkish speakers took up the word, but the creative move they made was to re-spell it in accordance with the orthographic conventions of their own languages. Instead of just reproducing the Turkish grapheme <ç>, they used whatever grapheme stood for the same phoneme (or the closest sound to it) in their own system, e.g. <ch> or <tsch>—hence we saw *chapulling* in English, *tschapulieren* in German, *chapulo* in Spanish, *chapule* in French. It could be argued that by 'nativizing' the spelling, using locally familiar orthographic conventions (which would also convey to English/German/Spanish/French readers how to pronounce the word in speech), these supporters of the protest were underlining their message of solidarity. Re-spelled, the word no longer looks 'Turkish' or 'foreign', and that symbolically suggests that the same applies to the political struggle which gave the word its current meaning: 'we are all part of this movement, wherever we live and whatever languages we use'.

In other cases, however, writers do deviate from the conventional orthography of the language they are writing in, deliberately making it look different from the standard written form, and thus unfamiliar or 'foreign' to readers who are used to reading texts in that form. This strategy is particularly common where writers want to make clear that what they are representing is not the standardized language variety normally used in writing, but a non-standard dialect. The writing that results from using spelling for this purpose is sometimes called **eye-dialect**—dialect which can be identified using visual rather than aural clues.[6]

Below are three short extracts from literary works written in Scots dialect rather than standard English. The first two are taken from poems written approximately 200 years apart, while the third is more recent, and comes from a novel. (Glosses in standard English are given below each extract.)

Robert Burns, *To a Louse* (c. 1785)

O wad some Pow'r the giftie gie us/ To see oursels as others see us

(*'if only some power would give us the gift of seeing ourselves as others see us'*)

Tom Leonard, *The Six O'Clock News* (1984)

thi reason/ a talk wia/ BBC accent/iz coz yi /widny wahnt/mi ti talk aboot thi/trooth wia/voice lik/ wanna yoo/scruff.

(*'the reason I talk with a BBC accent is because you wouldn't want me to talk about the truth with a voice like one of you scruff'*)

Irvine Welsh, *Skagboys* (2012)

Ali's propped herself up against ma legs, ah kin feel her back restin oan ma shins. Her braids ur that black and shiny ah huv an urge tae touch them [...]

(*'Ali has propped herself up against my legs, I can feel her back resting on my shins. Her braids are so black and shiny, I have an urge to touch them'*)

There is no standard orthography for (modern) Scots: though its long history of being written has produced conventions which many writers observe, there is still more variation than would be found in a fully codified variety. Even in these three short extracts, it is apparent that our three writers have different ways of spelling the same common words. For instance, Burns writes the preposition 'to' as *to*, whereas Leonard writes *ti* and Welsh spells it *tae*; for the pronoun 'I' Leonard uses *a* whereas Welsh prefers *ah*. It is true that these writers come/came from different parts of Scotland (Ayrshire, Glasgow and Edinburgh, respectively), but the differences in the way they spell are related only tangentially, if at all, to regional differences in pronunciation. None of these extracts is a systematic representation of the way Scottish speech sounds. Rather, what differentiates them is the extent to which the writer has tried to make the text *look* different from standard written English.

The most 'extreme' deviation from the familiar standard English norm is seen in Leonard's poem. Some of the non-standard spellings in this extract do represent distinctively Scots pronunciations of words, like *wi* for 'with', *widny* for 'wouldn't' and *aboot* for 'about'. Others, however, do not. The words *is*, (be)*cause*, *me* and *you* sound much the same in Scots as in other varieties of English: by choosing to use the unfamiliar, quasi-phonetic spellings *iz*, *coz*, *mi* and *yoo*, Leonard is making the text overall look more different than it would if he only respelled words that sound significantly different in Scots. The effect is to make the reader continually aware of being addressed in a non-standard rather than standard English voice. In other contexts, this strategy has been criticized as patronizing: where it is only used in the fictional dialogue given to working-class or ethnic minority characters, for instance, it may reinforce stereotypes of those groups as 'illiterate' or comical. But in this case that objection is neutralized by the fact that the poem is actually *about* the social meaning of accent and dialect differences. The speaker points out that those who 'speak with a BBC accent' are accorded a level of authority and trust which non-standard Glaswegian speakers do not enjoy, because they are 'scruff' (unkempt, common, working-class).

Irvine Welsh's narrator is also a working-class, non-standard Scots speaker (though not an uneducated one: in this novel he is a university student). To remind us of that, Welsh has used non-standard spellings for common words that tend to recur regularly in any long text, like the verbs *can*, *are* and *have* (spelt *kin*, *ur* and *huv*), prepositions 'to' and 'on' (*tae*, *oan*) and pronouns (*ah*). Otherwise, the spelling is standard English. Because he was writing a long novel rather than a short poem, Welsh was probably more concerned than Leonard about maintaining the intelligibility of the text, and also its narrative pace (unfamiliar word-spellings take longer to process, and beyond a certain point there is a risk readers will perceive them as a distraction from the story). Then again, the poet Burns used much the same strategy in the eighteenth century as Welsh does in the twenty-first: in the extract quoted he too reserves non-standard spellings for high-frequency items where there is a difference between English and Scots, such as 'would' (*wad*), 'give' (*gie*) and reflexive pronouns ending in –self/selves (*oursels*).

THE POLITICS OF SPELLING AND SPELLING REFORM

We said at the beginning that spelling and script choices are not purely technical, but may be matters of social, cultural and political significance. In a poem like Tom Leonard's, for instance, spelling is clearly being used to make a statement that is both artistic and overtly political. But spelling can also be political on a larger scale, when choices are made, not just by one writer or for one text, but for a whole language and a whole society.

As an example, we can go back to Atatürk's momentous decision to reform Turkish (the word often used to describe this in Turkish, *devrim*, primarily means 'revolution'). In this case, language reform was part of a larger programme of economic, legal, social and cultural measures which were intended to transform post-Ottoman Turkey into a modern, secular state. But the linguistic transformation came at a price, disconnecting future generations from a major part of their cultural heritage—the thousands of texts, spanning many centuries of history, written in a script that is no longer intelligible to the great majority of Turks. Though it might be argued that the replacement of Arabic with Roman script had practical benefits—it facilitated the development of a highly efficient, almost perfectly phonemic writing system for Turkish—it was clearly also an ideological move. Since Arabic script has a strong association with Islam (the Qur'an is written in it), abandoning it was a powerful symbol of secularism, and since the major languages of western Europe are written in Roman script, adopting it was a powerful symbol of Turkey's orientation to the 'modern' west. The reform was a radical break with the past, whose effects are still felt almost a century later. Some commentators on Turkish politics argue that the contemporary revival of Islamism and 'neo-Ottomanism' (a newly-discovered fascination with the Ottoman era) expresses resistance to the secularizing and westernizing policies which Atatürk pursued with such determination.

The reform of Turkish was unusually radical. More often, reform is a piecemeal, long-drawn out process: as Sebba observes, 'orthographic wars are often fought letter by letter, diacritic by diacritic, taking no prisoners' (2007: 133). He goes on to examine several cases where even proposals for relatively minor reforms have caused 'public uproar' (an example is the opposition provoked by recent proposals to modernize German orthography). While opponents commonly give pragmatic reasons for resisting change, the deeper motives for resistance are often emotional: language is a powerful symbol of national identity and culture, and any attempt to change established norms risks being interpreted as an attack on culture and tradition. According to Sebba (2007: 155):

> Successful reforms of orthographies, whether marginal modifications or total replacements, are rare. Conservatism is almost always the most attractive option for the majority of language users, who will be already-literate adults. The exception to this is where changes are motivated by a desire for symbolic renewal, as in the case of the script change from Cyrillic to Roman in Moldova and parts of Central Asia. Here, the reform could be presented as a part of being reborn as a new nation, looking West instead of East (or North) towards Russia.

These comments suggest two important reasons why Atatürk's reform of Turkish was implemented successfully, without causing much social friction: the literate population at the time was fairly small, and the reforms aimed to create a new, modern, nation. ('Atatürk', the nickname given to Mustafa Kemal, means 'the Father of the Turks'.) Equally, Sebba's comments suggest some reasons why proposals to reform English orthography (of which there have been many) have never come to anything, and are unlikely to do so in the future. Though the opacity and complexity of English spelling slows down the acquisition of literacy among native English-speakers and causes endless frustration for foreign learners, everyone who has succeeded in learning to read and write English has an investment in retaining the system they know. (Think how much more effort it took to decode the non-standard writing in the last section than it would have taken to read a similar quantity of conventional English text.) Millions of people around the world are literate in English, and the quantity of writing in circulation in English is vast. Proposals for an Atatürk-style reform of English would provoke global resistance.

SCRIPTS IN DISCOURSE: ICONIC CHARACTERS AND 'FAUX FONTS'

Imagine a situation where someone who doesn't know Arabic, but has seen the Arabic script before, is shown the following line and asked to say what language it is:

وات لانغويج دو يو ثينك ذيس إيز؟

Most likely, they would say: 'It's Arabic'. But they would be wrong. It is actually English—the English question 'What language do you think this is?' written in Arabic script. And it could easily have been one of the other languages that are, or used to be, written in Arabic script, such as Persian, Urdu, Pashtu, Sindhi or Ottoman Turkish. Cases where a script is only used to write a single language are rare (though one example is the Hangul alphabet, used exclusively for Korean), but many scripts are prototypically associated with just one of the languages which are written in them. People who do not read the script in question tend to assume that anything written in it must be an example of the 'prototype' language—if it's Arabic script it must be

Arabic, if it's Cyrillic it must be Russian, etc. The Roman alphabet does not have a strong association with any single language, but specific languages can be evoked by using certain characters and diacritics. The point is illustrated in the following tweet posted by a young Egyptian:

> Güte nacht boys and girls of the world. Gute doesn't actually come with the ü on it. But it looks more German. I'll go to bed now.

The symbolic meanings of scripts can be exploited in discourse by creating 'faux fonts', using letters and other graphic devices to convey the idea that the text is 'foreign', though the message will only make sense if it is decoded in the intended reader's own language. The designers of the poster advertising the (English language) film *Borat: Cultural Learnings of America for Make Benefit Glorious Nation of Kazakhstan* created a faux-Russian effect by replacing some of the Roman letters with similar-looking Cyrillic ones: 'Borat', for instance, was written BORДT. This is 'false' Russian because it has no regard for the way letters relate to sounds in real Russian. The Cyrillic letter < Д > is the equivalent of English <D>, not <A>. <B> is equivalent to <V>, and <R> is not even part of the Russian alphabet.

Figures 4.2 and 4.3 show two examples where orthographic features other than letters are used to create the 'foreign' effect. In Figure 4.2, a faux-Devanagari script has been created by

working with written discourse

Figure 4.2

Figure 4.3

using a horizontal line to connect the top part of the letters. In Figure 4.3, the use of a faux-Arabic script together with a stylized representation of a hookah (water-pipe) signals to patrons of the establishment that they are entering a 'Middle Eastern' place.

WHEN SCRIPT 'DEFINES' A LANGUAGE:
SERBO-CROATIAN AND *UR-NAGARI*

In 1999, a Serbian film called *Rane* (*The Wounds*) was shown in Zagreb, the capital of Croatia. A dramatic depiction of the brutality of everyday life in the Serbian capital Belgrade in the 1990s, in a region torn by civil war and rising corruption and crime, it was greeted by the audience in Zagreb with gales of laughter. Why? Because the film was subtitled. The audience found this absurd, because no speaker of Croatian needs subtitles to understand dialogue in Serbian. The two are mutually intelligible; only a few years earlier, they had been defined officially as varieties of a single language, 'Serbo-Croatian' (or 'Croato-Serbian').

The foundations of Serbo-Croatian as a shared literary language for Serbs and Croats were laid in 1850, when a number of intellectuals and writers from Serbia and Croatia signed the so-called Vienna Literary Agreement. This initiative reflected the Romantic nationalism of the period, expressed politically in a desire to unite the 'South Slavs' in one country. That country came into being under the name 'Yugoslavia': it existed for most of the twentieth century, before disintegrating in the 1990s. Serbo-Croatian was one of Yugoslavia's three official languages (the others were Slovene and Macedonian): two variants—Serbian and Croatian—were recognized from the outset, although, as noted earlier, they are mutually intelligible, and according to many linguists less different from each other than the regional dialects of German. But where nineteenth-century nationalists arguing for political unity had emphasized how similar they were, when the dissolution of Yugoslavia started, the emphasis shifted to their differences. By the beginning of the twenty-first century, Serbo-Croatian had given birth to four different languages, still mutually intelligible but ideologically and politically distinct: Serbian, Croatian, Bosnian and Montenegrin.

Since the linguistic differences among the four are relatively slight, one way of reinforcing their separate identities was through script choice. Croatian and Bosnian are written exclusively in Roman script (locally known as *latinica*). In Serbia, on the other hand, the constitution grants official status only to the Cyrillic script (ћирилица), but in practice there is still **digraphia** (the use of two scripts to write one language; in this case the two are Cyrillic and Roman). Montenegrin, whose standardized form is still in the process of being codified, is also defined as a separate and distinct language by an orthographic intervention. While its advocates prefer Roman to Cyrillic script, both alphabets have been expanded by two letters to represent the previously non-standard phonemes /sj/ and /zj/ (ś, ź in the Roman alphabet; ć and з́ in Cyrillic).

Hindi and Urdu, two major languages of the Indian subcontinent, have also featured frequently in discussions of digraphia, and have been described as varieties of one language, differentiated above all by the scripts normally used to write them. Hindi, used in India, is written in Devanagari script, which has religious associations with Hinduism; Urdu, which became the national language of Pakistan following partition and is also spoken by some communities in India, has associations with Islam and is generally written in Perso-Arabic script.

Recently, however, Rizwan Ahmad (2011) has documented some interesting innovations made by Indian Muslim writers who want to write—and to make clear they are writing—Urdu in Devanagari script. These writers are using a diacritic called a *bindi* ('dot') to represent some distinctive Urdu sounds. They also use a grapheme which corresponds to the 'neutral' vowel sound schwa (written in the IPA as ə) in positions where it cannot appear in Hindi/ Devanagari orthography: what this grapheme represents is the Perso-Arabic letter 'ain <ع>, which is used in writing Urdu, though in fact it is a 'silent' letter, corresponding to a sound which is not pronounced in speech. By inserting this redundant grapheme, Muslim writers are inscribing Urdu in a script which has traditionally been taken to define whatever appears in it as *not*-Urdu. Ahmad believes this marks a cultural change in progress: in time, he suggests, the Arabic script may no longer be perceived as '*the* differentiating element between Urdu and Hindi on the written level', while Devanagari may cease to be regarded as 'completely antithetical to Urdu and [...] Muslim identity' (2011: 179).

TECHNOLOGY, ORTHOGRAPHY AND CREATIVITY: FROM *FRANCO* TO *FAKATSA* GIRLS

As we pointed out in Chapter 3, the way people write is affected—both enabled and constrained— by the affordances of different technologies and media. This point applies to scripts and spellings as much as to other aspects of written language. A good illustration is the development of *Franco*, which is one of the labels used by young Egyptians for the Romanized Arabic (Arabic written in Roman script) that has emerged in the era of digital communication.[7]

Using the Roman alphabet (sometimes in a modified or expanded form) to transcribe or transliterate languages which are normally written in another script is not in itself a new practice. But the development of Romanized Arabic was, at least initially, a response to a novel phenomenon: the advent of new communication technologies—especially mobile phones offering SMS—which at the time restricted users to the code known as ASCII ('American Standard Code for Information Interchange'). ASCII was based on the 26 letters of the English alphabet (in both upper and lower case), along with numerals and punctuation marks: since non-Roman scripts were not supported, users of Arabic had to find ways of writing that employed the Roman alphabet, supplemented by other ASCII characters where an Arabic letter had no Roman equivalent.

In the case of Arabic, the characters used to supplement the alphabet were numerals. Occasionally, the apostrophe is used as a diacritic. Some numerals were chosen for their visual similarity to the Arabic letter they corresponded to (see Figure 4.4). A different logic is exemplified by the number 5, which is used by some writers to transliterate < خ > (a letter corresponding to the sound whose IPA symbol is x: it also occurs in German, where it is written <ch> (as in the German word for 'eight', *acht*)). Using the number 5 to represent this sound in Romanized Arabic is motivated by a principle which is apparently as old as the alphabet itself: *acrophony*, naming the letters of an alphabet in such a way that the initial sound of the letter's name is the sound represented by that letter.[8] The Arabic word for 'five', *khamsa*, starts with /x/, and that became the value of <5>.

ء	ع	غ	ط	ظ	ح	خ	ص	ض
2	3	3'	6	6'	7	7'	9	'9

Figure 4.4

Not everyone uses <5> for < خ >, however: it can also be written as <kh> or <7'>. This kind of variability is one of the characteristics of 'alternative' orthographies like Franco, differentiating them from conventional, standardized orthographies. Different conventions and symbols have evolved in different parts of the Arab world, and even in a single country like Egypt there are variations (like the three transliterations of < خ > listed above). Yet this variation appears not to affect the average user's ability to decode messages. Ordinary people seem to have less difficulty with variable, non-standard spellings than state institutions and members of cultural elites. This should remind us that standardization, the process by which languages are codified and given a set of fixed rules, often has more to do with political needs (like the need to draw boundaries between nations, or between the 'educated' and 'uneducated' classes in a society) than it does with genuine communicative needs.

Today Arabic script is well supported by digital technology, but Romanized Arabic has not disappeared. It is still used in CMC by many, mostly younger, Arabs, but it has also become a sort of alternative transcription system that can be found alongside Arabic script on music CDs or film posters (Yaghan 2008: 46). What began as a *technologically imposed* rather than entirely voluntary practice (romanizing Arabic to make it usable on computers and mobile phones) is now being voluntarily maintained as a part of (youth) culture. It has come to be seen as an additional linguistic/semiotic resource which writers can exploit for various purposes (we return to this topic in Chapter 10).

By contrast with Romanized Arabic, whose conventions were originally developed to solve a practical problem of communication, other digital-age alternative orthographies have been created in the absence of any communicative need. An example is *Leetspeak*: 'Leet' (written 'l33t' or '1337') is an alternative alphabet for writing English—a language that has been fully supported on the internet from its very beginnings—by replacing English letters with other, similar-looking ASCII characters. It was developed in the 1980s on bulletin board systems (BBS), possibly as a way of bypassing text filters when discussing certain topics, and also as a way of affirming the writer's status as a savvy computer user (the name 'leet' comes from the word *elite*). Like Franco, l33t/1337 is very variable. As an illustration of what it looks like, we offer one possible l337 rendering of the title of our book:

\/\/0R|{1|\|9   \/\/17#   \/\/R1773|\| d1$(0|_|R$3

A final example of orthographic creativity online comes from the work of Carmen Vaisman (2011), which describes the way a group of Israeli teenage girls use typographic resources to perform a particular subcultural identity in their Hebrew language blogs. Members of this group are known as *Fakatsa* girls, and are stereotyped as shallow and brainless fashion victims. They have responded by embracing their identity with pride, and performing a cute, 'girly' femininity online, using the typographical options made available by the medium. Their strategy is similar to the one used in l337: some of the Hebrew letters in words (though never all of the letters or every word) are replaced with ASCII characters, primarily those that bear some visual resemblance to the letters they replace. According to Vaisman, this playful use of typography serves both practical purposes (like making it difficult for the girls' parents to monitor their online activities) and symbolic ones (Vaisman describes it as 'a self-aware performance of a desirable, stylish girlhood' (2011: 192) and suggests that it challenges 'traditional Jewish and Zionist gender expectations' (181)). Like the Gezi Park protestors who were 'çapuling every day', *Fakatsa* girls use language creatively to turn a stigmatized identity into something positive.

ORTHOGRAPHY AND PERSONAL IDENTITY

In previous sections we have seen that orthography may be among the resources used to con-struct identity in anything from a whole society (like post-Ottoman Turkey or present-day Montenegro) to a small subculture (like the Leetspeakers and *Fakatsa* girls). It can also have this function for individuals. Later in this book, for instance, we will refer to the work of the US scholar danah boyd. The way we have just written her name breaks an orthographic rule of English, which says that the initial letters of personal names should be capitalized. The person who copyedits our text may query this departure from convention, but we thought it was more important to respect boyd's own view, as set out in her essay 'What's in a name?' (www.danah.org/name.html):

> It's my name and i should be able to frame it as i see fit, as my adjective, not someone else's. Why must it follow some New York Times standard guide for naming? The words that i choose to describe myself should be framed in writing and in speech in a way that feels as though i own them, as though i can relate to them. This is not to say that i wanted a unique symbol to stand for my name, simply that i wanted to write it in a fashion that showed the beauty of my mother's consideration. Of course, as i get older, i end up having a deep engrained individualization of my name. i really don't like when people remove the 'h' or capitalize my name – it's not how i've cho-sen to identify.

ACTIVITY

Visit danah boyd's website and read the whole essay from which the passage quoted above is taken. What are her reasons for not capitalizing <d> and <b> in her name?

As you will probably have noticed, there is an obvious example of non-standard or deviant orthography in the passage quoted above; you may also have noticed instances where boyd does not deviate from standard conventions in the way you might have expected her to. How would you explain the pattern of deviation/non-deviation?

Now do an internet search on 'The artist formerly known as Prince', who at one point decided to change his *mononym* (i.e. the one-word name 'Prince', which he had used in preference to his full name 'Prince Rogers Nelson'), to an unpronounceable logo ('Love Symbol #2'). What were his reasons and how do they compare to danah boyd's?

SUMMARY

One of the main tasks of the elementary school is to teach us how to write and spell 'correctly' in our first language, and the importance of 'getting it right' is also emphasized when we study a foreign language. We are accustomed to thinking of spelling and punctuation as mechanical aspects of writing, governed by strict rules which we should strive to obey consistently. In this chapter, however, we have stressed that there is more to orthography than mechanics, and that some writers in some contexts are more interested in being creative than in 'getting it right'.

Like the different languages, semiotic modes and registers whose uses we discuss in other chapters, different ways of representing languages graphically are meaningful resources for written expression (indeed, unlike the others just mentioned, they are unique to writing). When you are analysing written discourse, therefore, it is always worth asking how these resources are used in the text or texts you are working with. Not all texts will use them in interesting ways, but in this chapter we have considered several cases where they are clearly of interest for the purposes of analysis, because their use is an integral part of what the text communicates. If a writer has chosen to use Franco (rather than Arabic script), eye-dialect (rather than conventional standard English), a 'faux font' or an extraneous diacritic, that is a meaningful choice, and some account of it needs to be given. This is a point we will return to in the next part of the book, where we consider different approaches to the analysis of written discourse, and look more closely at what the task involves.

FURTHER READING

Mark Sebba's book *Spelling and Society* (2007) argues that orthography should be studied as a social practice, and provides many examples of the way script choices and spelling may be linked to group and/or individual identities. Non-standard orthography was the subject of a special issue of the *Journal of Sociolinguistics* edited by Alexandra Jaffe in 2000, while the edited collection *Orthography as Social Action* (Jaffe et al. 2012) examines the social significance of different orthographic practices in a variety of contexts. Two recent, accessibly-written books about English spelling are David Crystal's *Spell It Out* (2012) and Simon Horobin's *Does Spelling Matter?* (2013).

NOTES

1 http://youtu.be/64q2GIqH7S8
2 http://youtu.be/URjXx1eDJ0U
3 Phonemes are abstract units in a sound system; when sounds are transcribed exactly as they are pronounced, *phonetically* rather than phonemically, this is indicated by enclosing them in square brackets. For instance, the English phoneme /k/ at the beginning of a word like *cat* might be transcribed phonetically as [kʰ]: this shows a small phonetic detail—the aspiration of the sound when it occurs in initial position—but it is still the same phoneme as the final /k/ in *black*, which is not aspirated.
4 There is also a set of special signs by which short vowels can be indicated, but they are only used in certain cases. Their use in the text of the Holy Qur'an is obligatory, but otherwise they are mostly found in educational and/or children's literature, or more sporadically in contexts where their absence might lead to ambiguity.
5 Hanley and his associates carried out research in which they compared children acquiring literacy in English with peers who were acquiring it in Welsh (which has a highly transparent phonemic orthography). Both groups were growing up in the same part of Wales, and receiving the same overall education in the same school system—the only difference was whether their parents had opted for English or Welsh-medium schooling. The finding that Welsh learners' progress was significantly faster is therefore strong evidence that English's orthography makes it harder to learn.
6 Some writers reserve the term 'eye-dialect' for cases where the spelling is non-standard but does not represent a dialectal pronunciation (e.g. writing *iz* for *is* and *yoo* for *you*); they prefer to call spelling which does imitate local/non-standard pronunciation (e.g. *aboot* for *about*) 'phonetic'.
7 The name 'Franco' has historical echoes of the Crusades, when foreigners from the west were generically referred to as 'Franks'. Other names used for Romanized Arabic by Arabic speakers include

'Arab<u>ish</u>', 'Arab<u>lish</u>' and 'Arab<u>izi</u>', all of which are compounds that signal 'foreignness'—the three terms just cited specifically link this way of writing to Eng<u>lish</u>, or in Arabic *ingil<u>izi</u>*.

8   In the earliest known alphabet, Phoenician, the first letter, *aleph*, represents the glottal stop. According to some interpretations, it was adapted from an Egyptian hieroglyph that represented an ox, the original word for which, *'alp*, was pronounced with an initial glottal stop. The Phoenician alphabet gave rise to the Greek and later to the Roman and Cyrillic alphabets: a modified form of the Phoenician *aleph* became the Greek *alpha* (Aα) and Roman and Cyrillic <A>, standing not for the glottal stop, but for the following vowel, /a/. Turned upside-down, the letter A still resembles a simplified representation of an ox head.

Approaches

5 Approaches to written discourse: an initial orientation

The purpose of this short chapter is to help readers navigate through the 'Approaches' part of the book. In it we explain our aims and the way we have organized our material; we draw attention to some questions or themes which recur in several chapters; and we say something about those approaches which do not get a chapter of their own.

AIMS AND ORGANIZATION

The approaches discussed in Part II are defined using a mixture of criteria, and in practice they can be combined in various ways—for example, a study might use both critical discourse analysis and corpus methods, and it might also deal with multimodal and/or multilingual data. This means that the following five chapters are not completely separate and self-contained discussions: though each one sets out to cover the essentials of the approach which is its topic, that approach may also be revisited and discussed further in later chapters.

The order of the chapters reflects the way the field has developed over time. We begin with critical discourse analysis (CDA), an approach which dates back to the 1970s, and move on to approaches using the corpus methods which have been developed since the 1980s (the use of corpora in the study of language has a much longer history, but the methods discussed in Chapter 7 were made possible by computing technology which only became widely available in the 1980s). Multimodal approaches have their roots in work done in the 1990s (some of it by scholars who had also been involved in the earlier development of CDA), but they were taken up more widely, and developed further, during the first decade of the twenty-first century. A similar point could be made about discourse analytic approaches to computer-mediated communication (CMC). These began to emerge in the 1980s, soon after the emergence of CMC itself, and a substantial body of research was published in the 1990s; but their most rapid evolution (reflecting the equally rapid evolution of the technologies and communicative practices they deal with) has taken place more recently. Finally, the analysis of multilingual written discourse has only really begun to coalesce as a distinctive area of research during the last few years: interest in it has clearly been motivated in part by observations made in earlier work on CMC, where writers are freer than they once were (or than they would be in traditional print forums) to produce complex multilingual texts.

Our main aim in these chapters is not to survey the entire body of work that has been done using a particular approach, but rather to show what is involved in actually *using* the approach in question—what kinds of questions analysts ask about their data, how they go about doing the analysis and what kinds of conclusions they draw. The best way to do that, we think, is not to summarize a large number of studies, but to work through a small number of examples in detail. For a more comprehensive overview of the literature on a particular approach, you can consult the 'further reading' section that appears at the end of each chapter.

MAKING CONNECTIONS: THEMES, THREADS AND QUESTIONS

Most of the approaches we discuss in Part II can be applied to spoken as well as written discourse. In this book, we concentrate on the latter, choosing written examples to illustrate each approach. But one question which is implicitly raised in many or most chapters is what difference it makes, methodologically and analytically, whether discourse is written rather than spoken. Some of the challenges confronting analysts of spoken interaction (e.g. decisions about how to transcribe the data for analysis) do not arise in the case of writing; but other challenges may be more acute. For instance, analysts of conversation can look for evidence about the interpretation of utterances by examining participants' responses to what has previously been said. Whether/how speaker A's contribution was understood by speaker B will be apparent in speaker B's response. With writing, on the other hand, interpretation is typically a 'private' process occurring at a distance from the context of production; analysts may have only the text itself to work with, and no way of knowing how their own interpretations relate to the interpretations made by readers.

Of course, there are exceptions to the generalization just made, such as the interactive forms of writing (chat, IM, etc.) which are facilitated by new digital media. *Mediation*, the effects on written discourse of being produced in and for a particular medium, is another theme that will recur in the following chapters. Although only one chapter (the one on CMC) actually announces its subject as (a subset of) media discourse, all chapters in Part II contain some discussion which is relevant to that theme.

Many of the examples we analyse in Chapters 6–8 are drawn from the output of what were traditionally called the 'mass' media (they include newspaper reports, magazine articles and advertisements). In choosing these we are not just following our own interests, but consciously echoing the preoccupations of many analysts who have used the approaches under discussion. Though the advent of digital technologies has changed the media landscape, discourse analysts continue to be interested in studying the kinds of media output (whether printed, broadcast or circulated via the web) which are addressed to a mass audience. In some cases, this kind of output may be used in research simply because it offers a large and easily accessible source of data, but in most cases researchers' interest in it has more to do with their understanding of the media as key social and political institutions. Research motivated by that understanding has often focused particularly on the discourse of the news media, whose role is not only to inform audiences about recent events, but also to act as a forum for political debate; consequently, they have considerable power to shape the political agenda and influence public opinion. How this is done and what its consequences are have been important questions for analysts who adopt a 'critical' stance.

Not all media discourse analysis is 'critical': some analysts have more straightforwardly descriptive goals. Colleen Cotter (2003: 417) makes a distinction between what she calls 'sociolinguistic' and 'discourse analytic' approaches, which roughly corresponds to the difference between 'descriptive' and 'critical' aims. (She also points out that there are 'non-linguistic' approaches, developed in social science disciplines like communication, media studies, sociology and politics, which use content analysis (see Chapter 1) as their main tool for analysing media texts.) What Cotter labels 'sociolinguistic' approaches are concerned with the description of style and register variation (see Chapter 2): researchers seek to identify the linguistic features and structural patterns which are characteristic of a media genre like 'news story' or 'editorial'. From our point of view, this approach would also count as 'discourse analytic', since the object of analysis is 'language in use'. However, Cotter classifies approaches as 'discourse analytic' rather than 'sociolinguistic' where they do not just set out to describe the characteristic linguistic features of media texts, but also ask questions about how a story is framed, how the reader is positioned in relation to the text, and how linguistic choices may point a reader to a particular interpretation. These approaches are most likely to be used by analysts who define discourse not only as 'language in use', but also as a politically consequential form of practice (see Chapter 1 for different definitions of 'discourse').

In the following chapters we will have something to say about both the approaches Cotter identifies, though we will acknowledge—as she does—that in practice they are often combined. One point that we hope will emerge from the overall presentation of media discourse in Part II, however, is the difficulty of generalizing, either *about* 'media discourse' (which is not a single, homogeneous category: there are important differences among the various genres analysts have examined as well as between the outputs of the 'old' and 'new' media), or *from* media discourse to discourse in general. Although we have already remarked that some researchers do this, we do not believe that texts drawn from media sources such as newspapers should be treated simply as 'representative' examples of written language. It is necessary to be attentive to the way writing is shaped by the specific demands of the medium, the conditions in which text-producers operate, and the conventions of usage which have developed in particular genres and/or communities over time.

That point also applies to the (many) forms of writing which do not fall into the category of 'media discourse', but which have also been of interest to discourse analysts: for instance, personal letters, diaries and other 'everyday' written genres, stories written by young children, educational materials and students' essays, religious tracts, political leaflets, posters and banners, academic and scientific articles, business communications, official documents, public signage and graffiti. Some of the items on this list have already been mentioned in Part I (e.g. the discussion of postcards in Chapter 2); others (e.g. academic/scientific writing, signage, graffiti, personal letters) will feature later on in the book. But there are, we should acknowledge, some categories of writing that we do not discuss in any detail; there are also some approaches to written discourse which do not get a chapter to themselves.

There is, for example, no single chapter dealing with ethnographic approaches. In linguistic anthropology the term 'ethnography of speaking' has commonly been applied to the study of the speech events, genres and styles which are characteristic of a particular community; but some scholars prefer the broader term 'ethnography of communication', which allows for the possibility of applying ethnographic methods to the study of communicative practices that do not rely on the spoken word. It is certainly possible to study people's *writing* practices ethnographically: we have already observed (see Chapter 2) that this is an important element of work in the 'new literacy studies', and we will give further examples of this kind of work in the following chapters.

What makes ethnographic approaches to writing distinctive is their emphasis on literacy *practices*—things people do with reading and writing—and on placing those practices in their wider sociocultural context. Typically, an ethnographer does not just study the outcome of the literacy practice being investigated, namely the texts people produce and consume; s/he also observes them engaging in the practice, and talks to them about what it involves and what it means to them. For example, one classic ethnographic study of literacy practices, Shirley Brice Heath's *Ways With Words* (1983), contrasted the way reading and writing were used and understood by young children and their adult carers in three different communities in the south of the USA: the study showed how some home-based literacy practices prepared children directly for the kind of reading and writing they would do at school, whereas others emphasized skills that were not explicitly recognized and valued in the classroom. Heath wanted to challenge 'deficit' accounts which explained educational underachievement among poor and minority children as a consequence of their being members of an 'oral' or 'non-literate' culture, brought up in homes where they were not exposed to books. Her observations of family life showed that these accounts were inaccurate: reading and writing were part of the home culture in all communities, but their meaning and the way they were engaged in differed. Other ethnographers have examined the meaning, uses and consequences of literacy in communities where it is a recent historical development. In Chapter 11, for instance, we discuss the anthropologist Laura Ahearn's research on the practice of writing love letters in a village in Nepal (Ahearn 2001, 2003). Though Ahearn does analyse a sample of villagers' love letters, analysing them as linguistic artefacts is not her primary aim. The main story she wants to tell is about the effects of love letter writing (which at the time of her fieldwork was a new practice in the village), both on the individuals who engaged in it and on the life of the community as a whole.

Ethnographic research on writing is sometimes done by people who are or have been members of the community whose practices they are studying. Some work on news discourse, for instance, has been produced by 'journalinguists', that is, linguists who have been journalists themselves and who are able to make use of inside knowledge of the professional culture (a recent example is Cotter 2010). Similarly, some ethnographically-informed studies of writing in educational contexts have been produced by teachers or former teachers. An interesting example is the work of the applied linguist Suresh Canagarajah (1999), which draws on his experience of teaching English to Tamil students in his native Sri Lanka. Canagarajah makes ingenious use of data whose significance an 'outsider' researcher could easily have overlooked. Having noticed that his students regularly engaged in defacing their textbooks by writing and drawing on them in class, Canagarajah analysed their additions to and comments on the text as a form of resistance both to the content of their US-produced coursebook (which was remote from the concerns of Sri Lankans), and to the 'official' discourse of English language education. By looking at the products of this 'unofficial' literacy practice, he was able to find evidence of attitudes which students might not have expressed directly to a researcher.

Ethnographic approaches are used in a range of ways by researchers working with written discourse, and our discussion of studies that make use of them may be of interest to readers who want to include an ethnographic element in their own research (though it needs to be borne in mind that full-scale ethnography requires an investment of time which is not practicable for most student projects). However, the examples already mentioned illustrate why ethnographic approaches do not feature as the subject of a separate chapter in Part II. Ethnography is not so much a *kind* of discourse analysis as an approach that may be *combined* with discourse analysis. The central characteristic of discourse analysis itself is close and systematic attention paid to the language of a text, and in this section we will concentrate on the tools and techniques that are most useful for that purpose. At the same time, we will not suggest that discourse analysis should focus exclusively on the text, giving no consideration to anything beyond the words on the page or the screen. On the contrary, the importance of putting texts in context, and seeing them as the products of certain social and linguistic practices, is a recurring theme in the following chapters.

Another approach, or set of approaches, which we do not deal with in a specific chapter are those which belong to literary stylistics (the study of the language of literature) or poetics (the study of verbal art). This is too large and varied a subject to be dealt with in a single chapter: it is often considered as a field of study in its own right, and in many institutions it is taught separately from discourse analysis. However, some of the approaches we discuss can be and have been applied to literary texts. For example, though our discussion of CDA in Chapter 6 takes its examples mainly from news and advertising, the same linguistic framework which is used to analyse those genres has also been applied (sometimes by the same scholars) to novels and other works of fiction (e.g. Fowler 1996; Halliday 1971). Corpus methods, discussed in Chapter 7, are also used by analysts of literary discourse. In fact, today's corpus methods have historical roots in the kind of textual scholarship which was originally as much a 'literary' as a 'linguistic' enterprise. Before the advent of the computer software which is used to do the job now, scholars painstakingly compiled concordances—lists of every use of a specific word or expression in a text or a collection of texts—as an aid to elucidating the meaning of a text, tracing its provenance and relationship to other texts, identifying features of an author's individual style, and—in some cases—establishing who the author might have been. The texts for which this task was undertaken were typically works of special cultural significance (e.g. religious texts or the works of a 'great author' like Shakespeare). Today's technology makes it feasible to do it for a wider range of materials, but it can still be used for the purposes mentioned above. (The use of corpus methods to establish authorship made headlines in 2013, when a crime novel by the previously unknown 'Robert Galbraith' was revealed as the pseudonymous work of the much more famous J. K. Rowling.)

Certain kinds of literary texts may be amenable to analysis using the other approaches we discuss in Part II. Multimodal approaches are potentially useful for analysing examples of literary discourse where written text is integrated with visual illustrations (obvious examples include children's picture-books and adult graphic novels). Approaches developed for analysing computer-mediated discourse are relevant for work on literary genres produced in and for new digital media—an example we discuss in Chapter 9 is the Japanese *keitai* (mobile phone) novel—while approaches to multilingual discourse are relevant for analysing texts in which writers have made creative use of more than one code or script.

As well as showing readers how to use particular approaches to written discourse analysis, we want the chapters that follow to give a sense of what those approaches can be used for. This is not only a matter of the kinds of written texts they can most fruitfully be applied to, but also of the kinds of questions they are best equipped to address. Different approaches suit different kinds of questions: when you choose an approach, or a combination of approaches, the most important thing to consider is whether it will enable you to answer the question you are interested in. In the following chapters we will choose our examples to demonstrate this point about the relationship between research questions and analytic frameworks or techniques. We begin with an approach—CDA—where that relationship is very clear, since the critical stance which defines the approach prompts those who use it to ask a particular set of questions about discourse, power and social control.

6 Critical discourse analysis

Critical discourse analysis (CDA) is an approach that highlights the social, ideological and political dimension of discourse. Its practitioners regard discourse in the same way as critical social theorists like Foucault (see Chapter 1)—as something that does not just describe a pre-existing reality, but actively shapes our understanding of reality. As Norman Fairclough explains (1995: 219), 'it is mainly in discourse that consent is achieved, ideologies are transmitted, and practices, meanings, values and identities are taught and learned'. 'Central to CDA', say Meriel and Thomas Bloor (2007: 4), 'is the understanding that discourse is an integral aspect of power and control'.

One strand of research in CDA studies the way power is exercised in spoken interaction, especially in institutional settings like police stations, law courts, classrooms and workplaces. But written discourse may also be 'an integral aspect of power and control'. As a concrete example, we may return to an example from Chapter 1: the construction of 'obesity' in contemporary news reports. In the examples we reproduced, obese people were represented in a number of negative ways—for instance, as too ignorant to feed their children properly and as a burden on the public healthcare system. These media representations do not exercise power over obese individuals as directly as, say, insults hurled at them in the street, or lectures delivered to them by healthcare professionals, but they do contribute to the 'blaming and shaming' of the obese, which is a powerful mechanism of social control. To the extent that they shape our view of the world, they help to create a social climate where it is acceptable for the obese to be bullied, lectured or discriminated against.

Media discourse has been a major preoccupation in CDA. The size of the audiences the mass media can reach, together with the authority accorded to certain outlets (e.g. 'newspapers of record' or national broadcasters like the BBC), makes them particularly influential in shaping public opinion and setting the agenda for political debate. In modern societies, the media also provide the main channel through which politicians and government representatives communicate with the public; 'political discourse' is to a large extent also 'media discourse'. Many CDA studies have examined the part played by media/political discourse (largely news and current affairs) in shaping opinion on issues like industrial relations (Glasgow Media Group 1980), nuclear warfare (Chilton 1985), 'race' and immigration (van Dijk 1991), and the environment (de Beaugrande 2004). Another strand of work examines the construction of gender and other identities in popular genres like lifestyle journalism, advice literature and advertising (e.g. Benwell 2003; Cameron 2006a; Lazar 2000; Machin and van Leeuwen 2010).

This list of topics might suggest that critical discourse analysts have a particular political agenda. Few of them would deny that: for some, it is actually part of the definition of their approach. Norman Fairclough and Ruth Wodak (1997: 258–9) say that CDA 'intervenes on the side of dominated and oppressed groups and against dominating groups', adding that it 'openly declares the emancipatory interests that motivate it'. Teun van Dijk (2003: 352) has described CDA as a 'dissident' research paradigm whose goal is 'to understand, expose and ultimately resist social inequality'. Statements like these have sometimes prompted the criticism that CDA is more like propaganda than analysis. To be academically legitimate, analysis must be 'objective' and 'value free': by 'openly declar[ing] ... the interests that motivate it', CDA fails to meet that criterion.[1]

This criticism raises a larger question which has been much debated among researchers in the humanities and social sciences: whether any analysis can be truly 'objective', done without preconceptions or biases. CDA is on the side of this argument which maintains that 'objectivity' is an illusion: analysts are part of the social world they study, and it is impossible for them to approach their data without any preconceptions at all. In addition, one of CDA's central principles is that no representation of reality is neutral—in discourse there is always a point of view. It follows that no analysis can be neutral either: an analysis, after all, is itself a representation. Rather than pretending to be 'objective', critical discourse analysts argue that it is better to make your own position explicit, so that readers can take account of it when judging your analysis. This is an ongoing debate, and we will return to it at the end of this chapter. First, though, we will take a closer look at what is involved in actually doing CDA.

LOOKING AT LANGUAGE 'CRITICALLY': THE LINGUISTICS OF CDA

In Chapter 1 we made a distinction between discourse analysis and 'content analysis': the latter is concerned only or mainly with *what* is said/written in a text, whereas the former also involves paying close attention to the way in which propositions are expressed, on the basis that the linguistic choices writers make are crucial for an analysis of what the text communicates. Content analysis can certainly be done from a 'critical' perspective, but CDA is a discourse analytic approach, which places emphasis on examining the language of texts systematically and in detail. It is therefore necessary to consider which aspects of language are most significant for the purposes of 'being critical'—that is, identifying the ideological presuppositions of a text and understanding how it constructs a particular version of reality.

We will begin with two general points. First, a critical analysis will be most compelling if what it shows is a *pattern* in the text, or in a set of related texts. An argument that media discourse portrays immigrants as alien and threatening cannot convincingly be based on a single sentence in one news report: it needs to be supported by evidence that certain words or metaphors which imply otherness and threat (e.g. references to 'swarms' of migrants who are 'invading' a territory or 'swamping' the native population) recur in a sample of reports. Second, a critical analysis will be more interesting and revealing if it focuses on what is *covert* in the text. Applying CDA to something as overtly racist as the heading 'Keep Britain White' in a leaflet distributed by a fascist organization will not add anything to the obvious interpretation: there is no 'hidden agenda' to be uncovered through linguistic analysis. Analysts who use the tools of CDA to study racism are usually more interested in the subtler strategies which speakers and writers use to express sentiments not unlike the one in the fascist leaflet *without* appearing overtly racist.

In sum: the linguistic features of most interest for CDA are those which could potentially be involved in a non-neutral pattern of representation which is not immediately obvious on the surface. Patterns of this kind may be found by examining the vocabulary or the metaphors used in a text, its grammar at the level of phrases and sentences, its textual organization (structure 'above the sentence'), its framing in relation either to other texts or to familiar cultural 'scripts' or 'schemas', and the way in which it addresses and positions the recipient. Which of these features will be associated with interesting patterns will vary from one text to another: since it is not usually feasible to look at everything in exhaustive detail, deciding what to concentrate on is a matter for the analyst's own judgment.

Another decision analysts have to make is what linguistic framework to use when describing the features of a text. Historically, there has been a strong association between CDA and one particular descriptive framework, the 'systemic functional linguistics' (SFL) developed originally by the British linguist Michael Halliday. In the 1970s a group of British-based researchers used this framework to describe what they argued were ideologically significant patterns in the wording and grammar of headlines and news reports. This enterprise was labelled 'critical linguistics' (Fowler et al. 1979), and the kind of analysis it involved became one element of the broader 'critical discourse analysis' that developed subsequently. The link to SFL has been maintained by some influential figures (e.g. Norman Fairclough and Gunther Kress, who was one of the original 'critical linguists'), and the concepts and terminology of SFL are therefore encountered frequently in the literature of CDA. However, not all practitioners of CDA today are followers of Halliday: our own view is that the insights CDA produces when applied to data do not depend on adhering rigidly to the SFL framework or using only the terminology that belongs to that framework.

It will be apparent from this discussion that what is involved in doing CDA will vary depending on the material being analysed: you cannot expect to find exactly the same patterns in every text or every kind of discourse. To give a broad sense of the kinds of patterns critical analysts look for, however, and to show how those patterns can be interpreted, we will now consider some examples of CDA, focusing on two of the written genres which have been studied most frequently: news journalism and advertising.

LANGUAGE IN THE NEWS: WORDS, GRAMMAR AND FRAMING

News reporting is a narrative genre, preoccupied with the representation of actions/events and the people involved in them. In addition, as Allan Bell points out (1991), news 'stories' (a term journalists and editors prefer to 'articles') resemble other kinds of stories, in that events are not simply recounted, they are structured and presented in a way that indicates what the point or angle of a story is, what information is more/less important, and what evaluative stance is being taken by the teller. It is therefore of interest to look at the placement and framing of information (in news stories the headline and first-paragraph 'lead' summarize the point of a story and act as a frame for the more detailed narrative that follows), the words and metaphors chosen to describe people and their actions, and the way grammatical choices contribute to the construction of a stance by, for instance, directing attention towards or away from particular actors, and assigning responsibility or blame to them. It is also often of interest to look beyond the individual text, considering how it is linked to other related texts and to the wider context in which the story is being placed.

Consider, for instance, the extract reproduced below: it is the opening of a news report published in a British national newspaper, the *Daily Mail*, in December 2012:[2]

Shop forced to call police after druid refuses to pay because cashier wouldn't ask for the money in WELSH

A druid refused to pay for his items at a small shop in a North Wales town because staff refused to tell him the total in Welsh.

Archdruid Dr Robyn Lewis, 83, was at the Spar store in Pwllheli where he wanted workers to speak to him in the native language.

However, the owner of the shop said that the situation had been "completely blown out of proportion."

Police were called after Dr Lewis – former Archdruid of the Gorsedd, a group that promotes Welsh literature, poetry and music – was given the option of paying £58.62 for his shopping or leave. But the first officer that arrived on the scene could not speak Welsh and so back up had to be called to deal with the situation.

[...]

Dr Lewis says that he wanted to be answered "in my own language, in my own country."

Conrad Davies, who owns the Spar shop, said that the cashier had been left upset by the incident.

Note: 'druid' is defined by the Concise Oxford Dictionary *as meaning (1) an ancient Celtic priest, magician or soothsayer; (2) a member of a Welsh druidic order, esp. the Gorsedd.*

Describing an incident where the police were called to deal with a conflict between a customer and the staff of a local shop, this report observes all the usual journalistic conventions: it begins with a first-paragraph 'lead' summarizing the key points of the story, and goes on to offer the standard information on where the events took place, who was involved, what the conflict was about, and how it unfolded. The text does not, on the face of it, take sides. Later in the report there are quotes from both the customer and the shop's owner; the newspaper makes no overt comment on the issue at stake in the dispute, whether customers are entitled to insist on being addressed in Welsh rather than English. Nevertheless, your intuitions as a reader may tell you (as ours tell us) that the newspaper's sympathies lie more with the supermarket staff than the customer. What is it about the language of the report that creates that impression?

One obvious thing to look at in this connection is the words used to describe people and actions. An example that stands out is the naming of the customer in the story as a *druid* or *archdruid*. It is especially significant that he is introduced using the term 'druid' rather than any of the other expressions that would be equally accurate (e.g. 'a customer', 'an 83-year-old man' or 'Dr Robyn Lewis'). Not only does the choice of 'a druid' establish Dr Lewis's 'druid' identity as the most relevant identity for the purposes of the report (a view underlined by the accompanying photograph, which depicts him wearing the ceremonial robes of an archdruid of the Gorsedd, an organization devoted to Welsh literature, poetry and music), it also sets up an interpretive frame in which his central action (refusing to pay for his shopping unless the server asks for the money in Welsh) will be understood with reference to his status as a 'druid'. Although it is reasonable to make some connection between the two things—Dr Lewis's insistence on being addressed in Welsh in shops and his involvement in the Gorsedd are both motivated by a strong commitment to the Welsh language and Welsh culture—it is less obvious that 'druid' is Dr Lewis's primary identity when he is shopping for groceries. The other participants mentioned are identified using role-descriptors like *cashier, staff, workers, supermarket manager*, rather than other terms which might also apply to them, but which are irrelevant in this context (e.g. *grandmother, chapel-goer* and *rugby enthusiast*). By repeatedly identifying Dr Lewis as a 'druid' in the grocery-shopping context, the text is representing him in a different way from the other participants, and, arguably, in a less favourable way. For although he is indeed a druid in the second sense listed by the dictionary (a member of the Gorsedd), most *Mail* readers' understanding will probably be closer to the first sense, 'an ancient Celtic priest, magician or soothsayer'. Contemporary 'druids' are widely regarded as an eccentric fringe-group whose beliefs and practices are both ridiculous and faintly sinister. By emphasizing Dr Lewis's status as a druid, the report implicitly invites readers to view his insistence on speaking Welsh in the same way; it also implies that support for the Welsh language is a 'fringe' rather than main-stream position.

Another indication that the newspaper is covertly taking sides can be found in the verbs used to label the actions taken by participants in the story. The actions taken by representatives of the shop are most frequently described using verbs that suggest a reasonable and considerate attitude. Initially it is said that staff '*refused* to tell [Dr Lewis] the total in Welsh', but this adversarial stance soon yields to a more placatory one, conveyed here by the verb *give* [*the option*], and later, by the statement that the manager was called in an effort to *appease* Dr Lewis and *resolve* the situation. Dr Lewis, on the other hand, continues to *refuse*.

It is also noticeable that the action ultimately taken by staff is described in a way ('shop *forced* to call police') which seems to dismiss in advance any potential criticism of this response as disproportionate. Here it is not only the choice of the verb *force* which is significant, but also the choice of grammatical verb form: this sentence is in the passive voice (the equivalent sentence in the active voice would be '[someone/something] forced the shop to call the police'). In an active sentence which describes an actor ('agent') performing an action, the agent will usually be the grammatical subject, and in English, the normal or 'unmarked' position for the subject of a sentence to occupy is the first slot, before the verb that denotes the action (e.g. 'the police [subject] arrested [verb] a druid [object]'). In a passive sentence, by contrast, the object or recipient of the action becomes the grammatical subject and moves into the slot before the verb, while the agent is either relegated to a 'by' phrase (e.g. 'a druid was arrested by the police') or left out altogether ('a druid was arrested'). 'Shop forced to call police' is an example of an *agentless passive*, which does not explicitly specify who or what forced the shop to call the police. This means that the reader has to infer the identity of the agent using clues in the surrounding discourse or assumptions that make sense in context. In this case, 'shop forced to call police' is immediately followed by 'after druid refuses to pay'. The most obvious inference is that the responsibility lies with the druid: it was his behaviour that forced the shop to call the police. The agentless passive contributes to the impression that Dr Lewis was at fault whereas the shop workers and manager were just reacting in the way any normal, reasonable person would react.

The grammatical 'packaging' of information about who did what to whom is worth examining when you are analysing a text critically; but it is also important not to assume that grammatical constructions like the agentless passive have only one possible motivation or meaning. Though style-guides often advise writers to avoid the passive voice because it obscures who is responsible for an action, this is not always sound advice. Formulating a sentence in the passive rather than the active is a way of putting the focus on the object rather than the agent of an action: writers may choose to do this for a variety of reasons. For instance, in the headline PRESIDENT KENNEDY ASSASSINATED, what motivates the choice of the agentless passive is not a desire to deflect blame from the assassin. Rather, it reflects the writer's understanding of what the key piece of information is—that the President of the USA has been killed. Putting 'President Kennedy' in the subject slot underlines that the story is about him.

So far, we have argued that the lexical and grammatical choices made in the *Mail* are not neutral with respect to the participants and actions described. Despite its appearance of factuality, the text represents the incident in a way that implicitly 'takes sides'. Why, though, has the *Mail* chosen to represent reality in this way? What is it taking sides about?

First, we might notice that the *Mail* is on the side of authority—the staff of the shop rather than the customer who refuses to obey the rules. Numerous CDA studies have looked at the reporting of events which involve a challenge to authority, such as industrial disputes, political protests and demonstrations, and they have found that it is most common for the authorities to be presented as reasonable while the challengers are portrayed as uncooperative or aggressive 'troublemakers'. For example, the Glasgow Media Group (1980) found that television news reports dealing with strikes consistently represented managers as making 'offers' while striking workers were said to make 'demands' and 'threats'. This is an instructive example because news broadcasters in Britain (unlike newspapers) have a legal obligation to present a 'balanced' view. It is therefore unlikely that the pattern reflected a deliberate bias; it is more likely that this perception of industrial conflict has been incorporated into our common-sense view of reality, so that we do not notice any bias in the lexical choices which express it. By contrast, if a news bulletin reported that striking workers had 'offered' to return to work in exchange for a 5% pay increase and managers had 'demanded' they return without any increase, that would probably be perceived as taking the strikers' side.

But one man's personal protest in a local shop is hardly comparable to the challenge posed by a strike or a mass demonstration. Why should a national newspaper treat it in a similar way, or indeed report it at all? To see what else might be at stake here, we need to shift the focus of analysis from the language of the text to the wider context, relating this report to other reports that appeared in the same newspaper around the same time, and to relevant contemporary political developments.

The *Mail* is a right-of-centre newspaper, sometimes dubbed 'the voice of "middle England"'. It champions conservative values—it is for 'Britishness', the monarchy, law and order, traditional sexual morality and respect for/obedience to authority, and against internationalism, republicanism, multiculturalism, permissiveness and 'political correctness'. It is particularly hostile to the kind of identity/diversity politics which enables minorities (ethnic, religious, sexual or linguistic) to assert their rights at the expense (as the *Mail* sees it) of the majority's traditions and values. This stance has led the *Mail* to make an issue of the promotion of Welsh in Wales, portraying it as a threat to the position of English as Britain's *de facto* national language, and an attack on the rights of English-speakers. Shortly before the article about the supermarket incident appeared, the newspaper had alleged that in some schools, young children who had limited proficiency in Welsh were being refused permission to go to the bathroom if they made the request in English. Regular readers of the newspaper would have placed the apparently much more trivial supermarket story in the same frame, understanding it not as an isolated case, but as another piece of evidence in an ongoing argument about the threat posed by Welsh language activism.

This is an example of **intertextuality**. The term, already established in literary criticism (where it refers to the way in which texts habitually cite, allude to and otherwise reference other texts), is used in CDA to capture two main ideas. The first is that readers do not treat each text they read as a discrete item, but rather interpret texts in the light of other relevant texts they have encountered (e.g. texts which deal with the same or similar themes, or which are part of a 'chain' in which each item links back to the preceding ones). These intertextual connections are potentially relevant for analysis because they are among the resources readers may be drawing on in making their own interpretations. The other idea is that many or most texts refer to and are partly assembled from other texts. This point does not just apply to literature. Many news reports are compiled from the contents of press releases, government briefings, written records of Parliamentary debates, official reports or the texts of speeches politicians have yet to deliver (this is the source of all those news items that begin 'the prime minister is expected to say...'). It is also common for news stories to contain reported speech and direct quotation from participants, eye-witnesses and spokespersons. From a 'critical' perspective, an interesting question concerns the extent to which, and the ways in which, these various source texts are altered and reframed in the process of assembling a new text from them, and how the alteration/reframing might relate to the ideological motivations of the text-producer.

ACTIVITY

Sometimes it is easier to see how linguistic choices contribute to the stance taken on events and participants in a news story if you compare two reports of the same news event. Below is a version of the 'druid' story that appeared in the *Huffington Post*, a 'liberal' newspaper which only appears online.[3] Paying close attention to the linguistic choices made in this text, consider (a) what evidence there is that the two versions of the story were compiled using the same sources; and (b) how the *Post's* presentation of the story differs from the *Mail's*.

Police were called to a shop in Wales after an Archdruid refused to pay for his goods because the cashier did not speak to him in Welsh.

Dr Robyn Lewis, a former Archdruid of literary group the Gorsedd, told the *Cambrian News* he felt "humiliated" after officers were called to the store merely because he "wanted to be spoken to in his own language".

The ruckus occurred at the Spar in Pwllheli, after the 83-year-old was told to pay £58.62 for his groceries. He told the BBC he was shocked to hear the amount spoken in English rather than the Welsh number "pum-deg-wyth punt, chwedeg-dau".

The Archdruid was aggravated further when a police officer arrived, who also had no knowledge of Welsh. After backup was called, the situation was resolved: in Welsh of course.

In the activity above you will probably have identified some significant differences in the lexical and grammatical choices made by the *Post* as compared to the *Mail*, but you may also have found the *Post's* attitude to Dr Lewis's protest difficult to pin down. While contrasting linguistic choices may sometimes suggest diametrically opposed positions on a story, their effects are often more subtle than that: CDA approaches to news discourse have been criticized for relying too much on the assumption that there is, as Allan Bell puts it (1991: 214), 'a clearly definable relation between any given linguistic choice and a specific ideology' (a point also made in our discussion of agentless passives above). Another criticism sometimes made of CDA, that it implicitly presents readers as passive consumers of texts, manipulated or even brainwashed by the ideological biases embedded in the language of the news, is also debated in relation to the next genre we consider, advertising.

ADVERTISING: SCHEMAS, STEREOTYPES AND MODES OF ADDRESS

Advertising is a very varied discourse genre, which circulates in every medium and borrows features from many different linguistic registers. What defines it and makes it recognizable is its purpose, which is to sell a product and/or promote a brand. Because it has this promotional function, discussions of the language of advertising often focus on the rhetorical strategies which are used to present the brand or product in a positive way. But the language of advertisements is varied, and can include ways of representing a product which do not on the surface appear particularly positive. Among the most recognizable current British advertising slogans, for instance, are these two:

> You either love it or you hate it

> It does exactly what it says on the tin

The first slogan, advertising a savoury spread, concedes that many consumers think the product is revolting; the second, advertising a range of home improvement products such as varnish and wood-stain, says merely that if you buy the brand in question it will do the job it is meant to do. Not only do these slogans appear to be 'talking down' the product ('lots of people hate it'; 'it's just varnish'), they are presenting it in a way that makes advertising seem superfluous. If you love a product you don't need to be persuaded to buy it, and if you hate it no amount of promotion will persuade you. So why bother to advertise at all?

One answer might be that memorable slogans are always effective: simply making people aware of the existence and name of a product or brand tends to increase its sales. Another answer, however, takes us closer to the concerns of CDA. Arguably, the advertising slogans quoted above are persuasive not because of what they explicitly say about the *product*, but because of what they implicitly say about the *consumer*. They construct an identity for the consumer, addressing her or him in a way that solicits recognition, identification and approval. 'Yes, I'm that kind of person, and I think it's a good kind of person to be'. The first, 'love it or hate it' slogan might be saying something like: 'you're the kind of self-confident individual who knows what s/he likes, and has strong tastes rather than bland ones'. The second, 'does exactly what it says on the tin' slogan communicates something like 'you're a no-nonsense, down-to-earth type who just wants to get the job done; we know you won't be taken in by extravagant claims, so we're not going to make them for our product'.

The goal of advertising, and more generally of consumer capitalism, is not only to sell products but also to create consumers. In affluent societies, people do not buy only the things they really need, but also use consumption as a form of self-expression: while they do make choices partly on the basis of price and quality, they also consider what a product or a brand communicates—what kind of self it expresses. Creating an identity for the consumer which can be expressed through a certain product or brand is therefore part of the business of the advertising text. The more we identify with the positions advertisers construct for us textually, the more likely we are to see their products as appropriate and desirable expressions of our individual tastes and personalities.

Of course, we aren't really being addressed as individuals. Though many advertisers implicitly or explicitly congratulate us on our individuality, they have an interest in appealing to large numbers of consumers: they use market and other research to put people into categories on the basis of social/demographic characteristics (e.g. age, gender), lifestyles, attitudes, values and aspirations. If we are going to apply CDA to advertising texts, one question we might ask is how the linguistic choices made in these texts do the work of constructing and addressing the various categories or types of consumer identified by advertisers. A related 'critical' question is to what extent these textual constructions depend on and recycle dominant ideologies, so that in identifying with the positions on offer, consumers are also 'buying into' certain kinds of power and inequality.

One way in which identities or positions may be constructed in advertising texts is by offering the consumer an actual person to identify with. This may be a fictional character (like 'Katie', a housewife and mother whose domestic life was depicted in a long series of British TV advertisements for stock-cubes), or it may be a celebrity who is paid to endorse a company's products. In recent years, for instance, both print and television advertisements in L'Oréal's 'because you're worth it' series have featured well-known actresses and media personalities, including Cheryl Cole, Jane Fonda, Eva Longoria and Andie McDowell, all telling us how effective they have found the company's skin and haircare products. In digital social media the people advertisers recruit to influence our habits of consumption are our own friends and social contacts: the idea is that if we see on Facebook that our friends have 'liked' a brand, product or cultural commodity, we are more likely to want to check it out, and perhaps to 'like' it ourselves.

This kind of marketing is based on the principle that individuals tend to adopt the tastes and preferences of the people or groups they identify with. Identification is based on a combination of feeling that you *are* like someone (they represent some aspect of your actual self) and feeling that you would *like* to be like them (they represent your desires and aspirations). The use of peer-influence in social media has more to do with the first, similarity element, while in celebrity endorsement advertising it is the second, aspirational element which is foregrounded: the women in the L'Oréal campaign, for instance, are unlike the consumer in the sense that they are not just 'average looking'. At the same time, L'Oréal's advertisers clearly believe that consumers' identification depends on the featured celebrities resembling them in certain key respects: if you are marketing products to older women you need an older celebrity like Jane Fonda, and if you want women of all ethnicities to buy your products you should not feature only white celebrities. And it is taken for granted that people are more likely to identify with a celebrity of their own sex.

It is not surprising that this principle should be observed in beauty product advertising, since the products themselves are targeted towards one sex. But it may also be applied when the same product is being marketed to consumers of both sexes. Below we reproduce a case in point: a pair of celebrity endorsement advertisements produced in the mid-1970s for a revamped version of a popular British small car, 'the new Mini'. The featured celebrities, the actor James Bolam and the singer Lulu, were both popular British performers who had risen to prominence in the 1960s, and personified the qualities associated with that era, such as youth, modernity, individual style and classlessness (both are working-class northerners—Lulu is Scottish and James Bolam is from northeast England). Both were therefore good choices to endorse the Mini, itself an icon of the 'swinging 60s'. But one difference between them was crucial for the advertisers: their gender. The 'new Mini' campaign was addressed to both women and men (its unisex appeal was part of the Mini's 'modern' image). But the advertisers evidently felt that targeting both sexes effectively required separate 'male' and 'female' advertisements. The two celebrities were intended to represent the kind of man and the kind of woman a male or female reader of the text would be likely to identify with.

The advertisements were designed for publication in printed magazines such as the glossy supplements found in Sunday newspapers, where they would have occupied a double-page spread. For the purposes of this discussion, we are not going to consider the original layout or reproduce the visual images that appeared in each advertisement (the two images in fact were much more similar than the accompanying words—both were photographs showing the celebrity with a Mini). Rather, we will concentrate on the written text, and especially on the differences between the 'male' and 'female' versions.

Text 1: "I didn't know what I'd been missing"

"Don't know about you, but it's years since I drove a Mini. When I got a new one, I hardly recognised it."

No wonder, James. It's changed a lot.

Take the Mini 1000 in the picture with James Bolam. One of the new Minis.

New contoured seats. New soundproofing for a quieter drive. New improved suspension. New luxury trim. New wall-to-wall carpeting. New re-positioned controls.

The marvellous economy and low running costs haven't changed; nor has the infectious fun of Mini motoring.

As James Bolam puts it:

"If you're like me you probably always thought of the Mini as a bit out of the ordinary. The new ones are out of this world."

See for yourself at your Austin or Morris showroom.

And a word to James. Welcome back.

Text 2: "It's like falling in love all over again"

Once upon a time, Lulu drove a Mini.

And loved it so much she nearly cried when she sold it.

Recently we showed Lulu a new Mini Clubman. She said it was like falling in love all over again.

The new Clubman has new soundproofing for a quieter drive. It has an improved suspension for a smoother ride. There are new contoured seats, a luxury interior trim and wall-to-wall carpets. We've fitted new, easy to operate and good to look at controls.

Some things Lulu found easy to recognise. Like the Mini's economy and the sheer fun of Mini motoring.

As the lady said: "This thing's bigger than both of us".

Your local Austin or Morris showroom will happily arrange a re-introduction for you.

Meet a new Mini. Try a second honeymoon.

Both texts follow the same narrative schema, in which someone who once drove a Mini, but has not done so for many years, rediscovers the pleasures of their youth by trying out the new, improved version of the car. But in text 2, there is another narrative schema which is not present in text 1: Lulu's relationship to the Mini is framed as a fairy-tale romance. The text begins with the formulaic fairy-tale opening 'once upon a time', and continues with the information that Lulu 'loved' her Mini and 'cried' when she sold it. Her first encounter with the new Mini is equated with 'falling in love all over again'; later the text proposes that consumers ask a car salesman to 'arrange a reintroduction', after which, ideally, there will be a re-marriage and 'a second honeymoon'.

The way the car itself is described also differs in the two texts. Text 1 emphasizes the new Mini's enhanced technological features (contouring, soundproofing, suspension), whereas text 2 says more about the way these features make the car look and feel. In text 1 the controls have been 'repositioned', while in text 2 they are 'easy to operate and good to look at'. Another difference is grammatical: the description of the new Mini's features in text 1 takes the form of a series of units which are marked as complete by capitalization and punctuation marks, but are syntactically noun phrases rather than complete sentences containing verbs (e.g. 'New contoured seats. New soundproofing for a quieter ride'.) In the corresponding section of text 2, however, they have been expanded into complete sentences ('*The new Clubman has* new soundproofing for a quieter ride...*there are* new contoured seats').

Text 1 is presented as a three-way conversation between James Bolam, the reader and the narrative voice representing the maker of the product. James Bolam twice addresses the reader directly, using the pronoun *you*, and is addressed directly himself. In text 2, by contrast, Lulu is almost entirely mute. The narrative voice speaks for her and about her, reporting what she thought, felt and said: there is only one direct quotation of her words, prefaced by 'as the lady said'—and ironically the words that follow are not Lulu's own, but a recognizable allusion to a line in the film *Casablanca*.[4]

How should we interpret these differences? On the assumption that the most fundamental distinction between the two texts is that text 1 features a male celebrity whereas text 2 features a female celebrity (and that this is a strategy for constructing each text's primary addressee as either a male or a female consumer), we might reason that the discourse differences just outlined relate to gender, and argue that the texts

- Represent men and women as different in their desires and preferences—both in general terms (e.g. women are more concerned with romantic love) and more specifically in what they want from their cars (e.g. men care about technology/performance, women care about a car's looks and how easy it is to drive).
- Represent men and women as different in the way they use language. This point relates to the observations made above about the more active speaking role given to James Bolam in text 1, and the use of incomplete versus complete sentences in the description of the car's features. The latter might seem to have nothing to do with gender, but there is a potential connection. The incomplete sentences of text 1 exhibit what some linguists call 'economy', whereas the complete sentences of text 2 exhibit 'elaboration'. In English-speaking cultures, there is a folk-belief that men are more economical than women with words, and that this is a desirable masculine trait. Saying only as much as needs to be said, in the least elaborate way possible, is a characteristic of the hero in popular genres like action films and westerns. Perhaps, then, this feature of text 1 reflects the advertisers' desire to create a 'masculine' voice with which male readers will identify.
- Address men and women readers differently. The combination of direct address and economy (if we accept the interpretation of this as a marker of masculinity) positions the reader of text 1 as a participant in 'man-to-man' conversation. The female reader of text 2, by contrast, is not positioned as a participant in any kind of conversation: rather, the text casts her from the first as someone being told a story.

Overall, we might conclude that commonplace ideological beliefs about gender are being reflected and reproduced in this campaign through (a) the way the advertisements *represent* men and women, and (b) the way the advertisements *address* male and female readers.

You might wonder whether the points we have just made have any relevance for analysts looking at advertising today. Sexist attitudes and gender stereotypes may have been rife in the 1970s, but hasn't the world moved on? In the following activity we ask you to consider that question.

ACTIVITY

Find two recent/current print or billboard advertisements promoting a similar product or service, where one appears to target a male consumer and the other a female one. For instance, you might choose advertisements for a category of products that comes in distinct 'male' and 'female' versions (e.g. moisturizer, shampoo, razors), or one that comes in multiple varieties/ brands, some of which are marketed more to men while others are marketed more to women (e.g. soft drinks, breakfast cereals, cars). Or you may be able to find a case like the Mini campaign, where there are two gender-specific versions of the same message (this sometimes applies to public health messages, such as government-sponsored TV ads about diet, smoking or drinking). When you have chosen your examples, consider the following questions.

1 How does each text construct the target consumer?
2 What similarities and differences are there in the way the two texts represent the product or service being advertised (or in the case of public information texts, the attitude/behaviour being promoted)?
3 If there are differences, do you think they are related to gender, or that they reproduce particular ideologies of gender? Why or why not?
4 Do these twenty-first-century examples have anything in common with the 1970s examples discussed above? How are they similar and how are they different?

BEING CRITICAL OF CRITICAL DISCOURSE ANALYSIS

At this point we want to go back and consider our analysis of the Mini advertisements more critically. What we said about these texts is an example of the kind of interpretation that some-times prompts complaints of ideological or political bias on the part of the analyst ('you're seeing sexism where none exists'). For instance, someone who disagreed with our interpreta-tion might say: 'yes, these texts are differentiated by the gender of the celebrity, but that doesn't mean every other difference between them must be related to gender'. Or 'these ads are clearly tongue-in-cheek, so what they're saying about men and women could be intended ironically'. Or 'how do you know that readers identify with these celebrities or these representations of their gender'?

How might we respond to these points? To our first hypothetical critic, we would have to admit that our interpretation is based on treating the relevance of gender as a given, but we would want to ask: 'if the differences are not about gender, what else might they be about?' A challenger who offered no convincing alternative account would be suggesting that the differences between the two texts were just random phenomena of no significance, and in some cases (like the use of a 'romance' schema in text 2 but not text 1) that does not seem very plausible.

The 'irony' challenge is interesting, because nowadays it is common for accusations of sexism to be met with the argument that the disputed utterance or text, though offensive if taken at face value, was in fact intended ironically: it is not *enacting* sexism, but on the contrary, poking fun at it. In advertising there is a specific version of this tendency which Judith Williamson (2003) has dubbed 'retrosexism', where stereotypically sexist scenarios are used, but are pointedly located in the past (e.g. a subservient housewife is dressed in 1950s clothing and placed in a 1950s kitchen). The advertiser can then claim, if challenged, to be making an 'ironic' comment on the sexist attitudes of the period depicted in the advertisement, which by implication has nothing to do with the present. Williamson thinks this is an unconvincing defence. She argues that what this kind of advertising really expresses is nostalgia for a pre-feminist era when gender roles and relationships were more straightforward. It might also be pointed out that recycling a proposition 'ironically' still involves restating it. If a stereotype or prejudice is really outmoded or unacceptable, it tends not to be restated, 'ironically' or otherwise—there is no genre of 'retroracist' advertising, for instance. So, while the humour that is an element of many advertisements should certainly be addressed in any critical analysis of the text, part of being 'critical' is to consider the way humour can be used to make objectionable representations more acceptable, and to counter potential criticisms (in that critics can be accused of simply lacking a sense of humour).

The last of the critical questions listed above, 'how do you know whether readers identify with the celebrities in the text, or accept the propositions about gender in the text?', brings us up against the limits of CDA, and indeed of written discourse analysis more generally. The meaning of a text is not fully determined (though it is to some degree constrained) by the content, structure and form of that text: in the final analysis, it has to be produced by the recipient (we will have more to say about this in Chapter 8). In cases like print advertising, analysts usually have no access to either the process of interpretation or its outcome (whereas in interactive discourse the recipient's following contribution offers evidence of how s/he interpreted previous ones). We therefore do not know whether what we find in a text using discourse analytic methods is either noticed or understood in the same way by (other) readers of the text. We can only make claims about what is 'there' to be noticed, and proposals about how it is likely to be understood. Similarly, we usually have no access to the intentions of the author of a text, or their reasons for making particular linguistic choices.

Some analysts have tried to address these limitations by supplementing analysis of the text itself with other kinds of information. For instance, ethnographic research on the institutional practices of journalists or advertising agencies may show that certain features of news or advertising discourse arise less from purely ideological considerations than from the way the text-production process works (e.g. see Bell (1991) and Cotter (2010) on news, and Myers (1998) on advertising). Another 'supplementary' research strategy involves using methods designed to probe the reception of a text by specific audiences. As part of a project dealing with the representation of poverty in late twentieth-century Britain (Meinhof and Richardson 1994), Kay Richardson carried out focus group research to investigate the way different groups of viewers interpreted a television documentary series on the subject (she found that their interpretations were affected by whether they had personal experience of poverty). Deborah Cameron (2006b, and see also Chapter 8) examined evidence relating to the interpretation of advertisements which had attracted complaints of sexism or homophobia, using the written judgments produced by the Advertising Standards Authority (ASA), which adjudicates such complaints in Britain. Today, when most print and broadcast media outlets also publish online, and encourage interaction via their websites, the comments posted about a text may be a useful source of evidence about the way readers have interpreted it.

Critics may also dispute the claims being made about a text by asking questions about CDA's methodology. They may ask, for instance, whether the examples being used to illustrate a pattern are representative of the data sample as a whole, and if the pattern itself has any significance, or if it could be the result of chance. Those questions could be asked about our observation that the two Mini advertisements describe the car's features differently, using incomplete sentences in the male text and complete ones in the female text. Since we only looked at one pair of texts, we cannot show that this difference exemplifies a larger-scale pattern: the fact that the same information was formulated more 'economically' in the male text might be just a coincidence (it could equally have been the other way round, it just happened not to be in these examples). If that were the case, it would undermine our proposal that economy features were used to construct a 'masculine' voice.

This is the kind of issue that can sometimes be addressed by using the methods of corpus linguistics. By comparing the texts you are interested in with a reference corpus, a comparable but larger body of text which can be searched and manipulated using computer software, you can find out whether something you see in your sample—such as an association between economy features and male speakers or male addressees—exemplifies a more general pattern of usage, and whether the differences you claim are analytically significant are also statistically significant (i.e. very unlikely to have occurred by chance). You can also compile your own corpus (of news articles, or advertisements, or whatever you want to focus on) and use software packages designed for corpus analysis to look for linguistic patterns which you might not notice if you relied only on your own intuitions. Increasingly, critical discourse analysts are among those turning to corpus methods (e.g. see Baker 2006; Koller and Mautner 2004; Stubbs 2004), on the basis that adopting those methods can make critical analysis more 'rigorous', less vulnerable to the objection that the analyst is seeing patterns where none exist, or offering purely subjective interpretations. Corpus-based discourse analysis (including the 'critical' variety) is the subject of the next chapter.

SUMMARY

This chapter has discussed CDA as a politically committed approach to discourse analysis, characterized by concerns about discourse as a site where ideologies, power relations and forms of social control are reproduced, and particular accounts of reality are 'naturalized' (made to seem normal, desirable or inevitable). We have considered some of the linguistic features and patterns which are commonly examined when CDA is applied to written texts (e.g. lexical and grammatical choices, the use of familiar cultural schemas, modes of address which position the reader in a particular way), looking at examples drawn from two written genres that have been studied extensively by CDA practitioners, news reporting and advertising. We have also discussed some of the criticisms levelled at CDA, and considered what kinds of claims can or cannot be based on this kind of analysis. Since CDA is often used in conjunction with other approaches (e.g. corpus-based and multimodal discourse analysis), it will be discussed further in several of the following chapters.

FURTHER READING

Bloor and Bloor (2007) is an introductory textbook devoted to CDA, dealing with both spoken interaction and written text. Fairclough (1995) is a book-length survey by one of CDA's most influential figures, while van Dijk (2003) is an article-length survey by another leading theorist and practitioner. News discourse is treated from a CDA perspective by Fowler (1991); two other books on the language of news (though they do not deal exclusively with 'critical' concerns) are Bell (1991) and Cotter (2010). Advertising is the subject of Cook (2006) and Myers (1998), while Lazar (2005) is a collection illustrating the application of CDA to gender issues. CDA work on a range of topics can be found in the journals *Discourse & Society* and *Critical Discourse Studies*.

NOTES

1   On this debate, see Widdowson (1995) and Toolan (1997).
2   www.dailymail.co.uk/news/article-2254205/Police-called-Welsh-druid-refuses-pay-corner-shop-cashier-asked-money-ENGLISH.html, accessed 29 December 2012.
3   www.huffingtonpost.co.uk/2012/12/28/welsh-archdruid-spar-english-language_n_2376424.html, accessed 7 February 2013.
4   We are not suggesting that any of the words in the texts represent any actual utterance produced by either celebrity: we assume the texts were composed by copywriters.

7 Corpus-based discourse analysis

In this chapter we examine an approach which is defined by its use of analytic methods developed in the field of corpus linguistics. *Corpus* (the plural form is *corpora*) is a Latin word meaning 'body'. In linguistics, it has historically been used to refer to a 'body' of data—a sample of utterances or texts—which provides evidence about the language it comes from. The term can still be used with that general meaning, but today it is most often used to refer to a particular kind of sample: a large collection of authentic linguistic material which is stored in computer-readable form and can be analysed using computer software.

The use of corpus methods adds a *quantitative* dimension to discourse analysis, using statistical techniques to identify patterns in the data being analysed. That is not to say the approach is purely quantitative: qualitative analysis is also needed to interpret the patterns and explain their significance in context. But since discourse analysis is traditionally thought of as a qualitative approach, it might be asked why some analysts—in fact, a growing number—have found it helpful to adopt quantitative methods.

One argument which is often made is that quantitative methods eliminate a potential source of inaccuracy, unreliability and bias, namely over-dependence on the analyst's intuitions about what patterns are most common or most significant in a sample of discourse. Statistical analysis can reveal patterns which are not obvious to a human analyst, whether because they are too subtle to be noticeable or because a researcher's unconscious preconceptions cause them to be overlooked. Another argument is that by using computer software, analysts can deal with much larger quantities of data, and so put forward more convincing evidence in support of their claims. Both points have been emphasized by corpus analysts who adopt a 'critical' stance, and who want to argue that certain patterns of language-use are ideologically significant. As we saw in Chapter 6, this argument is vulnerable to the objection that it is based on a selective reading of the evidence (i.e. it relies too heavily on a few examples which support the analyst's interpretation), or that the analyst has not examined enough data to be able to show that there is a systematic pattern. That kind of objection can be countered by offering statistical evidence that the pattern occurs systematically and frequently (or significantly more frequently than would be expected by chance) in a large sample of discourse data.

In the following discussion we will expand on the points just made by looking in more detail at the principles that inform corpus-based approaches, the kinds of questions they can be used to address, and the insights they have produced when applied to written discourse. We should note, though, that our discussion will not contain detailed instructions on how to do corpus analysis: this is a case where the skills involved are best acquired through hands-on practice, and the most useful sources of practical advice (other than an experienced tutor) are the guides and manuals designed for a particular corpus or piece of software. We will refer to several specific corpora, and to some 'generic' software (programs which can be used with many different corpora), but in a single chapter of a textbook it is impossible to cover all the resources readers might want to work with. More technical information is given in some of the texts listed as suggestions for further reading; we have also included a section listing some widely-used resources (corpora and software programs) and how they can be accessed.

CORPORA: A BRIEF INTRODUCTION

In its current form, corpus linguistics is a product of the digital technology that became widely available in the 1980s. Though the basic goal remains the same as it was before computers existed—to identify patterns in the structure and use of language by systematically examining a collection of real examples—technology allows this to be done on a much larger scale. If your aim is to make general statements about some aspect of language structure or usage, then arguably size does matter: a sample consisting of millions of words is preferable to a sample of a few thousand. By pre-digital standards, almost all electronic corpora are large. But their exact size and composition depends on the purpose for which they were compiled.

The 'prototypical' kind of corpus is intended to provide linguists with a representative sample of a whole language or linguistic variety (most often a national standard variety, such as British or US English). Corpora of this general or *reference* type tend to be large in size (100 million words or more) and varied in composition (i.e. they include a range of different text-types). An example is the British National Corpus (BNC), which contains around 100 million words of British English, most of it dating from the 1980s and early 1990s. Though some of it is conversational speech, most of the sample is written text, drawn from sources that include published fiction and non-fiction books, newspapers and other periodicals, academic writing, student essays, and letters. Another large corpus, the Bank of English, is mainly British, but includes a substantial proportion (around 30%) of material from US and other non-British sources; unlike the BNC, it has continued to be expanded since it was first compiled. For the USA, a widely-used resource is COCA, the Corpus of Contemporary American English, and there is an expanding series of million-word corpora belonging to the 'ICE' ('International Corpus of English') project, representing various geographically-defined varieties (e.g. Canadian, East African, Irish, Jamaican, New Zealand, Sri Lankan).

Other corpora are smaller and more specialized. Some are designed for historical research on the usage of a particular period, or the development of a language over time: the Helsinki Corpus of English Texts, for instance, contains texts spanning the period between the mid-eighth and late eighteenth centuries. Other corpora concentrate on a particular discourse genre. Among written genres, academic/scientific writing is well represented in collections such as the Reading Academic Text Corpus, which is made up of articles and doctoral theses in subjects ranging from agricultural botany to history, and the even more specific ALIBI corpus, which consists of 308 biomedical research articles. There are also corpora containing written texts produced by learners of English as a foreign/second language, such as the Longman Learner's Corpus. And of course, there are corpora—including both large reference corpora and more specialized ones—for numerous languages other than English.

Purpose-built corpora typically contain not only the linguistic material itself, but also other information which is relevant for analysis. It is common for texts to be 'tagged' with **part-of-speech** information (i.e. each word is assigned to a class such as 'preposition', 'verb' or 'noun'), which makes it possible to investigate the patterning not only of specific words and phrases, but also of items or sequences with particular grammatical characteristics. Corpora also include 'metadata' (i.e. supplementary information *about* the data, like the source and publication date of a text and demographic information on the writer's date/place of birth, gender, etc.). This is useful where a researcher compiling a sample from a large corpus wants to ensure its composition is socially as well as linguistically 'balanced' (e.g. includes equal numbers of male- and female-authored texts), or if the researcher wishes to exclude texts produced outside a certain time-frame.

There is a difference between a corpus, which is specifically designed for linguistic research, and a digital text *archive*, which is intended only to store text: the contents of an archive may be haphazard and unstructured, and will lack the metadata and annotation features mentioned above. For certain purposes, however, archives can be useful data sources. For instance, the website LexisNexis offers access to the full text of articles from a range of newspapers; individual newspapers may also have searchable electronic archives. Examples of other specific text-types, ranging from recipes to Supreme Court judgments, may be available in usable quantities on publicly-accessible websites. Such archived material can be used to build your own corpus, which can then be analysed using tools designed for the purpose. However, researchers using archived data to build a corpus will have to make decisions about how to sample the material in the archive, and they will also have to 'clean' the data (e.g. get rid of anything which is not part of the text itself, and convert all items into a format their software will work on) before it can be analysed.

Some linguists argue that the term 'corpus' should not be applied to just any collection of linguistic material, but only to what one textbook-writer calls 'a collection of texts or part of texts upon which some *general linguistic analysis* can be conducted' (Meyer 2002: xi, emphasis added). For this writer, other kinds of corpora do not provide a solid basis for linguistic generalizations. However, what counts as an appropriate data sample depends on the question being investigated. Some of the questions investigated by discourse analysts do require a large balanced sample from which to generalize (e.g. the work on register variation discussed in Chapter 2), but many are questions about a specific aspect of language-use in a particular context or genre. In those cases, a reference corpus compiled to facilitate 'general linguistic analysis' may not provide the necessary data. For instance, Jennifer Rey (2001) examined changes over time in the dialogue given to male and female characters in *Star Trek*, using a corpus of scripts from the original TV series and two of its later spin-offs. She could not have found these in any pre-existing reference corpus, but they were clearly the most appropriate data for the study she wanted to do, which was not about English 'in general' but specifically about the dialogue in *Star Trek*. Corpus *methods* can be used to find patterns in a data sample whether or not those patterns can be generalized beyond that sample. Which leads us to the next question: what *are* 'corpus methods', and what can a discourse analyst use them for?

CORPUS METHODS

We said earlier that corpus methods are used to identify patterns in data samples. One type of pattern which analysts often look for relates to *frequency*: how often a particular form (a word, lemma[1] or grammatical feature) appears in the sample under investigation. (This would usually be expressed not as a raw number of tokens of the form in question, but in terms of its percentage contribution to the sample or its occurrences per million words). The overall frequency of a single item is not usually very informative on its own, but it becomes more significant when comparisons are made with other items. For instance, you might compare the frequencies of two expressions which have the same meaning or referent, but whose connotations are different, or which belong to different 'discourses' in the sense of 'verbal representations that construct reality in certain ways'. Examples might include word-pairs like *gay* and *homosexual*, or *fat* and *obese*. Paul Baker (2006) gives the more complex example of the various multi-word expressions that centre on the item *wheelchair*, e.g. *confined to a wheelchair* and *wheelchair bound*, *wheelchair user*. As he points out, the first two belong to a discourse that constructs disability as a form of disadvantage or deficiency, whereas the third belongs to a discourse in which that construction is resisted. Looking at frequencies in a large general corpus might tell us something about which discourse is the dominant one. As well as looking at their relative frequency, it is possible to look at the *dispersion* of contrasting terms across the different subcategories of texts in a large corpus, to see if the terms appear in the same types or if each tends to predominate in certain types.

Another purpose for which frequency information can be used is to identify important themes or concepts in a discourse sample. Once again, though, the importance of a word or expression is not determined by its absolute frequency (the highest-frequency items in most English corpora will be grammatical function words like *the*, *and* and *to*); what you really want to know is whether its frequency is higher than would normally be expected. That of course presupposes that we have some measure of its expected or 'normal' frequency. For that purpose, the most commonly-used measure is the frequency of the item in a large representative sample of the language variety in question. To gauge whether something appears with higher than expected frequency in a specific sample, you compare its frequency in that sample with its frequency in a larger reference corpus. If you use a program such as AntConc or WordSmith, the method can be employed to identify certain items as 'keywords' (i.e. items which are significantly more frequent in your sample than in the sample you are comparing it with), and to produce a 'keyness' score for each. The results can then be rank-ordered, allowing the analyst to select items for more detailed examination.

A detailed examination of items in a corpus looks not only at their frequency, but also at their contexts of use and their relationships with other items. In that connection, one common analytic procedure involves examining the *concordances* of a word, lemma or phrase. A concordance is a list of every occurrence of the item you are interested in, and what corpus analysis programs typically produce is known as a 'KWIC' ('key word in context') concordance. Each occurrence of the search-term is displayed in a single line of text, with the search-term in the middle, and a few words of preceding and following text on either side, as shown in the example in Figure 7.1. (Here we should point out a potentially confusing feature of the terminology we are using: a 'key word in context' is simply the word or other item you have requested concordances for, and need not be a keyword in the other sense outlined above.)

The patterns a discourse analyst would be looking for in a set of KWIC concordance lines are about meaning in context, and their identification is not a mechanical process, it is an interpretive one. This is illustrated in Paul Baker's analysis of the use of the words *refugee* and *refugees* in a corpus of newspaper articles taken from the online archive Newsbank (Baker 2006: 76–84). He found that the concordance lines for *refugees* frequently included quantifying expressions (usually denoting large numbers, e.g. 'tens of thousands'), and expressions which metaphorically equated refugees with an undifferentiated mass or an uncontrolled flow of

```
telligence might be obtained immediately after an  incident.
. General Fay is also believed to be examining an  incident at Abu Ghraib last October in which several Iraqi
ce. Last November, Colonel Jordan investigated an  incident involving Specialist Armin J. Cruz and Specialist
9th Military Intelligence Battalion, described an  incident of sexually tinged abuse against an Iraqi woman b
, including dereliction of duty, stemming from an  incident on Nov. 8 in which prisoners were stripped, hoode
anuary. In one instance, the transcript shows, an  incident of abuse was reported -- but apparently to a staf
abuse cases at Abu Ghraib. The diary mentioned an  incident in November 2003 involving a detainee that Sergea
  forced nudity was such accepted practice that an  incident report written by two of the soldiers now charged
lly resumed sovereignty in June. It was the first  incident of its kind in front of the embassy office, thoug
ison under Saddam Hussein. Mr. Amin mentioned one  incident that took place in the 1980's, in which, he said,
estigation of detainee abuse began. In the second  incident, he refused at least seven times to follow a plat
etainee who had been shot. He did not report that  incident. Sgt. Neil Wallin, another medic, recorded on Nov
hraib but was kept off the prison roster. In that  incident, the Navy personnel initially denied any abuse. B
er detainees. A civilian interpreter reported the  incident, fearing that the humiliation could incite other
ng shot. A subsequent Army investigation into the  incident, which took place nearly four hours after a major
ional step of a suspension in connection with the  incident. General Karpinski was quoted in The New York Tim
  and translator, intelligence officials said. The incident is being investigated by the C.I.A.'s inspector g
, Specialist Graner's lawyer, said he doubted the  incident took place and questioned Specialist Sivits's ver
  before interrogation. The three prisoners in the incident involving Specialist Cruz were not considered pot
  82nd Airborne Division, which was accused in the incident, also declined to comment on the case beyond the
  investigation. According to the four Iraqis, the incident began in Falluja after Friday Prayer on Jan. 2. W
upset this had happened.'' Captain Reese said the  incident occurred after an attack on the International Com
d he believed that the officer did not report the  incident to anyone else, so the report went nowhere. ''I t
ce, but it harshly criticized the handling of the  incident. Among the problems cited were overcrowding, lack
o embarrass him.' '' Mr. Stefanowicz reported the  incident, and Specialist Spencer was moved out of the inte
nger, to review the military's findings about the  incident in light of the scandal over the treatment of pri
ling that the man had severe facial injuries. The  incident was described in testimony at a closed hearing ea
of the soldiers involved and other details of the  incident. Spokesmen for the XVIII Airborne Corps did not r
ges to emerge during the prisoner-abuse case. The  incident also drew attention because the detainee was bein
ed during apprehension." But the murkiness of the  incident, which is also being investigated by the C.I.A.'s
ges to emerge during the prisoner-abuse case. The  incident also drew attention because the detainee was bein
g that he was, in fact, ''the perpetrator in this  incident,'' Special Agent Pieron said. He said he believed
n operations to ensure that similar ''disgraceful  incidents'' would not occur again. ''Such practices do not
at some point. Other abuses appeared to stem from  incidents inside the prison. An American interpreter who al
ng we can say,'' she said. Most of the Abu Ghraib  incidents were reported before January, said military intel
y Rumsfeld had actual knowledge of these horrific  incidents in the prison system that were the direct result
stan where two prisoners died in December 2002 in  incidents that are being investigated as homicides. For bot
and,'' he said. ''I believe that we have isolated  incidents that have taken place.'' After nearly four hours
ners Is Seen as a Pervasive Pattern, Not Isolated  Incidents In the weeks since photographs of naked detainees
that between October and December 2003 ''numerous  incidents of sadistic, blatant and wanton criminal abuses w
soldier poured cold water on him. Among the other  incidents cited by military personnel: a man was shoved to
el said that so far there were some 30 reported    incidents of mistreatment, and 66 confirmed abuses so far.
military personnel. At least four of the reported  incidents of abuse had occurred in the high-security sectio
ere transferred to Abu Ghraib, but at least seven  incidents said to be cited in the documents took place at t
oldiers or officers, personnel issues or specific  incidents of wrongdoing at Abu Ghraib and elsewhere in Iraq
a fact that he was participating in numerous such  incidents.'' Two weeks ago, Specialist Sivits abruptly left
ral Jacoby on June 24. The memo suggests that the  incidents experienced by the officials occurred earlier in
her the members of the task force involved in the  incidents are under investigation. The Pentagon has also sa
ther any action had been taken to investigate the  incidents. The situation of the p
tements have been verified, though several of the  incidents were military or civilian. Col. Jill E. Morgenthaler, chief of public affai
e was encouraged in order to get information. The  incidents form the basis of the charges against seven membe
repeated inquiries for more information about the  incidents. Captain Wood had served 10 years in enlisted ran
```

Figure 7.1

liquid (e.g. 'flood', 'streaming', 'overflowing', 'swelling', 'heaving'). Baker argues that these are not random choices, but reflect a consistent tendency for news reports to treat the movement of people seeking refuge as a kind of natural disaster which threatens the safety of the communities they move to. Other recurring patterns represented refugees as tragic victims, passive recipients of others' charity, criminals and (occasionally) terrorists.

One conclusion that might be drawn from these findings is that *refugee(s)* in English news discourse has what is called a 'negative semantic (or discourse) prosody': its meaning tends—at least in the context of news reporting—to be negative rather than positive or neutral. This is not something you would necessarily discover by just looking the word up in a dictionary. A dictionary would treat *refugee* as simply a category label referring to people seeking refuge from persecution, war or natural disaster. But by looking at concordance lines in a corpus, it becomes possible to see that in actual usage the word *refugee* is not just a neutral category label: it is recurrently linked to negative concepts like natural disaster and crime.

Other patterns corpus analysts look for involve statistical relationships among linguistic forms. One such relationship that is often investigated is the **collocations** of a word or other expression, that is which other words/expressions it is most strongly associated with or most often found in close proximity to (within a certain number of words: the number or 'span' considered can be varied by the corpus user). Relationships based on proximity can sometimes be spotted in KWIC concordances, as with Baker's observation that *refugees* was often preceded by a quantifying expression. But it is also possible to search for the most significant collocations of an item using more sophisticated measures. Another kind of relationship that can be investigated is the tendency of certain features (which need not be single words or phrases) to cluster together in a sample. This approach was used in the corpus-based work on register variation which was discussed in Chapter 2. What Biber and his colleagues labelled a 'dimension of variation', like 'involved—informational', was defined not by the presence/absence of any single feature, but by the co-occurrence of a cluster of features; these clusters also turned out to be significantly more frequent in some registers than others. For instance, conversation and personal letters included high frequencies of a cluster of 'involved' features such as first- and second-person pronouns and 'private' verbs like *know*, *think* and *feel*; expository writing, by contrast, showed low frequencies for this set of features.

In the rest of this chapter we will consider some studies in which questions about written discourse have been investigated using corpus methods. The specific examples we have chosen as illustrations come from three more general categories:

1. 'Descriptive' studies, where corpus methods are used to establish what linguistic characteristics are found in texts of a particular register or genre. An example already mentioned is the work of Biber and others on register variation; below we will look more specifically at some corpus-based studies of written academic genres.
2. 'Sociolinguistic' studies, where corpus methods are used to investigate similarities and differences in the written discourse produced by or for members of different social groups, such as younger and older people or women and men. Rey's study of gender differences in *Star Trek* dialogue is an example; but whereas she examined scripted dialogue as evidence of the writers' ideas about male and female speech, we will consider some research in which the question was whether men and women write differently.
3. 'Critical' studies, where corpus methods are used to identify ideologically significant patterns in discourse. Baker's analysis of news reports about refugees is an example of this kind of research; our discussion will focus on a study—in fact, a student project—examining news reports on sexual violence in conflict situations.

DESCRIBING GENRES: ACADEMIC WRITING

Academic writing is an important research topic, of interest to researchers who study professional discourse, scientific registers, and academic literacy (the teaching of writing in and for higher education). Corpus methods have been widely used in these areas of research, and the resources available are quite extensive: as we mentioned above, academic writing is often included in reference corpora like the BNC, and there are also numerous specialist corpora devoted to it.

A theoretical framework that has been influential in research on academic writing is the 'genre theory' associated with John Swales (e.g. Swales 1990). Rather than treating 'academic discourse' as a single undifferentiated entity, genre theorists treat it as a collection of genres which are recognized and referred to by expert members of the academic discourse community—for instance, 'essay', 'report', 'thesis', 'abstract', 'article', etc. For researchers who are interested in describing academic genres, an important question is *how* members of the community recognize a text as an example of a particular genre. Do the texts produced by expert academic writers, or accepted by them as legitimate, show genre-specific patterns of language-use, and if so, what are those patterns? To answer those questions, many researchers have turned to corpus methods.

One advantage that is often claimed for corpus methods is that they can reveal patterns which are not intuitively obvious, or which run counter to prevailing assumptions. In the case of academic writing, it is commonly assumed that writers aim to be as 'objective' and impersonal as possible; but corpus-based research suggests that the reality is more complicated. On one hand, work like Biber's on register variation shows that academic discourse contains fewer markers of overt stance-taking than most other registers. On the other hand, research examining academic and scientific writing in detail suggests that certain kinds of stance-taking are important features of these registers, where they are used to construct authority and credibility. In a discussion of stance-taking in experimental research reports—a particularly 'fact-oriented' genre which we might expect to be strongly influenced by the scientific norm of 'objectivity'—Susan Hunston points out that scientists reporting new research findings are trying not just to disseminate facts, but also 'to persuade the academic community to accept the new knowledge claims' (Hunston 1994: 192). The genre, in other words, has a rhetorical as well as an informational function.

In academic discourse, one of the commonest forms of stance-taking is *epistemic*, to do with the status of knowledge. Linguistic markers of epistemic stance are used to indicate the degree of a writer's commitment to the truth of a proposition, the validity of a claim or the significance of a finding. They include both forms that weaken the degree of commitment or certainty expressed (e.g. hedges like the adverb *possibly* and the modal verbs *may* and *might*) and forms that strengthen commitment (e.g. 'boosters' such as *obviously* and formulas presupposing the truth/validity of a claim, like 'as we have shown...'). Both types can serve the persuasive purpose of presenting the writer as a knowledgeable member of the academic community. Markers of uncertainty may be used to signify an appropriate degree of caution or modesty in making claims, while expressions of certainty can be used to display the writer's awareness of what is accepted by the community as established knowledge.

The following examples show how the same stance-taking device can fulfil the various functions just outlined. In each of the four sentences reproduced, the writer has used a *that*-complement clause preceded by a word that conveys a greater or lesser degree of commitment to the assertion which follows. In the first two examples the stance being taken is cautious (the italicized words are hedges); in the second two it is confident. (Examples 1, 3 and 4 are taken from Gray and Biber (2012); example 2 is from Hyland (2012).)

1. It is *possible* that the data were too noisy to detect an underlying trend.
2. Although it *seems* that some group II introns are spliced efficiently under physiological conditions only if aided by trans-acting factors, it remains *plausible* that others may actually self-splice in vivo.
3. It is *known* that adolescents of this age rapidly move from one mood state to another.
4. It is *clear* that the performance difference grows with the number of processors used.

Research suggests that stance-taking is a feature of academic writing which less experienced writers often struggle with. For example, Ken Hyland (2012) looked at the use of stance markers in a 630,000-word corpus of project reports written by undergraduate students in Hong Kong, comparing their work with that of expert academic writers, as represented in a larger corpus of published research articles. Overall, he found the students used stance-markers less frequently than the experts; there were also differences in the way they used them. The student reports contained far fewer hedges marking caution or uncertainty than the published articles; conversely, the frequency of boosters was significantly higher in the student than the expert corpus.

This statistical finding prompted Hyland to look more closely at the way boosters were used in student reports. He found that examples like the following were fairly typical (2012: 146–7):

5. High EQ is *definitely* an advantage in any domain of life and *we all know* that a person with high EQ can *certainly* manage their own feelings well and deal effectively with others.
6. The *remarkable* inertness of the nitrido function in technetium complexes towards proton-active reagents permits an *extraordinarily* wide variety of substitution reactions.

These examples show that the students not only use boosters more frequently than expert writers, they also use stronger boosters (e.g. *definitely/certainly* rather than *clearly/evidently*). Instead of projecting the desired qualities of confidence and authority, these terms make the writer appear dogmatic or over-enthusiastic. As Hyland comments, in expert academic writing 'persuasion is accomplished by a more calculated and measured expression of attitude' (2012: 148). To students, however, it is often unclear what will be judged as appropriately 'measured'. Hyland speculates that this may pose particular problems for writers who are taking on the discourse conventions of a non-native language and culture.

In some contexts, the stances taken in academic discourse may have ethical implications. In biomedical science, there is ongoing debate about the involvement of commercial stakeholders like pharmaceutical companies in conducting or funding research on the safety and effectiveness of their products. The producer of a drug or treatment has a commercial interest in its success, and there is concern that in some cases this has led commercially-funded researchers to deviate from the norms of transparency and accountability (e.g. by not publishing all their results, or not describing their methods fully so that other scientists can try to replicate their findings). Alan Gross and Paula Chesley (2012) conducted a corpus study to investigate whether the same kind of bias might also affect the language used to present findings in published reports.

The question Gross and Chesley asked was whether studies funded by a commercial stakeholder were 'more likely to report their results in a way that encourages readers to give more credence to their claims than their evidential base permits' (2012: 90). One way to give a claim more credence than the evidence warrants is to be sparing in the use of hedging devices which indicate uncertainty or caution. This strategy is less noticeable than its opposite (using boosters), since it is a matter of what writers leave out of their discourse rather than what they put into it. But if there is in fact a pattern, comparing the statistical frequency of hedging in reports of industry-funded and non-industry-funded studies should reveal it. Gross and Chesley used the ALIBI corpus of biomedical research articles to test the hypothesis that articles reporting the findings of industry-funded studies would show lower frequencies of hedging than those reporting the findings of non-industry-funded studies. Their analysis supported the hypothesis: articles reporting industry-funded research had significantly lower hedging scores.

Once again, though, qualitative analysis can be a useful supplement to statistical findings. At the beginning of their article Gross and Chesley discuss an example which, on the face of things, does not fit the pattern. It comes from an industry-funded study, but the stance adopted is cautious, marked by repeated hedging (shown here in italics):

7. It is *possible* that any *apparent* differences between JUPITER and each of the prior trials *may* simply reflect the play of chance.

In a purely quantitative analysis of hedging frequencies, this example would just become part of the aggregated score for all reports on industry-funded studies. If there were enough examples like it they would make the pattern appear weaker. But a qualitative analysis, focusing more closely on what this statement is being used to communicate in context, reveals that the example is not an exception to the overall trend, but exemplifies that trend in a different way.

JUPITER was the name of a trial conducted on a new statin—a cholesterol-lowering drug—to investigate how effective it was in preventing strokes. The results of the trial were more positive than those of earlier trials, and suggested that the drug was highly effective. But a subsequent meta-analysis (a type of study which puts together the findings of many different studies) concluded that if all the trials were taken into account, the new drug was no more effective than existing statins. The hedging in example 7 can be analysed as a strategy for addressing this criticism. The writers concede that the positive results of the JUPITER trial 'may simply reflect the play of chance', thus appearing to take a cautious position on their own positive claims for the new drug; but they are also implicitly urging caution about the less positive conclusions drawn in the meta-analysis. Acknowledging an opponent's argument as one 'possible' interpretation of the facts at hand can be a rhetorically effective way of defending your own position, since it logically implies that other interpretations—including your own—are also 'possible'.

This example suggests that a purely quantitative approach to hedging (i.e. just counting frequencies) does not capture the full range and complexity of their uses in biomedical research articles, and may not tell the whole story about the bias being investigated. While statistical analysis of large samples can uncover patterns that could not be identified in a single text or a small number of similar texts, it is often helpful for our understanding of a pattern to examine individual examples (and apparent counter-examples) in more detail, relating them to the whole text they are part of and to the larger communicative and social context.

INVESTIGATING DIFFERENCES: GENDER AND WRITING

Comparing the patterning of linguistic features in two or more datasets is a common procedure in corpus studies. The two studies discussed in the last section both compared the frequency of certain stance-markers in two sets of texts differentiated by a particular characteristic—in Hyland's case, the writer's degree of expertise, and in Gross and Chesley's, whether or not the writer had received industry funding. And corpus methods have often been seen as well-suited to the investigation of a more general and much-debated question: whether and how men and women differ in their use of language. If you want to answer that question 'objectively', it might seem that taking large samples of the language produced by each sex, and systematically comparing them using quantitative methods, is the obvious way to go about it. But in practice this is far from straightforward, as is illustrated by a long line of corpus studies looking specifically at male–female differences in *writing*.

An example that pre-dates the digital era is Mary Hiatt's *The Way Women Write* (1977). Hiatt's corpus consisted of 100 passages taken from popular fiction and non-fiction texts written by men and women, which were analysed using a combination of qualitative and quantitative methods. Hiatt reported that the women writers in her sample used shorter and less grammatically complex sentences than the men, more adverbs describing feelings and fewer describing actions, and more parentheses. She also discussed some less tangible qualities she perceived in the women's texts, such as a less authoritative and more moderate tone, and a tendency towards conformity rather than individuality of style. Influenced by the early femi-nist work of Robin Lakoff (1975), who had argued that women were socialized to adopt a 'powerless' register of language, Hiatt speculated that the distinctive features of women's writ-ing were effects of their subordinate status.

Since Hiatt's time there have been changes both in researchers' ideas about language and gender and in the technology they can use to test those ideas; but the belief that it is possible to generalize about 'the way women write' has persisted. In 2003, for example, a group of comput-ing scientists specializing in automated text categorization reported on an algorithm they had developed which, they claimed, was able to categorize texts as either male- or female-authored with an 80% rate of accuracy (Argamon et al. 2003). They developed the program using a large (25 million word) subset of the BNC: like Hiatt, they sampled both fiction and non-fiction, tak-ing an equal number of male- and female-authored texts from each category. They then carried out statistical analyses on a large number of linguistic variables, looking for the ones that most reliably discriminated the male- from the female-authored texts. Unlike Hiatt, they concen-trated on the high-frequency grammatical items that can be expected to occur regularly in any text, no matter what it is about. They found that several of these were good discriminators of gender, in the sense that their frequencies, while high across the sample, showed statistically significant differences in the male and female sub-samples. For example, high frequencies of personal pronouns, especially *I, you, she* and their variants, emerged as markers of female authorship, while high frequencies of determiners (e.g. *a* and *the*), quantifiers (e.g. *many, sev-eral, 57*) and nouns postmodified by prepositional phrases with *of* (e.g. 'a shelf of books') emerged as markers of male authorship.

To explain these findings, Argamon et al. suggested that there was an underlying difference in men's and women's orientation to the entities (people, objects, concepts) which are encoded linguistically using nominal expressions. Men and women did not differ in the overall fre-quency with which they use nominal expressions, but they did differ in the kinds of expressions they favoured. The researchers argued that men's more frequent use of determiners, quantifiers and 'of' **postmodification** reflects a male tendency to specify the properties of objects. Women's more frequent use of personal pronouns reflects a female tendency to focus on people and relationships. As the researchers pointed out, some of the items they identified as gender-markers are also markers of the 'involved—informational' contrast that is one dimension of register variation in Douglas Biber's model. In terms of that model, it could be said that women's writing is more involved and men's is more informational.

In August 2003, what was described as a 'simplified version' of Argamon et al.'s program was installed on a publicly accessible, interactive website, which its creators called 'the Gender Genie'. Visitors were invited to paste a sample of written text into a box, and receive an instant verdict on whether the text had been written by a man or a woman. In addition to making judg-ments about the authorship of the text submitted, the Genie solicited feedback from each user on whether it had guessed correctly. Continuously updated statistics on its success rate were made available for inspection. These were not as impressive as the 80% accuracy claimed by Argamon et al.: sometimes the rate of correct guesses fell as low as 51%—roughly what you would get by guessing at random. One problem might have been that the Genie was using a 'simplified' version of the original algorithm. Another, however, is suggested by the experiences of users who submitted multiple examples of their own writing for analysis.

For a while, the Genie was very popular, and many users discussed their experiences with it in blog-posts and forums. A study based on a sample of 100 such discussions (Cameron 2007) found that many users reported the same thing: the Genie had identified their gender differently depending on the type of text they put in. Blog-posts and poetry were generally judged to be female, whereas extracts of academic writing were almost always judged to be male. This is, of course, anecdotal evidence, but it points to a recurring problem in corpus studies whose aim is to identify 'general' differences between men's and women's writing: these studies may be failing to differentiate between the effects of *gender* and those of *genre*.

Consider, for instance, Hiatt's claim that female-authored texts in her sample contained more adverbs describing emotional states (e.g. 'she thought to herself, *sadly*') while male-authored texts contained more adverbs describing action (e.g. 'he moved *quickly* towards the controls'). The (invented) examples we have just given to illustrate this difference suggest a possible reason for it: perhaps the male- and female-authored texts belonged to genres which differed in the relative emphasis placed on feelings or on actions. In Chapter 2, we noted that Biber's examination of the 'involved—informational' dimension of register variation had found clear differences between different genres of popular fiction. Romance fiction, which is centrally concerned with feelings, had a much higher frequency of involvement markers (and a lower frequency of informational ones) than science fiction, which deals with themes like technology and the exploration of distant worlds. Another difference between these genres is that romance writers are overwhelmingly female, while most science fiction writers are male. If the fiction sampled for a corpus reflects this social fact, so that male examples are dominant in some genres and female ones in others, it will be difficult to separate the variables of gender and genre. The finding reported by Argamon et al.—that women's writing is more involved and men's more informational—may reflect not basic gender differences in orientation to the world, but rather a feature of the sample, whereby each group is over-represented in those genres where an 'involved' or 'informational' style is the norm for writers of both genders.

This issue does not just arise with fiction. In a study of a corpus of blogs which took its cue from Argamon et al.'s work, Susan Herring and John Paolillo (2006) found that within the category 'blog' there was a genre distinction between 'diary' blogs (where material is drawn from the blogger's own life) and 'filter' blogs (which reproduce or link to other web content). In Herring and Paolillo's sample, the diary and filter blogs differed in their frequencies of involved and informational features; there was also a gender difference, in that more women produced diary blogs and more men produced filter blogs. However, the linguistic differences correlated more closely with the diary/filter distinction than with the female/male distinction, leading the researchers to conclude that genre had more influence than gender on writing-style in blogs.

Of course, it might be argued that genre preferences are themselves evidence of 'deeper' gender differences: perhaps men and women choose to specialize in the types of writing that are closest to their 'natural' ways of using language, or that make best use of their linguistic skills. But it could also be argued that the division results from longstanding cultural assumptions or prejudices about what is 'gender appropriate', which affect men's and women's opportunities as well as their personal choices, making each sex more likely to study certain subjects, take up certain occupations, and write certain kinds of texts.

An attempt to probe some of the internal complexities of the relationship between gender and writing in very large samples has recently been made by David Bamman, Jacob Eisenstein and Tyler Schnoebelen (2012), whose corpus was compiled using data from the microblogging site Twitter: they sampled more than 9 million tweets produced by over 14,000 individual users during the first six months of 2011. Their analysis showed that the frequencies of some items strongly predicted the writer's gender. For male writers, these predictors included a high frequency of references to named entities (e.g. *Facebook*, *i-Phone*), hashtags (the # symbol used to mark a searchable keyword on Twitter), numbers and taboo words; for female writers, they included non-standard words (both 'pronounceable' deviant spellings like *luv* and 'unpronounceable' emoticons or abbreviations like *lmao* ['laughing my ass off'], *omg*), and punctuation marks (? !). As the researchers comment, however, it is not obvious how all of these relate to the 'involved—informational' dimension of variation which was a focus of earlier studies like Argamon et al.'s and Herring and Paolillo's.

Further analysis led Bamman et al. to conclude that there were not just two gendered styles, a male and a female one; there were *multiple* gendered styles. When they put the users in their sample into clusters (grouping people together on the basis that they had similar frequency scores for the items which had been identified as gender-markers), they could see that both female and male clusters were differentiated by other variables, such as age and ethnicity. They also found differences related to individual tweeters' social networks. Individuals whose patterns of language-use did not conform to the overall pattern for their gender tended to belong to mixed-gender social networks, whereas those whose language conformed closely to the overall pattern for their gender had social networks whose members were predominantly of that gender. Rather than explaining the 'gender-untypical' tweeters as just statistical 'outliers', however, Bamman et al. suggested that they might be men and women who took a consciously critical attitude to mainstream gender norms and constructed their own gender identities differently. The point that masculinities and femininities come in different varieties is often obscured in studies that use statistics, because they commonly treat gender as a binary variable (in effect, they equate it with biological sex). In the Twitter study, however, the researchers designed their procedure to avoid making that assumption.

ANALYSING DISCOURSE CRITICALLY: CONTRASTING FRAMES IN NEWS REPORTING

The Twitter study just discussed is an example of what Baker (2006) calls 'corpus-*driven*' analysis: rather than testing some prior hypothesis about male/female differences, the analysts used the 'inductive' approach of letting statistical analysis identify the relevant features, and then asking what might explain them. However, 'corpus-*based*' analysis may use corpora and corpus methods in other ways. Rather than asking open-ended questions about what patterns are (statistically) significant in the corpus, an analyst might start with a pattern whose significance is assumed on some other basis, and look for examples of it in the corpus. The point might be to check the analyst's intuition, or some other researcher's claim that it exists and is significant, or it might be to get a sense of how common the pattern is and what contexts it is found in.

This approach is often used in CDA studies, where, as we saw in Chapter 6, analysts do generally approach data with some kind of agenda. In this section we discuss an example: a research project carried out for a Master's dissertation dealing with the representation of sexual violence in *New York Times* reports on two conflict settings, the Democratic Republic of Congo (DRC) and Abu Ghraib prison in Iraq. The researcher, Tamar Holoshitz, used the newspaper's searchable electronic archive to compile a corpus consisting of 89 articles on each setting, which she analysed using the concordancing program AntConc. Her analysis was guided by a set of questions which had been raised by previous (non-corpus-based) work on the representation of sexual violence (e.g. Clark 1998), and foreign conflicts (e.g. Chari 2010), in news reporting.

The DRC and Abu Ghraib were both cases where sexual violence was used in the context of a political and military conflict as a tactic to intimidate and control an 'enemy' population. In the DRC the tactic was used on a mass scale by armed militia groups against civilians, while in Abu Ghraib it was used on a smaller scale by members of the occupying US forces against Iraqi prisoners. However, the sexual and racial/national dynamics differed in the two cases. In the DRC, the violence was perpetrated by African men against Congolese women and girls. In Abu Ghraib, the abuse was perpetrated against men as well as (mostly) by them, and the abusers were Americans whereas the victims were Arabs. Tamar's argument was that these differences had led to the two cases being framed in very different ways by US news outlets—ways which reflected and reproduced a number of sexist and racist assumptions. In the DRC, the frame used was 'illustrative'—bearing witness to the horror by focusing on the number and suffering of the victims, but making no attempt to identify the perpetrators or explain their motivations, which were presented not as political, but as expressions of a 'savagery' that was endemic to the culture they came from. In reports on Abu Ghraib, on the other hand, there was very little focus on the victims, and the sexualized nature of the abuse was downplayed. The frame used was 'investigative', placing most emphasis on the efforts being made by the US military authorities to identify and punish those responsible. The abusers were presented as untypical individuals who had been driven to act in abusive ways by psychological and social problems.

This analysis may sound like the product of a qualitative, interpretive approach, and in many ways it was: unlike someone working with nine million tweets or a 100 million-word reference corpus, Tamar was able to read her entire sample, and the trends she discerned in doing so formed the basis of her argument. Her dissertation contains a number of close, qualitative analyses of specific extracts from the reports. However, she also wanted to be able to show that these examples were not totally unrepresentative of the sample as a whole, and for that purpose she found it useful to employ the techniques of corpus linguistics, such as identifying keywords in each sub-corpus (by comparing it with a larger reference sample of newspaper writing) and then looking at their concordances.

For example, analysis of the DRC sub-corpus showed that *women* was one of the top-ranked keywords. This might seem unsurprising given that the topic of the reports was violence against women, but it supported Tamar's intuition that the reports focused on the victims more than the perpetrators. When concordance lines containing *women* were examined, it also became clear how strongly the reports emphasized the high numbers of victims. There was a pattern whereby *women* was very frequently preceded by a quantifying expression such as *dozens/ hundreds/thousands of, more than N, at least N*. This led Tamar to look at the use of quantifying expressions in the Abu Ghraib sub-corpus, where she discovered that they were very rarely used in references to the victims: concordances for the lemma *prisoner* (the term most often used to denote victims) showed that only 21 out of 481 references included a quantifying expression. There was, however, another category of references in which precise quantification was common: references to the numbers of military personnel who had been interrogated about the abuse or charged with involvement in it. For instance:

> The inquiry ... implicated 29 other military intelligence soldiers. ... The report also stated that 11 military police soldiers—seven of whom have already been charged—were involved in abuses, and that two Army medics in Iraq failed to report misconduct they had witnessed.

This difference in the patterning of quantifying expressions across the two sub-corpora offered support for the argument Tamar had already begun to develop––that different frames were being used in reporting.

Another set of patterns Tamar investigated was suggested by previous CDA work on the representation of rape in non-conflict settings, which had noted a tendency for reports to downplay the responsibility of perpetrators by describing sexual assaults in the language of consensual sex or romance, or by implying that the victim's behaviour provoked the assailant. These patterns might be expected to be absent, or rare, in reports on a situation where the mass rape of civilians by soldiers was being used as an intimidation tactic, but in the DRC corpus Tamar found that rape, including the rape of very young girls, was frequently described using 'neutral' terms that included the item *sex* rather than terms that implied force or coercion, such as *rape* and *assault*. When she examined concordances for the lemma *sex*, the phrases she found included 'sexual activity', 'sexual contact', 'sexual relations', 'sex with underage partners', 'sex with a girl', 'sex with people under 18', and 'sex with minors'. There was also a reference to a militia group which was said to enlist children as young as eight, and train the girls to 'provide sex to militiamen'. As she commented, expressions like 'underage partners' and 'provide sex' are markedly non-judgmental in this context. It would be interesting to investigate whether the *New York Times* would use them to describe incidents taking place in the USA rather than the DRC (a question which could also be addressed using corpus methods, though they would need to be applied to a different sample from the one Tamar analysed).

The examples we have discussed show that corpus methods can play a variety of roles in discourse analytic studies. In the Twitter study, Bamman et al. began with statistical analysis and then tried to explain the patterns they found. By contrast, Tamar Holoshitz approached her data looking for certain patterns: she used corpus methods to investigate how frequently and systematically they appeared. Her argument depended on evidence produced by both quantitative and qualitative analysis. Either of these ways of using corpus methods may be appropriate for a particular purpose. Whether quantitative methods are useful, and what the balance between quantitative and qualitative analysis should be, will depend on the question you are trying to answer and the kinds of claims you want to make. We will return to this point in Chapter 12, on designing your own research projects. In the next chapter, however, we move away from the exclusive focus on language which is a characteristic feature of corpus-based discourse analysis, and consider some approaches which focus on the combination of language with other semiotic systems in multimodal texts.

SUMMARY

In this chapter we have seen that corpus methods offer powerful tools for finding non-obvious, meaningful patterns in language-use, and they allow analysts to work with much larger quantities of data than they could process otherwise. It should not be assumed that larger is always better—that depends on the research question—but sometimes a very large sample gives a more accurate and detailed picture than a smaller one would (the Twitter study discussed above is one illustration). As with any quantitative method, though, the decisions an analyst makes about the composition of the sample and what to look for in it are crucial for ensuring valid results. (There are also numerous technical decisions to be made about, for instance, choosing between different statistical tests and setting parameters for various operations, which we have not touched on here at all; they are discussed in some of the further reading sources listed below and in the bibliography.) And in discourse analysis, where context always matters, the interpretation of results will often require a more qualitative approach, in which specific examples are examined closely.

FURTHER READING

Paul Baker's *Using Corpora in Discourse Analysis* (2006) is an accessible textbook for readers who want to use a corpus-based approach: it gives more technical explanations than we have offered in this chapter, and some fairly detailed guidance on using certain resources (e.g. the BNC and WordSmith). It is especially useful for those who want to combine corpus methods with CDA (other books by the same author which show this combination in action deal with gender and sexuality (Baker 2008) and British media representations of Islam (Baker et al. 2013)). A more 'advanced' but very clear survey of corpus methods and the associated technical issues is Stefan Gries and John Newman's chapter 'Creating and using corpora' in Robert Podesva and Devyani Sharma's edited volume *Research Methods in Linguistics* (2013).

RESOURCES

This is a selective listing of (English language) corpora and software packages, with details of where they (and more detailed information about them) can be accessed. Some of the sources in the 'further reading' section above, or referred to elsewhere in the chapter, include more comprehensive lists, but while the information in books is accurate at the time of writing, in this area things change rapidly, as electronic resources are updated and added to. This section includes information on whether corpora and software packages are available free of charge, but even if they are not, students may find they have access to them under a licence or subscription purchased by the institution where they are studying.

Corpora

British National Corpus. Information on the BNC, including a reference guide to the corpus and details of how to purchase it, is available from www.natcorp.ox.ac.uk. The BNC can also be accessed at no charge through Mark Davies' website at www.corpus.byu.edu/bnc.

Corpus of Contemporary American English. COCA is a corpus which is only accessible via a web interface. It can be found, along with a full description, at www.americancorpus.org/.

ICAME. This stands for International Computer Archive of Modern and Medieval English, and is a collection of corpora available to buy on CD-ROM. See icame.uib.no/newcd.htm.

International Corpus of English. The ICE series of million-word corpora for varieties of English around the world is continuously being expanded. Individual ICE corpora are maintained in different locations: for information on what is available and where it may be obtained, see the ICE website at www.ice-corpora.net/ice/index.htm. Many ICE corpora can be downloaded free of charge; some are available on CD-ROM and require payment, though the costs are generally low.

Linguistic Data Consortium. This is a subscription-based service which makes a selection of corpora (in a range of languages) available to subscribers. Its website is at www.ldc.upenn.edu/

Analytic tools for use with corpora

AntConc Concordancer. This program is available in several versions designed for different computer operating systems (i.e. it can be used on a PC or a Mac). It is available from www. antlab.sci.waseda.ac.jp/software.html

WordSmith. This commercial software package is designed for use with Microsoft Windows. It can be purchased at www.lexically.net/wordsmith/

CLAWS. This stands for Constituent Likelihood Automatic Word-tagging System: it is a tool for automatically annotating corpora with part-of-speech information (which may be relevant if you are making your own corpus and you want to be able to search for grammatical categories rather than just words). See www.ucrel.lancs.ac.uk/claws

NOTE

1   A lemma is the 'canonical' form of a word, the generic item you would look up in a dictionary: for instance, the entry for *eat* would not just include the form *eat* itself, but also the other inflectional forms of the same verb—*eats, eating, ate* and *eaten*. For some analytic purposes you might want to separate these, but for others you would want to analyse them as a single unit.

8 Multimodal discourse analysis

Discourse is *multimodal* if, in the words of Gunther Kress and Theo van Leeuwen (1996: 183), 'its meaning is realized through more than one semiotic code'. In that case, Kress and van Leeuwen go on,

> the question arises whether the products of the various codes should be analysed separately or in an integrated way; whether the meanings of the whole should be treated as the sum of the meanings of the parts, or whether the parts should be looked on as interacting with and affecting one another.

In this chapter, we consider what is involved in analysing multimodal discourse 'in an integrated way', paying attention both to the workings of different semiotic systems and to the interactions between them.

Interest in multimodal analysis has grown since the 1990s, in part because of the rise of new digital media which make use of very complex semiotic combinations. Even a fairly ordinary Facebook page is likely to contain written language, graphics, still images like photographs and cartoons, and embedded links to clips containing speech, moving images and music. Analysts working with this kind of data need frameworks that can capture its complexity. But as we noted in the introduction, multimodality is not a product of digital technology, or even of the modern era. Many theorists would argue that it is actually a normal feature of *all* communication. Even in face-to-face spoken interaction, which is often considered the most 'basic' form of linguistic communication, language is not the only source of meaning: we also communicate using non-verbal signals such as posture, gesture, gaze and facial expression. Written discourse, similarly, always depends on visual as well as verbal resources: its meaning is not just in the words, but also in their appearance and spatial arrangement.

But if we accept the view that all communication is multimodal, it becomes problematic to talk about 'spoken' and 'written' discourse, since those terms privilege the linguistic over every other mode. A more useful way of proceeding, Theo van Leeuwen (2004) suggests, might be to distinguish between those communicative acts which are 'performed' and those which are 'inscribed'.[1] In the following discussion we will confine our attention to the 'inscribed' category, which includes writing. To show what is distinctive about multimodal approaches, we will focus on cases where written language is combined with visual images.[2]

In the last sentence we referred to 'multimodal *approaches*', making the point that there is more than one. The term *multimodality* has come to be closely associated with a particular approach, an offshoot of systemic functional linguistics (SFL) whose best-known practitioners include Kress and van Leeuwen. This framework has been very influential, especially for discourse analysts whose 'home' discipline is linguistics, and we discuss it in more detail later on.

But we begin by considering some other traditions in which the same kinds of questions have been addressed.

IMAGE, TEXT AND CONTEXT: SEMIOLOGICAL APPROACHES

One approach which has been strong in visually-oriented disciplines (e.g. art, architecture, graphic design, film theory and media studies) is known as **semiology** or **semiotics**—both terms meaning, roughly, 'the study of signs'.[3] *Semiology* has its roots in the work of the Swiss language scholar Ferdinand de Saussure, who is often described as the founder of modern linguistics. In his *Course in General Linguistics* (a text compiled by his students from lecture notes after his death, and published in French in 1916), Saussure defined a language as a system of signs, and linguistics as part of a larger 'science of signs'. *Semiotics* is the name for another theory of signs which was developed independently by Saussure's near-contemporary, the US philosopher and mathematician Charles Sanders Peirce.

Peirce's framework has been less widely influential than Saussure's, but one part of it which has achieved wide currency is his division of signs into three classes or types. An *icon* is a sign which conveys meaning through direct resemblance to what it represents: examples include figurative paintings or photographs of people, places and events. An *index* is a sign which communicates meaning through a natural association: for instance, human footprints in the sand index or 'point to' the presence of a person walking, though they do not directly depict a person walking. Finally, a *symbol* is a sign which communicates meaning through a purely conventional association. In Britain's Highway Code, for example, the road sign alerting drivers to a hazard is a triangle (a convention meaning that the sign is a warning) enclosing an exclamation mark (a convention meaning 'danger').[4]

In the case of linguistic signs, the relationship between form and meaning is typically conventional/symbolic. The arbitrary nature of the linguistic sign was pointed out by Saussure, who observed that there is no natural connection between what he called the *signifier*, for instance the sequence of English sounds /kæt/ ('cat'), and the *signified* that goes with it, the concept of a feline domestic animal. Rather than corresponding directly to objects in the world, signs acquire their meaning by contrasting with other signs in the same system. In the British Highway Code, for instance, triangular signs, which carry warnings, contrast with circular signs, which issue commands, and rectangular signs, which give information. There is nothing intrinsically 'warning-like' about a triangle: the designers of the code could have put commands in triangles and warnings in circles, or they could have used a rhombus and a hexagon. What is meaningful is the *difference* between shapes rather than the shapes in and of themselves. And Saussure argued that the same is true in languages: just as a triangle is different from a circle, so a *cat* is different from a *bat* or a *rat*.

Saussure was not directly concerned with what is now labelled 'multimodality'. But by formulating what could be seen as a general theory of signs, he provided a foundation for later work which did address the relationship between different semiotic systems. Just as today's multimodal analysis is in part a response to the rise of new digital media, so the semiological analysis produced in the mid-twentieth century responded to new developments in the mass media of the time—in particular, the increasing emphasis placed on visual communication, which could be observed both in print genres like journalism and advertising, and in the rise of a powerful new mass medium, television. In that context, one theorist who wrote extensively about the relationship of language to visual images was the French literary and cultural critic Roland Barthes. As well as having a strong influence on the study of media and popular culture, Barthes's semiology is acknowledged by scholars like Kress and van Leeuwen as an important antecedent of their own multimodal approach.

For Barthes, there is a key difference between verbal and visual communication: the meaning of images is inherently more open-ended than the meaning of words. When language is juxtaposed with an image, therefore, the function of the former is to 'fix' the latter's meaning. He explains this using the example of a verbal caption juxtaposed with an image of a plate of food:

> Shown a plateful of something ... I may hesitate in identifying the forms and the masses; the caption ('rice and tuna fish with mushrooms') helps me to choose the correct level of perception, permits me to focus not simply my gaze but also my understanding (Barthes 1977: 36).

Barthes called this relationship *anchorage*: the language 'anchors' or pins down the meaning of the image. He also argued that anchorage had become the dominant text–image relationship, superseding the older historical tendency for images to function as *illustrations* of a text, reiterating, condensing or highlighting something that had already been presented verbally. In the older tradition, the text took precedence; in modern media, images had become primary, but words were still needed to 'focus [the viewer's] understanding', to tell the viewer what to make of an image that might, in principle, mean many different things. Barthes also described a third possibility, *relay*, in which verbal and visual meanings complement one another: the text adds information which is not present in the image, as with film and comic strip dialogue.

In Barthes's example, the caption 'rice and tuna fish with mushrooms' elucidates the meaning of an image by offering a brief description of its content—in effect, it functions as a label. The same is true of the titles displayed alongside artworks in a gallery ('Girl with a pearl earring'), the captions given to photographs in news reports ('Demonstrators in Tahrir Square'), the headings preceding diagrams in instruction booklets ('Inserting and Removing the Battery') and the labels identifying figures and tables in academic texts ('Table 1: Ge'ez script: Tigrinya alphabet'). But the relationship between visual and verbal material is not always as simple as this—a point which is emphasized in the next approach we discuss, based on the principles of **pragmatics**, a branch of language-study which is concerned with the interpretation of discourse.

INFERRING MEANING: PRAGMATIC APPROACHES

The advertisement reproduced in Figure 8.1 comes from a series which appeared on billboards in the UK in 2000, advertising Gossard women's underwear. They all featured an image showing what appeared to be the aftermath of a sexual encounter (a bedroom scene, with a woman lying on the bed in the background and discarded clothing, including the product, in the foreground); they all featured the same tag-line, 'Gossard Find Your G-spot' ('G-spot' references both the initial letter of the brand name Gossard and a part of the female body which is supposed to be the site of intense sexual pleasure); and they all featured a short caption—in this case, 'If he's late, you can always start without him' (other ads in the series were captioned 'Moan, moan, moan' and 'Bring him to his knees').

Figure 8.1

The relationship between text and image in these advertisements is not easily accounted for using Barthes's framework, in which the open-ended meaning of a visual image is 'anchored', pinned down more precisely, by giving it a verbal caption. That assumption works reasonably well for captions which function as labels: if you just showed people the caption and asked them to guess what the image showed, most people would probably guess correctly that the caption 'rice and tuna fish with mushrooms' went with a picture of a plate of food, while 'Demonstrators in Tahrir Square' went with a photograph of people engaged in a political protest in Cairo. But if you showed people the Gossard caption, they would be unlikely to guess from the language alone what the accompanying image depicted. Though anyone who knows English can *decode* the sentence 'if he's late, you can always start without him', some of the information which is needed to interpret what it means in a specific context—like the identity of the person referred to by the pronouns *he* and *him*, and the nature of the activity which 'you can always start without him'—is not explicitly encoded in the sentence, and therefore cannot be retrieved by simply decoding it. Rather, it has to be *inferred* by the recipient, by putting the linguistic meaning of the sentence together with other contextual information. If the sentence is presented along with a visual image, readers will assume that the image should be treated as highly relevant information.

In the case of the 'If he's late...' advertisement, the image directs the viewer towards a *sexual* interpretation of the caption. Without the image, there would be nothing to prompt that inference: the sentence itself does not directly refer to sex, and if it had been juxtaposed with an image of, say, a group of smartly-dressed people sitting around a table in a board-room, it would be interpreted as a reference to business rather than sex (e.g. 'if [your male colleague/boss] is late [for a business meeting], you can always start [the meeting] without him'). But when the caption is read in conjunction with the visual representation of a bedroom scene, featuring an unclothed woman lying on a bed and scattered items of lingerie, the viewer is likely to interpret it as meaning 'If [your male sexual partner] is late [for an assignation], you can start [having sex] without him'. That was certainly the interpretation of a large number of people who made complaints about the Gossard campaign to the British Advertising Standards Authority (ASA). The ASA upheld their complaints, and forced Gossard to withdraw the advertisement. In its judgment it stated that the caption was 'an allusion to masturbation', and was 'likely to give serious or widespread offence' (see Cameron 2006b).

The account we have just given of how the Gossard advertisement communicates the meaning the ASA objected to draws on a pragmatic approach known as 'relevance theory' (Sperber and Wilson 1995), which emphasizes that communication does not rely only on participants' knowledge of a code or sign-system, but also depends on their ability to infer meanings which are not directly encoded in the message. This approach has been applied to advertisements by a number of analysts, one of whom—Keiko Tanaka (1994)—specifically argues that it is better equipped than semiology to explain how viewers make sense of texts like the Gossard poster. For a semiologist like Barthes, the meaning of a text is in the sign-system, and the task of the viewer—or the analyst—is to decode the signs that constitute the message. For a pragmaticist, by contrast, the text is only part of the story: its meaning is a puzzle which the viewer has to solve, and to do that it is necessary to go beyond what is encoded in the message. To interpret 'If he's late...' as an allusion to a practice that is neither mentioned in the caption nor shown in the image, viewers must draw on their cultural background knowledge, as well as putting together the verbal and visual clues made available by the advertisement itself.

A basic principle of pragmatics is that communication depends on the recipient of a message understanding not only the meaning of the message itself, but also what the sender intended it to communicate: the question is not just 'what does this say?' but also 'why is this person telling me this?' In the case of commercial advertising, one intention that can always be attributed to the sender of the message is the intention to publicize the advertised product and present it as desirable. But in many advertisements, including the Gossard series, that intention is not communicated directly. It is not immediately obvious what the advertised product is: the brand-name does not feature in the captions, but only in the less prominent tag-line 'Gossard Find Your G-Spot'—and even that can hardly be described as a straightforward exhortation to buy underwear. The strategy used in this campaign is one we mentioned in Chapter 6: creating desire for a product or brand by giving it a personality with which the target consumer can identify. The company explained when they launched the campaign that they were targeting 'liberated women with a wicked sense of humour'. The advertising trade journal *Campaign* commented: 'Gossard dares to suggest that women wear beautiful underwear for themselves rather than the men in their life'.[5] 'Suggest' is an apt word: what the advertisement 'suggests' goes well beyond what the words in it say and what the visual image shows. The advertisers are relying on the viewer to supply the propositions which the text itself does not, and on that basis to draw the correct conclusions about what the text is intended to communicate.

Why do contemporary advertisers habitually make the viewer do so much interpretive work? Keiko Tanaka offers one answer to that question. In most contexts, she suggests, it is advantageous for communicators to make their intentions overt, but advertisers have a motive for keeping certain intentions hidden—in particular, the intention to manipulate consumers' behaviour, which is often done by appealing to motives which are less than admirable, like snobbery, envy, greed and sexual desire. Though advertisers believe this to be an effective strategy, they also know that it will not be effective if it is made too obvious. Therefore they rely heavily on what Tanaka calls 'covert communication', where propositions are conveyed by implication rather than explicitly. The message contains clues, pointing the recipient towards a certain inference, but the inferred meaning is what pragmaticists call 'defeasible'. If called to account, the producer of the message can deny that they intended the message to have that meaning, and the recipient can deny that they interpreted it as having that meaning. This strategy is used frequently by advertisers when they are faced with complaints from people who find their messages offensive. For instance, the makers of the Gossard campaign denied that the caption 'Bring him to his knees' was an allusion to oral sex. They told the ASA that they intended it simply as a reference to the intensity of the desire a woman in Gossard underwear could arouse. If some viewers thought otherwise, that was their own interpretation.

Other explanations have been proposed for the characteristic inexplicitness of many advertisements. Analysts who emphasize the creative and playful qualities of advertising (e.g. Cook 2006) suggest that by making us work for the meaning of a message, advertisers are offering us an experience we find pleasurable, and flattering us by treating us as intelligent, sophisticated readers. It has also been argued that in a world where people are continually bombarded with all kinds of messages, inexplicitness is an effective strategy for attracting and keeping our attention: a complex message whose meaning is not immediately obvious arouses more curiosity, and demands more active and prolonged engagement, than one which can be interpreted without effort. But whatever motives we attribute to advertisers, it is clear that multimodality is a source of complexity which they can and do exploit, by setting puzzles whose solution depends on integrating visual and verbal meanings.

VISUAL AND VERBAL GRAMMAR: SYSTEMIC-FUNCTIONAL APPROACHES

Earlier we noted that Barthes's work has been acknowledged by Kress and van Leeuwen as an important precursor to their own, SFL-based approach to multimodality. The SFL approach resembles semiology (and differs from pragmatics) in being strongly code-based; but while Kress and van Leeuwen give Barthes credit for his systematic attempt to theorize the relationship between language and visual images, they also criticize him for 'miss[ing] an important point: the visual component of a text is an independently organized and structured message—connected with the verbal text but in no way dependent on it' (Kress and van Leeuwen 1996: 17).

This criticism is particularly directed towards Barthes's account of 'anchorage', which he regards as the predominant image–text relationship of the modern era. In this relationship, the verbal text is dominant, imposing a precise meaning on the inherently open-ended image. Kress and van Leeuwen argue that visual meaning is not subordinate to, or less precise than, verbal meaning. Each mode is, in principle, an autonomous system which communicates meaning independently of the other. What Barthes lacked, and what Kress and van Leeuwen aim to provide, is a fully elaborated account of the visual code, which works in a similar way to the linguistic code, but using a different set of semiotic resources.

To understand this argument it is necessary to place it in the context of the SFL framework which is the basis for Kress and van Leeuwen's approach. A key theoretical assumption in this tradition is that language is one of many 'social semiotic' systems—ways of making meaning which are shaped by the needs and the habitual activities of social beings in a social world. It is further assumed that these systems, since they are shaped by the same forces and fulfil the same functions, have fundamental things in common with each other: non-linguistic modes of communication work in a way which is analogous to the way language works. It follows that the different modes can also be analysed in similar ways—that it is possible to describe the 'grammar' of visual design (Kress and van Leeuwen 1996), or music (van Leeuwen 1999), using the same kind of descriptive apparatus that is used in SFL to describe the grammar of language.

The conception of 'grammar' which underpins this line of argument distinguishes practitioners of SFL from 'formalist' linguists (e.g. those who belong to the generativist tradition of

Noam Chomsky). For formalists, a grammar is a set of formal rules describing the structure of a language (e.g. what is or is not a permissible word order, and how various constructions, like questions or negatives, are formed). 'Functionalists', on the other hand, try to relate the structures found in languages to the functions they fulfil and the meanings they have evolved to express. Halliday, the founder of SFL, describes grammar not as a set of formal rules, but as 'a network of systems, or interrelated sets of options for making meaning' (1994: 15). By comparison with the formalist definition of grammar, which is specifically about the structures found in human languages, Halliday's definition is more easily extended to non-linguistic systems which are also 'sets of options for making meaning'.

In SFL it is postulated that any semiotic system will provide resources for making three kinds of meaning: *ideational* meaning (representing states of affairs in the world), *interpersonal* meaning (constructing relationships between the sender, the message and the receiver of the message) and *textual* meaning (signalling how the parts of a message relate to one another to form a coherent whole). The aim of analysis is to describe the options a given system makes available for each of these three 'metafunctions', and what contrasts in meaning are produced by different choices. The resources are different in different semiotic systems, but the meanings that can be made with them are comparable. As Kress and van Leeuwen explain, talking about language and visual communication (1996: 17): 'both realize the same fundamental and far-reaching systems of meaning that constitute our cultures, but ... each does so by means of its own specific forms'.

An example may help to make this clearer. In language, you can realize different interpersonal meanings through choices about whether and how to use personal pronouns. In that last sentence, for instance, we chose to use the second person *you/your*, which constructs a certain kind of relationship between writer and reader: alternatively, we could have used the third person plural, 'language-users can realize ... through their choices', or a passive form, 'interpersonal meanings can be realized through choices ...', which dispenses with pronouns entirely. These options are specific to language: pronouns are a linguistic resource which is not available to the producers of visual communications like photographs and paintings. However, the photographer or painter can realize similar contrasts in meaning using visual resources which are not available in language. In a photograph depicting a human subject, for example, different interpersonal meanings can be realized through different ways of positioning the subject relative to the viewer. The subject may be shown in close-up or from a distance, from above or below, looking towards or away from the viewer. The viewer's relationship to the subject will be different depending which of these options has been chosen.

Kress and van Leeuwen's grammar of visual design is a systematic attempt to describe the options available for meaning-making in the modern western tradition of visual communication, using SFL's three metafunctions—ideational, interpersonal and textual—as the organizing principle. Under the heading of ideational meaning (representing the world), they propose that images may be analysed as either *narrative* or *conceptual*. Narrative images are representations of actions or events, which typically show participants engaged in processes that unfold in time (these may include action processes, verbal processes and mental processes). Even if the image itself only captures a moment in time (like a news photograph), it is 'narrative' if its function is essentially to record the event or encapsulate the story which that moment is part of. Conceptual images, by contrast, are representations of some general (and by implication timeless) social reality which is being visually classified, analysed or symbolized. Examples of the classificatory and analytic types include maps, plans, diagrams, graphs, flowcharts and timelines (though a timeline is also in a sense a narrative, its function is not to visualize an event in time so much as to classify a process by showing it as a temporally ordered sequence of events). Conceptual images of the third, symbolic type are described by Kress and van Leeuwen (1996: 108) as being concerned with 'what a participant *means* or *is*'. Participants are not so much actors as carriers of symbolic attributes: 'they just sit or stand there, for no reason other than to display themselves to the viewer' (1996: 109). In the subtype of symbolic image which Kress and van Leeuwen label 'suggestive', 'detail tends to be de-emphasized in favour of "mood" or "atmosphere"' (1996: 110).

ACTIVITY

Would you analyse the Gossard poster reproduced above as a 'narrative' image or a 'conceptual' one of the 'symbolic' variety—or might it have elements of both? Does it make a difference to your answer whether you consider both the image and the verbal text?

Interpersonal meaning constructs relationships between the sender, the addressee and the message: as we have already noted, one linguistic resource for doing this is the system of personal pronouns, and the visual analogue is the way viewers are positioned in relation to an image. The analogy is perhaps clearest if we consider the ways in which an image may engage the viewer's *gaze*. An image in which the subject gazes directly at the viewer is termed a 'demand' by Kress and van Leeuwen, because it constructs the viewer in the same way the pronoun *you* does, as a direct addressee whose attention is being demanded. Where the subject does not meet the viewer's gaze, Kress and van Leeuwen call the image an 'offer', remarking that 'it "offers" the represented participants to the viewer as items of information, objects of contemplation, impersonally, as though they were specimens in a display case' (1996: 124). The Gossard image is an offer rather than a demand: arguably, it offers the viewer the position of a voyeur, watching (evidently without her knowledge, since she is facing away), a woman lying naked on a bed. The feeling of impersonality is reinforced by the use of *distance* in the image: whereas a close-up shot would produce an impression of intimacy, the long shot used here suggests a higher degree of social distance. A third element in the system is the perspective and angle from which the viewer is made to contemplate the image. The vertical dimension is about power: if we view an image from above, we will feel powerful in relation to it, whereas a view from below casts us as powerless. The horizontal dimension is about involvement: a frontal view suggests a personal connection with the subject, whereas an oblique view (as in the Gossard image) promotes detachment.

The other system of interpersonal meaning discussed by Kress and van Leeuwen is **modality**. The meanings realized through choices about modality relate to the truth or factuality of the message. In language, the statement 'it's going to rain' expresses a higher level of commitment to the truth of the proposition than, say, 'I think it's going to rain', 'it's probably going to rain', 'it might be going to rain', 'perhaps it's going to rain'. In visual communication, similarly, some representations are conventionally understood as more 'objective' or 'factual' than others. Visual modality is complex, however, because what counts as 'objective' or 'factual' will vary with the type of image and the means used to produce it. In painting, for instance, a high-modality (i.e. realistic or naturalistic) image will imitate nature in the way it uses colour: there will be a high level of colour differentiation and modulation (i.e. the use of different shades and tones)—though very highly saturated colour, as seen in some modern abstract paintings, has lower modality because it is too extreme to be perceived as natural. In scientific diagrams, on the other hand, naturalistic use of colour does not enhance credibility and truth value: the highest modality belongs to stark black and white.

Colour is one of several visual devices which can be graded from low to high modality. Others include *representation*—how abstract/concretely detailed the representation is; *contextualization*—how little or how much background is included; *depth*—how little/much use is made of perspective; and *illumination*—how little/much use is made of light and shade. One way to think about the differences here might be to imagine a representation of the same subject—say, Queen Elizabeth II—in three different visual genres: a cartoon, a portrait painted in oils, and a colour photograph. The cartoon would have lower modality than the portrait or the photograph (it would be likely to lack detail and depth), and the photograph would have higher modality than the painting. Of course, something would depend here on the style of painting or photography, but in general, contemporary viewers see even naturalistic paintings as more 'subjective' (i.e. more indebted to the artist's interpretation of reality) than naturalistic photographs.

Finally, Kress and van Leeuwen describe the way textual meaning, the overall coherence of an image, is produced by various characteristics of its composition. They propose, first, that the placement of elements in different parts of the visual field (left or right, top or bottom, centre or margin) gives them a particular information value. Specifically, they claim that if an image (or an image–text combination, like an advertisement or a magazine double-page spread) makes use of a left/right division, the left side will present 'given' information (something that is assumed to be part of the viewer's existing knowledge, or a matter of cultural consensus), while the right side will present 'new' information. Where a top/bottom division is used, the upper part will present the 'ideal'—the information which is taken to be more essential, general or abstract—while the lower part will present the 'real'—more specific and concrete information. If a centre/margin layout is used, the centre will contain the informational nucleus, and the marginal elements will be dependent on it or subordinate to it.

Two other elements of textual meaning are *salience* and *framing*. Salience is to do with the visual 'weight' of different elements in a composition: as with modality, salience has gradations which are signalled through the interaction of features like the size of the element, how sharply focused it is and where in the visual field it is placed. Highly salient elements tend to be larger, sharper and placed in the foreground and/or near the top. Framing is to do with the marking of boundaries, either within the image or between it and something else (like another image or a piece of text). If an element is clearly divided from the adjoining text, or enclosed by visible lines, that suggests it is a self-contained unit. In cases like the Gossard advertisement, where the verbal caption is not separated from the image but superimposed on it, the absence of strongly-marked boundaries tells us we are dealing with a single integrated communication.

In the approach to visual meaning that we have just summarized, Kress and van Leeuwen do two things which it is possible to separate out. First, they offer a structured account of the various choices which have to be made in the production of visual images, and which should therefore be considered when images are analysed. Second, they make a series of general claims about the meanings of particular choices (e.g. that something placed on the right side of the visual field will be marked as 'new' information). Some of these generalizations have been disputed: it is clear that they are not without exceptions (Kress and van Leeuwen often say themselves that they are only tendencies; they also make clear that they regard the conventions they are describing as historically and culturally specific rather than universal). But even if their claims about meaning do not all stand up to empirical scrutiny, Kress and van Leeuwen's framework still has the virtue of directing our attention to the choices that are potentially meaningful. Identifying a set of things to look at is a useful starting point for analysis, however we end up interpreting what we see. In the next section we will explore this point further by trying to apply their framework (and where appropriate, the other approaches discussed so far) to a specific example.

PUTTING IT INTO PRACTICE: A CARTOON CASE STUDY

The example we analyse in this section appeared on a website as part of a series entitled 'Cartoon Theories of Linguistics'. The whole thing is headed 'Phonetics vs. Phonology', and it consists of two images captioned, respectively, 'Phonetics' and 'Phonology'. For readers who are not linguists, we should explain that phonetics and phonology are two branches of linguistics which both deal with speech sounds, but from different perspectives. Phonetics aims to describe, concretely and in detail, the articulatory and acoustic properties of the sounds people produce when they actually speak, whereas phonology aims to theorize, more abstractly, the properties of the sound system which is represented in the speaker's mind. The cartoon takes the idea of phonetics and phonology as 'rival' approaches to speech sounds and turns it into an extended visual joke.

We can begin our analysis by examining the overall composition of this text. By following the normal, top-to-bottom reading path, the reader sees, first, the heading 'Phonetics vs. Phonology', then, the caption identifying the first image as 'Phonetics', then the image itself, and then the caption 'Phonology' followed by the second image. This ordering seems to go against Kress and van Leeuwen's claim that in a vertically-divided two-part composition, the upper element will represent the 'Ideal' and the lower one the 'Real': phonetics, placed at the top, is the subfield that deals with 'real' speech whereas phonology, which is placed at the bottom, is more abstract or idealized. (As we will see in a moment, some other features of the two images bear out the argument that the 'normal' placement of Ideal over Real has been reversed in this case—though some of those features also suggest a motive for the reversal.)

What kind of ideational meaning does this cartoon communicate—or to put it another way, what is it about? In Kress and van Leeuwen's terms, the two images are clearly of the *narrative* type: each image shows participants (two knights) engaged in an action process (jousting). But the meaning of the text overall is *conceptual* rather than narrative: it presents us with a two-part classification scheme differentiating phonetics from phonology. One piece of evidence for this is the spatial composition just described, which has the function of organizing the constituent parts into a coherent whole. The two images are the same size, and the positioning of the figures relative to one another is the same in both. This similarity underlines the point that the two images are intended to be alternative versions of the same reality—a point which also suggests a possible explanation for the failure of this cartoon to conform to the 'Ideal/Real' structure described by Kress and van Leeuwen. Perhaps 'Phonetics' comes first simply because its more recognizable portrayal of knights jousting is easier for the reader to decode; having decoded it, the reader will then be able to recognize 'Phonology' as a more abstract reworking of the same image.

Phonetics vs Phonology

Phonetics

Phonology

Figure 8.2 Cartoon theories of linguistics: Phonetics vs Phonology.

The other key piece of evidence for the cartoon being 'conceptual' is the linguistic element, the heading and captions. Although they are very short, the information they convey is crucial: without the words we might not guess that the images had anything to do with phonetics and phonology. What they literally (iconically) depict is not the study of speech sounds, but two knights jousting. The apparent mismatch between the verbal text (conceptual, related to phonetics/phonology) and the visual images (narrative, related to jousting) sets up a puzzle of the kind we discussed in relation to pragmatic analyses of advertising: to make the images relevant to the theme announced by the words, the reader has to infer what the connection might be. On that point, there is a clue in the main heading, 'Phonetics vs. [i.e. *versus*, 'against'] Phonology'. This formulation places phonetics and phonology in an adversarial relationship to one another, and the images also depict an adversarial contest. On that basis, the reader might infer that the intended meaning is something like, 'phonetics and phonology are like two knights battling for supremacy in a joust'.

In each image there is a speech bubble containing words which a practised reader of cartoons will understand that the knight on the left is addressing to the one on the right. In Barthes's framework, this is an example of 'relay', text being used to extend the meaning of an image. But in this case, the point of the dialogue is not primarily to add to our understanding of the visual narrative. Both bubbles contain the same piece of clichéd dialogue, 'take that, you scoundrel!' The aspect of the dialogue which adds most to the meaning is not its joust-related content but its linguistic form, which picks up on the 'Phonetics vs. Phonology' theme. In both cases, 'take that, you scoundrel' is written in the International Phonetic Alphabet (IPA), which represents all the speech sounds of the world's languages. There is a difference in the way the IPA is used in the two images, however, which is related to the difference between phonetics and phonology. The first speech-bubble text is a *phonetic* transcription of 'take that you scoundrel', which includes fine details like the aspiration of the initial /t/ in 'take' (rendered [tʰ]), and the lengthening of the vowel in 'you' ([ju::]). The second text is a *phonemic* transcription, which eliminates these details and represents only the abstract phonological units in the sequence 'take that you scoundrel'. The writer has also used the linguist's convention of enclosing phonetic representations in square brackets, whereas phonemic ones appear between slashes.

But what makes the cartoon funny, at least for linguists, is the way the same contrast between 'real/concrete' phonetics and 'idealized/abstract' phonology is systematically echoed in other differences between the two visual images. The most immediately striking difference is in the overall pictorial style: here Kress and van Leeuwen's account of modality offers some useful insights. The cartoon was produced using digital technology, but in the 'Phonetics' image, the maker has chosen to imitate the products of much older technologies (e.g. engraving, etching), and to use a number of the features which have high modality in that context. Though the image is black and white, shading is used extensively to pick out intricate details of the knights' armour, weapons and horses; in addition, 'classical' perspective and the inclusion of background landscape gives the impression of a three-dimensional reality. The 'Phonology' image, by contrast, uses a low-modality, abstract and schematic style of representation, with no depth, detail, background or shading. The knights, horses and lances are reduced to a series of black lines and geometric shapes on a white background. Analogous choices have been made about how to represent the dialogue visually. The dialogue in 'Phonetics' is enclosed in an elaborate frame whose design references the 'olde worlde' mediaeval setting, whereas the 'Phonology' equivalent is a simple, unadorned oval shape. The words in the 'Phonetics' image are 'mediaevalized' by setting them in an elaborate, quasi-Gothic typeface, while in 'Phonology' the typeface is functional, reminiscent of the Courier font which was originally designed for typewriters (a version of it is still used as a default 'plain text' font in some computer applications).

We chose this example because it uses so many different resources. Everything from the width of the lines that make up the images to the typefaces used for the dialogue has been marshalled to construct a sort of visual parody of the accusations that might be exchanged in a 'joust' between phonetics and phonology: phonetics is obsessed with fussy detail, while phonology is abstract to the point of unreality. Though cartoons are not generally thought of as 'difficult' texts—they are designed for instant impact rather than the extended contemplation we might devote to the ceiling of the Sistine Chapel—this example shows that they can be highly complex semiotic artefacts.

The cartoon was taken from a website, but for analytic purposes we detached it from that context and treated it in the same way we would have done if we had found it in a printed text like a book or a magazine. In the following activity, however, we ask you to think about websites themselves as complex semiotic artefacts. As many analysts have pointed out, they differ from printed texts in several ways. Some of the differences reflect the way we experience text on the printed page and on a screen. Whereas page-text tends to be dominated by the verbal mode, screen-text, it has been claimed, makes more extensive use of the visual mode. Website designers can also deploy a greater range of semiotic resources than print (e.g. they can include sound and moving images). And web-users have much more freedom to construct their own 'reading path', by following links from one page to another and one site to another. Few people would read a website, or even a webpage, in the way they would read a book—systematically, line by line and section by section. But in this activity we will ask you to suppress any inclination to follow your own path, and pay systematic attention to the design of a single page.

ACTIVITY

Go to the website of an organization such as a university, a language school, a government department/agency, a commercial company or a charity. (Note that for the purposes of this activity you are looking for a 'corporate' website which functions as the organization's public face; don't choose a website which is just an online interface for customers to purchase products.) Concentrate on the *homepage*—the page that serves as the visitor's gateway to the website as a whole. It will undoubtedly offer links to other parts of the site, but this activity focuses on how the homepage itself uses different semiotic resources, so you should confine your attention to what is visible on that page (you can scroll up and down the page, and note the presence of links that take the visitor to other pages, but don't click on the links).

Now analyse the homepage as a multimodal text, using the following questions as a rough guide (which ones are most relevant/interesting will vary depending on the characteristics of the page you have chosen; you should feel free to add questions and observations of your own).

1 Begin by making a note of your initial impressions of the page. What catches your eye? Where would you want to go from the homepage if we hadn't given you instructions to stay on it?

(Continued)

(Continued)

2   Now look at the semiotic resources used on the homepage. How many modes of communication are employed (e.g. language, visual images, sound) and what is the balance between them? Do any of the elements move or change (without the viewer's intervention?) What different types of image can you see (e.g. photographs, maps/plans, diagrams, logos) and what do they depict (e.g. buildings, landscapes, people, animals, objects, products, statistics)? Is all the text in a single language?

3   How is the homepage organized? How is the space divided up, and what is the function of the divisions? What have the designers chosen to place in which part of the visual field (e.g. top/bottom, right/left, margin/centre), and what effect does that have? How are contrasts of colour and typography used? How many and what kinds of links are there to other parts of the site or to external sites? What are the most salient items for the visitor, and what makes them salient?

4   If the homepage includes photographs, choose one to analyse in detail. Consider its ideational meaning (how it represents the external world) and its interpersonal meaning (how it addresses the viewer or invites the viewer to relate to it). If the photograph has a caption, how does the verbal meaning relate to the visual meaning?

5   How would you describe the relationship between the verbal and the visual elements of the homepage? Do they fulfil the same functions or different functions? Is one mode more important than the other?

6   What does the design of the homepage say about the organization the website belongs to? How do you think the organization wants to present itself, and what kind of person do you think its website is designed for?

Doing this activity will have prompted you to think about some of the characteristics of the discourse found in online environments, but the way we designed the task left many questions unaddressed. In the next chapter, we will turn our attention more directly to the topic of computer-mediated discourse, and the questions it raises for analysts of written discourse.

SUMMARY

Traditionally, written discourse analysis has concentrated on the language used in texts, but more and more analysts are now adopting approaches which also pay attention to the non-linguistic elements of meaning. One development prompting this increased interest in multimodal discourse analysis is the growth of new digital media which support complex semiotic combinations (e.g. the mixing of language, visual images and music found on many websites), but the use of more than one semiotic system is also a feature of some much older media genres (e.g. advertisements and cartoons). This chapter has focused on texts which combine written language with visual images, taking examples from both old and new media. As well as describing what is probably the best-known current framework for analysing this kind of discourse—the one developed by Kress and van Leeuwen, using the principles of SFL—we have examined some alternative approaches drawn from the fields of semiotics and pragmatics. Depending on the nature of the texts you want to analyse, all these approaches may have useful insights to contribute.

FURTHER READING

The Routledge Handbook of Multimodal Analysis (Jewitt 2009) is a useful collection for anyone wanting an overview of work in this area: the chapters deal with various aspects and types of multimodality, and the contributors represent more than one theoretical perspective. David Machin's *An Introduction to Multimodal Analysis* (2007) is designed to make current multimodal approaches accessible to newcomers, while a helpful introduction to semiotics/semiology can be found in *Semiotics for Beginners*, an online resource designed by Daniel Chandler which can be accessed at www.aber.ac.uk/media/Documents/S4B. If you want to know more about SFL, Thomas and Meriel Bloor's *The Functional Analysis of English* (2013) offers an up-to-date introductory-level treatment, while a more advanced SFL textbook is M. A. K. Halliday and Christian Matthiessen's *An Introduction to Functional Grammar* (2004).

NOTES

1   Van Leeuwen recognizes that there may not be an absolute divide between the two. Some communicative acts combine performance and inscription (e.g. an animated movie voiced by actors); some texts are inscriptions of a performance (e.g. transcripts of court proceedings) and some acts are performances of an inscribed text (e.g. stage plays). The key differences resemble those we discussed for speech and writing in Chapter 2.

2   We have chosen to concentrate on the combination of language and (still, two-dimensional) images because of the constraints of the medium we are working in: other combinations, such as writing and speech or moving images or music, are more difficult to represent adequately on the printed page, and raise issues of transcription which we do not have space to pursue here (but see our suggestions for further reading).

3   Today these terms are often used interchangeably. Where a distinction is made, it is usually on the basis that semiology draws on the ideas of Saussure whereas semiotics takes its concepts from the work of Peirce (see below).

4   Not all traffic signs are, in Peirce's terms, symbolic: iconic signs are also common. For instance, the signs that tell British drivers they are on a stretch of road where they may encounter old people, schoolchildren, deer or falling rocks are stylized pictorial representations of the hazard in question.

5   See www.campaignlive.co.uk/thework/56431/, accessed 6 April 2013.

9 Computer-mediated discourse analysis

The subject of this chapter is computer-mediated discourse (CMD)—discourse produced using digital technologies and media. Of course, this is not the first time CMD has been mentioned: we have mentioned it in some form in every one of the previous chapters, and we have also analysed examples. In this discussion, however, we look more closely at what is distinctive about CMD, and consider some of the approaches that have been developed to analyse it.

Paying attention to what is distinctive about CMD also entails paying attention to what is *not* distinctive about it, but is rather shared with other kinds of discourse. When a technology is new, it often prompts inflated claims about its difference from what preceded it, and the effects of that difference on individuals and society (Dennis Baron (2009) gives many historical examples of this tendency). Before we turn to this chapter's main question—how specific kinds of CMD can be analysed—we will briefly consider some of the claims that have been made about it as a general phenomenon, and suggest that these should be approached with caution.

COMMUNICATING IN THE DIGITAL AGE: EVOLUTION OR REVOLUTION?

Contemporary digital communication is sometimes talked about as if it represented a complete break with the past ('the digital revolution'). Without suggesting there is nothing new under the sun, it is important not to overstate the differences between 'then' and 'now'. It is always worth asking whether some new phenomenon is the product of revolution or evolution, categorically different from what came before or a 'scaling up' of already-existing trends.

It is often pointed out, for instance, that email and text messages can be exchanged more rapidly than 'snail mail', and that this influences what people use email/SMS for (e.g. arranging to meet at short notice). But it is less often remembered that postal services were not always as snail-like as they are today. A century ago in London there were several postal deliveries a day, and people often made short-term plans through a same-day exchange of letters. In his book *The Victorian Internet*, Tom Standage (1998) argues that some of the developments which we associate with the internet (including 'cyber-crime' and 'cyber-romance') can in fact be traced back to the invention of the telegraph in the nineteenth century. The adoption of a new transmission medium or delivery mechanism does not necessarily revolutionize what is communicated through it, as will be shown by some of the examples discussed in this chapter (e.g. email messages, mobile phone novels and online encyclopedias). Nor does technology change the fundamental purposes for which humans communicate.

The idea that digital communication is a new and revolutionary phenomenon has led some commentators to assert that it has profound effects on human cognition. Marc Prensky (2001) suggests that 'digital natives'—people who were born in the digital age and grew up with digital communication technologies—not only communicate but actually think in a different way from those without experience of digital technology, and even from 'digital immigrants', people who grew up before the era of computers but adopted new technology later in life. Prensky believes that education should be reformed to take account of the impact of technology on the minds of digital natives (though according to Bennett, Maton and Kervin (2008), the claim that there are cognitive differences between digital natives and others are as yet unsubstantiated by empirical evidence).

Another thing which digital communication is thought to have changed—usually for the worse—is the way language is used in other contexts; particular concern focuses on the supposed inability of young people (Prensky's 'digital natives') to write 'correctly' for academic and other formal purposes (Thurlow 2006). The US linguist Naomi Baron has linked the rise of new digital literacy practices with an attitude she calls 'linguistic whateverism'—'a marked indifference to the need for consistency in linguistic usage' (2008: 199). 'A generation of language users', she says, '...genuinely does not care about a whole range of language rules' (2008: 169).

Once again, though, research gives little support to the belief that practices like texting and online social networking are undermining linguistic standards—or, less pejoratively, changing writing styles—in other domains of language-use. Androutsopoulos (2011) mentions a study conducted in German-speaking schools in Switzerland, which compared students' out-of-school digital writing with their school essays: it found no evidence that features of their informal writing were being imported into their academic prose. From the perspective of sociolinguistics and discourse analysis, this finding is unsurprising: using different styles of writing for different purposes/in different settings is a normal part of language-users' **communicative competence** (their understanding of what is 'appropriate' in a particular communicative context). Work on written registers (see Chapter 2) shows that writing in all historical periods has exhibited variation linked to its audience, purpose and genre. There is no reason to think that today's writers are less sensitive to these influences than their predecessors were.

A final problem with the idea of digital communication as totally distinct from other kinds is that it can lead us to make an artificial division between the 'real' and the 'virtual' worlds. Here you might find it interesting to return to your notes on the activity in Chapter 3 which asked you to monitor all your communication for one day, and look at the connections between your online and offline activities. One kind of connection we hope you won't find is exemplified by the case of the triple-jumper Voula Papachristou, who was expelled from the Greek Olympic team two days before the 2012 London Games because of a racist tweet she had posted on her personal Twitter account. But you will probably find other kinds of connections: perhaps you had a conversation (offline) about something you saw on a website (online), or perhaps you sent a message or a Facebook friend request (online) to someone you met at a party (offline). For regular users, digital communication is not separate from everyday life, but an integral part of it.

In this chapter we will be less interested in arguments about whether CMD is good or bad, a product of evolution or of revolution, and more interested in understanding how current forms of it work and what people do with them. We will take it that CMD does not exist in a self-contained 'virtual world' unconnected to the 'real world', and that it is not so totally different from every other kind of discourse as to make the principles and approaches outlined in previous chapters irrelevant to it. We will also emphasize that 'CMD' does not name a single, homogeneous entity, but a diverse set of communicative practices and their textual products. In the next section, we will look at some ways of describing and classifying these practices/products.

DEFINITIONS AND CLASSIFICATIONS

The study of digital communication is an area in which terminology varies. Probably the most general of the terms in widespread use is 'computer-mediated communication' (CMC), which denotes all forms of communicative activity enabled by networked computers.[1] We have used that term elsewhere in this book, but in this chapter we will mostly refer to *computer-mediated discourse* or CMD (Herring 2001, 2004, 2007), a term that focuses attention on the discourse or texts which result from CMC as an activity. Other terms used by scholars in this field include *interactive written discourse* (Ferrara, Brunner and Whittemore 1991), *digital discourse* (Thurlow and Mroczek 2011), and *digital networked writing* (Androutsopoulos 2011). The proliferation of terms reflects researchers' ongoing attempts to grasp the complex, dynamic character of digital communication, and to deal with innovations like 'Web 2.0'—websites using technology that allows users to generate or share content, collaborate and network.

Whatever term we use, its scope has to be broad enough to encompass the whole array of practices and text-types that depend on digital technology: text messages (SMS), instant messaging (IM), chat, email, forums, blogs, tweets, Facebook statuses, photo and video sharing, users' comments on websites, hashtags, Wikipedia entries, online gaming, and so on. The diversity of this ever-expanding list has prompted numerous efforts to classify the forms of digital communication systematically. Here we will look at one of the most comprehensive and influential classification schemes, devised by Susan Herring (2007).

Central to this scheme is the concept of *facets*, which Herring borrows from library and information science. In ordinary usage, 'facets' are the individual sides of a many-sided object; in this scheme, they are individually describable attributes of a complex ('multifaceted') entity. Herring divides them into two groups, on the principle that CMD is 'subject to two basic types of influence: medium (technological) and situation (social)'.[2] Technological influences are about computer hardware, software, protocols, etc., while social influences are about the participants in communication, the purposes for which they communicate and the linguistic resources they use.

The most important technological/medium facets in Herring's scheme are:

1. *Synchronicity* (whether communication is synchronous or asynchronous, i.e. whether or not the participants are online at the same time)
2. *Message transmission* (one- or two-way)
3. *Persistence of transcript* (how long messages stay on the system)
4. *Size of message buffer* (number of characters per message)
5. *Channels of communication* (potential for multimedia content)
6. *Technological affordances of systems* (e.g. whether they permit anonymous messaging, private messaging, filtering and quoting)
7. *Message format.*

The social/situational facets include (but are not limited to):

1. *Participant structure* (one-to-one, one-to-many, many-to-many; public/private; degree of anonymity; group size, number of active participants,...)
2. *Participant characteristics* (demographics: gender, age, occupation, etc.; language proficiency, computer/ CMC skills; role and status in 'real life'; attitudes, beliefs, ideologies,...)

3. *Purpose* (of group, and goal of interaction)
4. *Topic or theme* (of group or exchanges)
5. *Tone* (serious/playful; formal/casual; cooperative/sarcastic, etc.)
6. *Activity* (debate, game, collaborative writing, information exchange, virtual sex, etc.)
7. *Norms* (of social organization, of appropriateness, of language,…)
8. *Code* (language variety; writing system; font…)

To illustrate how this scheme works when it is applied to a specific case, we will use it to describe the technological/medium facets of Facebook.

1. *Synchronicity*: Most Facebook activities are asynchronous, though there are functions (the main one being chat) that require users to be logged on at the same time.
2. *Persistence of transcript* is practically indefinite; unless users decide to remove it, their content is supposed to remain visible/accessible on their timelines for as long as Facebook exists. The same applies even to chat exchanges, which are integrated in the FB messaging tool.
3. *Size of message buffer* is very large, though that was not always the case. In the past, status updates were limited to 160 characters; this figure began to rise in 2009, and by the end of 2011 it was 63,206 characters—the length of a substantial book chapter.
4. *Channels of communication*: Facebook offers users opportunities to post text, photos, video and audio clips; they can also benefit from VoIP (Voice-over-Internet Protocol) technology, which is a part of FB chat.
5. *Filtering*: With its friendship request system, various privacy and security settings, and options to put friends in various groups according to what it is that we want to share with them, Facebook gives us a variety of filtering options—including the option of disabling other people's posts and comments on our timelines, hiding notifications about people we want to keep as friends but not see mentioned in our newsfeed, unfriending someone, or blocking them altogether. It is also possible to create an anonymous or fake profile on Facebook.
6. *Message format*: Like Twitter, Instagram, or Tumblr (and other blogging platforms), Facebook displays entries in reverse chronological order, with the most recent on top. Comments, on the other hand, are displayed with the first one on top.

What about the other, social/situational category? Compared to the technological facets, which tend to be similar (though not identical) across different Facebook profiles/pages, the situational facets are more idiosyncratic, making it difficult to produce a 'generic' description. Participant structure and characteristics, purpose of the group, goal of interactions, topics, tone, activities, norms and codes will all vary depending on whether a FB page is someone's personal profile, a celebrity's page, a fan page or a group page. Even in the case of an 'ordinary' person's page, these facets will differ depending on whether the user's profile is real or fake, how many friends they have, what their 'friendship policy' is (whether they add only people they know personally or accept all incoming friend requests), how often they post, what kind of things they post and what language(s) they post in.

Precisely because it does require you to be specific about the influences which are relevant in a particular case, Herring's classification scheme is a useful starting point from which to approach concrete examples of CMD. In the following activity, we ask you to try classifying some data using Herring's approach.

ACTIVITY

Read Herring's 2007 article, which is freely available online (http://bit.ly/13uRQ36). Now try to apply her model to your own data. There are several ways to do this; here we offer two suggestions:

1 If you are on Facebook, describe your own timeline and news feed (or the timeline of a FB group you belong to) in terms of the social/situational facets listed above. Depending on how dense your Facebook traffic is (how often you and your friends post), you will want to set a particular time-frame (e.g. 24 hours, three days, a week, a month).

Or alternatively:

2 Choose two different fan sites dedicated to the same person and classify them in terms of both technological and social facets. (You can either choose your own artist, or go to http:// gagafan.net and http://gagadaily.com, two sites dedicated to Lady Gaga.)

Which facets did you find particularly relevant for the production of the kind of discourse you encountered on the sites? Did you come up with other facets (not listed by Herring) that would be useful for your analysis? Compare your findings with those of other class members.

ANALYSING THE LANGUAGE OF CMD

What Jannis Androutsopoulos (2006: 420–1) calls the 'first wave' of linguistically-oriented studies of CMD began in the 1990s. The dominant approach was descriptive, conceptualizing the object of study as a distinct linguistic variety with its own features and rules—a sort of 'language of the internet' which could then be further subcategorized into the language of chat, email, instant messaging, etc. One influential advocate of this approach was David Crystal, who promoted the concept of 'netspeak' in his 2001 book *Language and the Internet*. The topics linguists investigated included differences between synchronous and asynchronous forms of CMC, its perceived 'hybridity' (the idea that it combined elements of spoken and written language), and the use of distinctive features, such as emoticons, abbreviations and variant (non-standard) spellings. These linguistic features were typically seen as reflecting the characteristics of the medium, rather than as resources drawn on by users of that medium.

If we try to apply this approach to an actual case, some problems with it become apparent. Below, we reproduce the opening sections from three email messages which were received by the same person on the same afternoon:

1. Hi,

   No worries, Prof. X has just sent me the page. Thank you though. [end]

2. Dear Colleagues

   I would like to draw to your attention that nominations are being invited for the position on the... [followed by another 15–20 lines]

3. We're offering the following courses in April. The full schedule for Trinity term will available by 12th April. [followed by a list of available courses and the closing line containing the explanation and links for registering for the course]

It might be asked: do these three texts collectively exemplify something it would make sense to call 'the language of email'? If you didn't already know they were email messages, could you identify them as such using purely linguistic criteria? The first one could be an SMS message, for instance, and the second a business letter or memo. The third one is harder to place: it is evidently an advertisement sent to the whole University community, but it seems to have been written in haste, since it lacks an opening salutation and contains an error which the writer has not edited out ('will available' instead of 'will be/become available'). If these three examples do not share many features with each other, while at the same time they do share a number of features with texts of other types (e.g. SMS message, memo), that might suggest that looking for a distinctive 'language of email' is not the most productive approach.

In his more recent work on this topic, David Crystal (2011) acknowledges the problem we have just pointed out: he warns against using the term *genre* as a label for 'the various entities which form Internet discourse', because it 'suggests a homogeneity which has not yet been established'. He goes on (2011: 9–10):

> Linguists have to demonstrate linguistic coherence, not assume it. We need a term that is theoretically neutral, from the linguistic point of view, and ... I propose to use *outputs*. I shall talk about email, for example, as being one of the outputs of Internet technology. The term implies nothing about its linguistic character, or how it relates to other outputs.

But although he has moved away from the idea of a single overarching 'netspeak', Crystal's approach still seems to assume the existence of (multiple) varieties defined by shared linguistic features. Along those lines, the chapter of his book that discusses Twitter offers 'some tentative stylistic generalizations' (2011: 39) about what he refers to as 'a variety in evolution' (52): the generalizations are based on analysing a sample of 146 tweets containing the word *language*.

While this descriptive approach is still being used by some scholars, its assumptions have been largely rejected by a new wave of researchers who draw on sociolinguistics and discourse analysis. These researchers are less interested in describing the 'language(s) of CMC' and more interested in understanding the practices of its users—the ways in which they manipulate linguistic and other semiotic resources to communicate, negotiate relationships and construct identities. According to Androutsopoulos (2006: 421), the new wave 'aims at demythologizing the alleged homogeneity and highlighting the social diversity of language use in CMC'. This, as he points out, avoids technological determinism by shifting the focus from the effects of the medium on language-use to the linguistic choices made by users of the medium: 'Characteristic features of "the language of CMC" are now understood as *resources* that particular (groups of) users *might* draw on in the construction of discourse styles in particular contexts' (2006: 421, emphasis added).

The shift Androutsopoulos describes has also had the effect of diversifying the methods analysts use. Textual analysis is often combined with ethnographic approaches, and quantitative with qualitative methods. The approaches discussed elsewhere in this book (critical, corpus-based, multimodal, multilingual, etc.) can all be applied to CMD. Often, combining more than one approach will be helpful in capturing the complex characteristics of texts produced on and for Web 2.0. Among these complexities we might list (though the list is not exhaustive): the mixing of languages, varieties and styles (including non-standard varieties and informal styles); multimodality (the use of multiple semiotic resources) and hypertextuality (the use of embedded links that lead to other texts and thus create different reading paths for users); and the dynamic (rather than static) nature of texts which are produced collaboratively and are inherently open-ended (e.g. comment threads or Wikipedia entries, which can be added to or edited).

Every instance of CMD is multifaceted, shaped by an array of technological and social factors, and this makes it impossible to construct a single, 'one-size-fits-all' method for doing computer-mediated discourse analysis. The methods an analyst uses will depend on the data s/he is analysing and the questions s/he wants to answer. In the following sections we will look at some studies which illustrate this point, using a range of approaches to address various questions about different kinds of CMD.

APPLYING ETHNOGRAPHIC METHODS TO CMD

In Chapter 2 we looked at some work on everyday or vernacular literacy which made use of ethnographic approaches. Similarly, Jannis Androutsopoulos (2008) advocates an approach to CMD which he calls 'discourse-centred online ethnography', combining systematic analysis of the discourse produced online with direct interaction between the researcher and the discourse producers.

Androutsopoulos used this approach to study German websites devoted to hip-hop culture: as well as analysing the discourse produced on the sites, he interviewed some active site-users. He was particularly interested in their attitudes to some of the linguistic features he had observed on the sites, such as the use of 'hip-hop related English' while writing in German, and the respelling of German words according to the conventions of hip-hop slang. He found that these linguistic variables had different social meanings and aesthetic values for different users, and were employed (or not) in a variety of ways to express different kinds of identity and group membership. One informant, Max, told him:

> I avoid using current slang expressions, which I often encounter on some other webpages. For this reason I assume that *Hauptschüler* are less comfortable on my page ;->

The term *Hauptschüler* denotes pupils from the lowest-status tier of secondary schooling in the German education system. Max's comment associates the use of hip-hop slang with a stigmatized social group, from which he evidently wishes to distance himself. This challenges the assumption that participants in online hip-hop culture must have a shared, positive attitude to hip-hop slang. Androutsopoulos summarizes: 'Rather than unanimously accepting hip-hop slang ... as "symbolic resistance" to mainstream language ... participants' attitudes seem to vary according to age and web experience' (2008: 14).

Textual analysis on its own would not have led Androutsopoulos to the conclusions he ultimately drew. In our next example, by contrast, textual analysis, of the corpus-based variety, was the most appropriate method for evaluating some claims that had been made about a new digital written genre, the Japanese *keitai* (mobile/cell phone) novel.

KEITAI NOVELS: CHALLENGING IDEOLOGIES OF LITERACY AND LITERATURE

In 2000, a Japanese man using the pen-name Yoshi, whose real identity is still a mystery, started posting his novel *Deep Love* on a website he had designed in such a way that his chapters could be delivered free of charge to the mobile phones of his followers. The site attracted over 20 million visits, and the novel was later published as a book that sold over 2.7 million copies; television, movie and manga versions of it were also produced. This first *keitai* novel gave birth to a whole cultural phenomenon. New sites were established where would-be authors disseminated their writings under one-word pseudonyms—initially to be read on mobile phones, but some examples followed *Deep Love* into print and onto the best-seller lists. Their success, however, prompted criticism from the literary establishment. *Keitai* novels are disparaged both for promoting low standards of literacy (they are said to deviate from standard Japanese prose style and to use 'immature' language) and for lacking literary merit (they are accused of having 'banal themes' and 'rough storylines without detailed description' (Nishimura 2011: 100)).

Yukiko Nishimura (2011) addressed the issue of literacy standards in a corpus-based study of the style and readability of seven popular *keitai* novels, which she compared to a sample of 88 print novels by authors of the same generation as the *keitai* writers. One of the variables her study examined was the distribution of parts of speech (word classes such as noun, verb, particle) in both narrative and dialogue. A comparison of the two samples did not reveal large differences, though the distribution of some sentence-final particles, interjections and auxiliary verbs did suggest a tendency for *keitai* novels to be more conversational in style than their conventional literary counterparts. Another variable Nishimura examined was the length of sentences. Perhaps surprisingly, the two samples did not differ much, though there was a more significant difference in their organization at a higher level of discourse structure: conventional novels favoured longer paragraphs whereas *keitai* novelists tended to break the text into shorter segments.

In her analysis of the novels' readability, Nishimura looked at the kind and number of *kanji* they contained (*kanji* are adopted Chinese characters representing words in written Japanese; the number and type of *kanji* a person knows has traditionally been regarded as an important measure of their level of literacy, and the charge of 'immature language' levelled against *keitai* novels refers in part to the writers' alleged preference for 'easy' *kanji*). Once again, though, analysis showed that the differences were small. The *kanji* used in conventional novels were slightly more complex, but the difference in reading level corresponded to less than one school grade.

To the extent that there are stylistic differences between *keitai* and traditional print novels, many of them can be related to differences in the context of production and reception. *Keitai* novelists publish their own work, without the involvement of intermediaries like editors and publishers; they also publish in instalments, uploading the text as they write it (in this respect, *keitai* novels resemble the many Victorian novels which were originally serialized in newspapers and magazines). *Keitai* novelists interact regularly with their fans during the process of writing, and this relationship to the audience is one reason for the more informal, conversational style of the novels. Another influence on the novels' style is the technological affordances of their medium: the use of short fragments rather than long paragraphs, for instance, is related to the small size of mobile phone screens.

What we might call the 'transgressive' character of *keitai* novels—the fact that, once published as books, they blur the online-offline distinction and trespass into the realm of 'real' novels, whose authors had different, more difficult trajectories—testifies to a cultural change in progress: literary canons are being reconfigured, and so are popular perceptions of what counts as a 'novel' and how one becomes a 'novelist'. Arguably, it is this cultural change that critics of *keitai* novels have issues with: their hostility to the genre is not motivated by 'objective' features of the novels' language, but is driven more by ideological considerations.

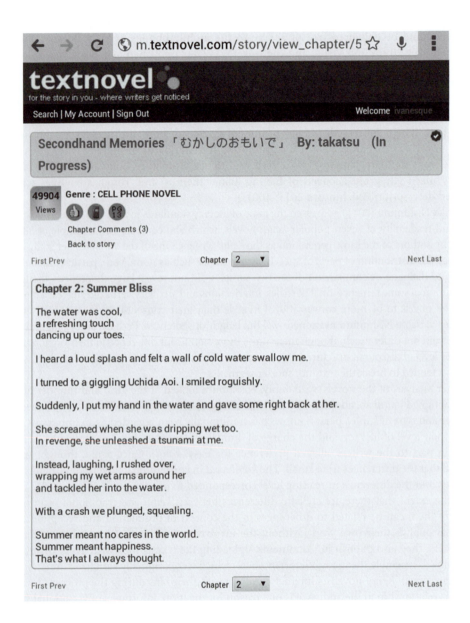

Figure 9.1

While the *keitai* novel has acquired some following outside Japan (in Figure 9.1 we reproduce a screenshot showing a chapter of *Secondhand Memories*, one of the most popular mobile phone novels on the English-language site textnovel.com[3]), both cultural and linguistic factors contribute to its remaining a largely Japanese genre.[4] In the next section we turn to a truly global phenomenon, Wikipedia, which we have chosen as an example of the kind of 'dynamic', collaborative and open-ended writing that 'Web 2.0' enables.

INVESTIGATING COLLABORATIVE WRITING ONLINE

Collaborative writing is not in itself a new phenomenon, but it has been taken to a new level by the advent of Web 2.0, and in particular of *wikis*, websites where users can add to and modify the content through their web browsers. To explore the way collaboratively-written texts evolve under these conditions of production, we will examine three versions of the same Wikipedia entry, the one that defines Wikipedia itself (Figure 9.2). (We have tried to represent some features of the original[5] which cannot be directly reproduced in print form: hyperlinks (which are blue on the website) are underlined, and links to yet-to-be-written articles (originally in red) are italicized. The short URLs given in parentheses lead to the archived versions.)

The first excerpt is the opening section of the initial entry that was written on 6 November 2001 by Larry Sanger, one of Wikipedia's two co-founders. The entire article was about 1,650 words long.

> **(1) 6 November 2001** (http://bit.ly/11wZPMV)
>
> **Wikipedia** is the name of an open content, WikiWiki encyclopedia found at http://www.wikipedia. com/, as well as of its supporting, very active encyclopedia-building project. The particular version of wiki software that runs Wikipedia is UseModWiki, for which *Clifford Adams* is responsible. The main and original wikipedia is in English (American, British, or other, depending on the participant), but there are a number of Wikipedias in other languages as well, the most active of which, as of September 2001, is the German-language Wikipedia.
>
> Wikipedia, like Nupedia, is supported by free software exponent Richard Stallman and the Free Software Foundation; Stallman is one of people who articulated the usefulness of a "free universal encyclopedia" (see his essay online, "The Free Universal Encyclopedia and Learning Resource") before Wikipedia and Nupedia were founded.

The second example, reproduced here in its entirety, is the first edit made to Sanger's original article. It represents one of the negative potential consequences of collaborative writing online: *vandalism*. Wikipedia defines vandalism as 'any addition, removal, or change of content in a *deliberate* attempt to compromise the integrity of Wikipedia'.

> **(2) 29 November 2001** (http://bit.ly/12D2IwY)
>
> **Wikipedia** is generously defined as some gay thing that you go to so you can ruin it for others. It is ancient greek in route and is for gays. And another thing, that like homosexuality, it is morally abhorent in the eyes of the Catholic Church. Giving the power to the people sucks.

This edit did not last long. Jimmy Wales, Wikipedia's other co-founder, restored the entry a minute after it was vandalized. Between that moment and 26 April 2013, the article was edited more than 30,000 times by more than 12,000 distinct authors, and its length expanded to more than 17,000 words. Below we reproduce the beginning of it:

> **(3) 26 April 2013** (http://bit.ly/13zLbos)
>
> **Wikipedia** (◀) ⁱ/ˌwɪkiˈpiːdiə/ or ◀) ⁱ/ˌwɪkiˈpiːdiə/ *wik-i-pee-dee-ə*) is a collaboratively edited, multilingual, free Internet encyclopedia supported by the non-profit Wikimedia Foundation. Wikipedia's 26 million articles in 286 languages, over 4.2 million in the English Wikipedia alone, are written

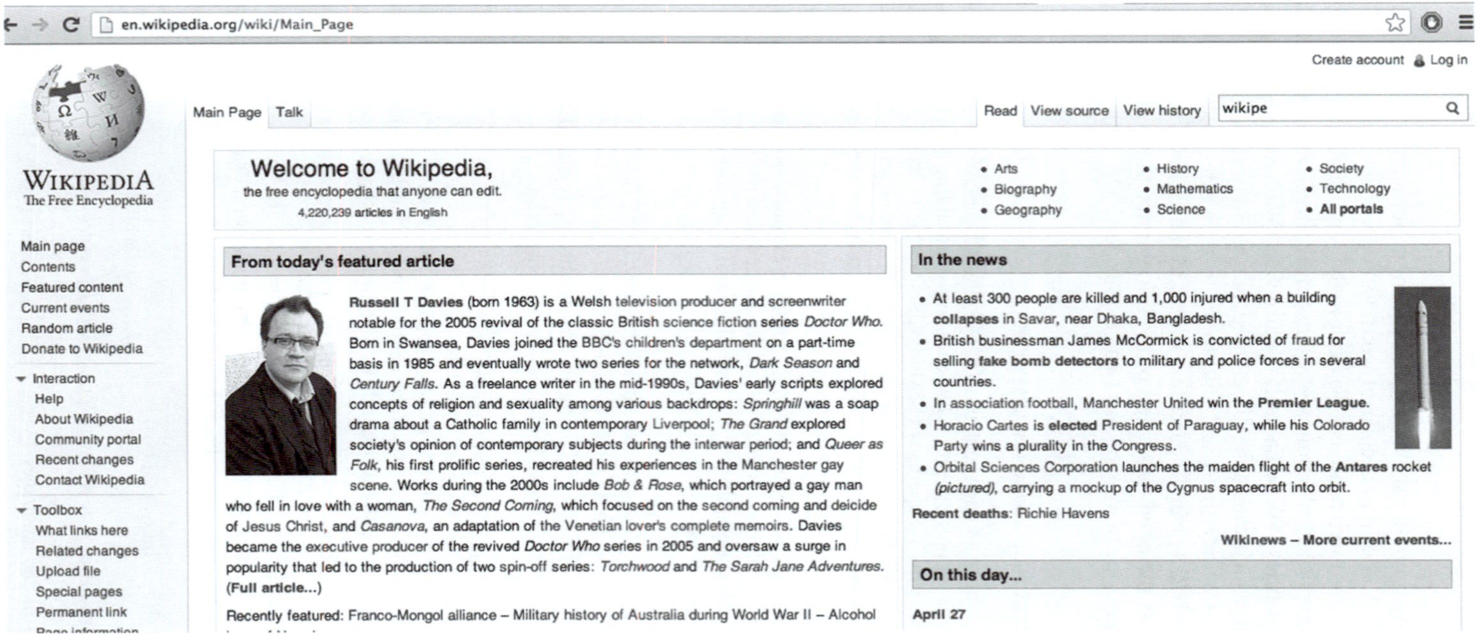

en.wikipedia.org/wiki/Main_Page
Create account
Log in
Wikipedia
The Free Encyclopedia
Main Page
Talk
Read
View source
View history
wikipe
Welcome to Wikipedia,
the free encyclopedia that anyone can edit.
4,220,239 articles in English
Arts
Biography
Geography
History
Mathematics
Science
Society
Technology
All portals
Main page
Contents
Featured content
Current events
Random article
Donate to Wikipedia
Interaction
Help
About Wikipedia
Community portal
Recent changes
Contact Wikipedia
Toolbox
What links here
Related changes
Upload file
Special pages
Permanent link
From today's featured article
Russell T Davies (born 1963) is a Welsh television producer and screenwriter notable for the 2005 revival of the classic British science fiction series Doctor Who. Born in Swansea, Davies joined the BBC's children's department on a part-time basis in 1985 and eventually wrote two series for the network, Dark Season and Century Falls. As a freelance writer in the mid-1990s, Davies' early scripts explored concepts of religion and sexuality among various backdrops: Springhill was a soap drama about a Catholic family in contemporary Liverpool; The Grand explored society's opinion of contemporary subjects during the interwar period; and Queer as Folk, his first prolific series, recreated his experiences in the Manchester gay scene. Works during the 2000s include Bob & Rose, which portrayed a gay man who fell in love with a woman, The Second Coming, which focused on the second coming and deicide of Jesus Christ, and Casanova, an adaptation of the Venetian lover's complete memoirs. Davies became the executive producer of the revived Doctor Who series in 2005 and oversaw a surge in popularity that led to the production of two spin-off series: Torchwood and The Sarah Jane Adventures. (Full article...)
Recently featured: Franco-Mongol alliance – Military history of Australia during World War II – Alcohol
In the news
At least 300 people are killed and 1,000 injured when a building collapses in Savar, near Dhaka, Bangladesh.
British businessman James McCormick is convicted of fraud for selling fake bomb detectors to military and police forces in several countries.
In association football, Manchester United win the Premier League.
Horacio Cartes is elected President of Paraguay, while his Colorado Party wins a plurality in the Congress.
Orbital Sciences Corporation launches the maiden flight of the Antares rocket (pictured), carrying a mockup of the Cygnus spacecraft into orbit.
Recent deaths: Richie Havens
Wikinews – More current events...
On this day...
April 27

Figure 9.2

collaboratively by <u>volunteers</u> around the world. Almost all of its articles can be edited by anyone with access to the site.[4] It has become the largest and most popular general <u>reference work</u> on the Internet,[5][6][7][8][9] ranking sixth globally among all websites on <u>Alexa</u> and having an estimated 365 million readers worldwide.[5][10]

Wikipedia was launched on January 15, 2001, by <u>Jimmy Wales</u> and <u>Larry Sanger</u>.[11] Sanger coined the name *<u>Wikipedia</u>*,[12] which is a <u>portmanteau</u> of ***wiki*** (a type of collaborative website, from the <u>Hawaiian</u> word <u>*wiki*</u>, meaning "quick")[13] and *encyclo**pedia***. Wikipedia's departure from the expert-driven style of <u>encyclopedia</u> building and the presence of a large body of unacademic content have received extensive attention in print media. In 2006, *Time* magazine recognized Wikipedia's participation in the rapid growth of online collaboration and interaction by millions of people around the world, in addition to <u>YouTube</u>, <u>MySpace</u>, and <u>Facebook</u>.[14] Wikipedia has also been praised as a news source due to articles related to breaking news often being rapidly updated.[15][16][17]

The open nature of Wikipedia has led to various concerns, such as the quality of writing,[18] the amount of <u>vandalism</u>[19][20] and the accuracy of information. Some articles contain unverified or inconsistent information,[21] though a 2005 investigation in *<u>Nature</u>* showed that the science articles they compared came close to the level of accuracy of *Encyclopædia Britannica* and had a similar rate of "serious errors".[22] *Britannica* replied that the study's methodology and conclusions were flawed,[23] but *Nature* reacted to this refutation with both a formal response and a point-by-point rebuttal of *Britannica*'s main objections.[24]

Over a decade of editing has left very little of the original version intact. The article has changed in both content and form, and expanded to more than ten times its original length. Wikipedia itself has also changed significantly since 2001: the difference between (1) and (3) mirrors the distance between what it was originally envisioned as and what it has now become. The latest version defines Wikipedia, embeds audio files to show how to pronounce the word, provides data about the number of articles and languages, highlights Wikipedia's history, explains the etymology of its name, and presents the main threads of appraisal, as well as criticism.

The stylistic development of Wikipedia over time is particularly interesting: although it is a free encyclopedia, entirely dependent on the work of volunteer writers and editors who are not required to be experts on the topics of the entries they work on, research suggests that on a number of stylistic dimensions, Wikipedia has become 'statistically indistinguishable' from a commercially-produced print encyclopedia. That is the conclusion reached by Emigh and Herring, whose analysis found 'evidence of increasing formality and homogeneity across the lifespan of a Wikipedia entry' (2005: 10)—an intriguing finding, since the open and democratic character of Wikipedia might lead us to expect the opposite, increasing stylistic heterogeneity and informality. However, Emigh and Herring suggest that Wikipedia users 'appropriate norms and expectations about what an "encyclopedia" should be, including norms of formality, neutrality, and consistency, from the larger culture' (2005: 9). The most active members of the Wikipedia community are diligent in monitoring Wikipedia's ever-evolving content, restoring or repairing entries after acts of vandalism, improving and enlarging articles, and eventually homogenizing them stylistically, all in accordance with the offline norms for an informative, balanced and 'well-written' encyclopedia entry. So, while one might expect Wikipedia to be a site of 'linguistic whateverism' *par excellence*, in fact it has been moving in the opposite direction.

The activity below asks you to look at another example of a large user-created content site, and compare it to Wikipedia.

ACTIVITY

Urban Dictionary, or UD (www.urbandictionary.com/) is a slang dictionary, a vernacular lexico-graphical project to which anyone can contribute. To collect data for your comparison of UD with Wikipedia, compile a list of words and look each one up in (1) UD and (2) Wikipedia. Start by looking up the definitions for the social networking sites Facebook, Twitter and Instagram, plus Wikipedia and Urban Dictionary (but feel free to add other words, concepts or names to your list). Now consider the following questions.

1 Many different authors are represented on the UD site, but is it an example of collaborative writing? How does it differ from Wikipedia in this respect?
2 What can you say about the language used on UD (e.g. spelling, punctuation, grammar, formality, politeness, consistency vs. individuality of writing style)? In what ways, if any, does the use of language differentiate UD from Wikipedia?

CONSTRUCTING IDENTITIES AND RELATIONSHIPS ONLINE

One of the most striking differences between the two sites you have just compared is the greater salience of the writer's individual voice in the UD entries compared to their counterparts on Wikipedia. Contributions to UD are more individualized because they are (normally) the work of a single author, and are not changed after they are posted. Wikipedia articles, by contrast, may be originated by a single author, but they are then refined through a collaborative process whereby other authors add, delete or change things, and editors make various revisions to the content, structure and style of the text. Over time, this process will tend to level out any stylistic idiosyncrasies, so that the voices of individual writers are no longer identifiable.

This discussion of writers' 'voices' brings us to two themes that have come to occupy a prominent place in the study of CMD. One is how writers discursively construct or 'perform' identities in online contexts, while the other is how they establish, maintain and negotiate relationships with others in those contexts. These questions have been around since the earliest days of the internet (e.g. see Turkle 1995), producing a vast scholarly literature. Here we will approach them from the perspective of discourse analysis; our data source is a tweet produced by a single individual along with the responses it prompted from her followers on Twitter.

Lena Dunham, the producer of the tweet, is a young American writer, director and actress, who is best known as the creator of the popular TV series *Girls*. She is also an active user of Twitter: by 25 July 2012 she had sent 6,420 tweets, and acquired more than a million followers (1,109,427). As a celebrity tweeter, Lena Dunham uses her Twitter account to create and maintain a particular persona. The tweet we reproduce below suggests that she is highly conscious of and reflexive about this: it is a 'meta-tweet', a tweet about tweeting.

5:46 a.m. – Feb 6, 2013

A typo in a tweet fills me with more shame than if my pants split at a presidential event of some kind

This is a comment on the practice of tweeting, in which the writer presents herself as a particular kind of tweeter, one who takes pride in her ability to craft messages and feels shamed by careless errors. (Evidently, she does not exemplify the linguistic 'whateverism' that Naomi Baron attributes to writers of her generation.) The meaning of the message is paralleled by its form: this is a complete, lexically varied and grammatically complex sentence, with no deviations from formal standard English, which uses 102 of the 140 characters Twitter sets as a maximum. The tweet is also witty, containing a figure of speech known as *hyperbole* (exaggeration). In this very short text, Lena Dunham constructs herself as a skilful writer/tweeter by simultaneously saying and doing: she both refers to the high standards she sets herself when writing/tweeting and displays those standards in the way she actually writes. Her use of hyperbole, which functions as a form of self-deprecating humour, prevents her from coming across as boastful or smug.

This tweet did not go unnoticed. More than 2,000 users retweeted it, and more than 1,000 marked it as one of their favourite tweets. Twenty-three users engaged with it by replying, marking their own tweets with '@lenadunham' to identify Dunham as the addressee. Below we reproduce these responses.[6]

1. 5:47 AM

    A: @lenadunham nersjknrjinevjaoe

2. 5:47 AM

    B: @lenadunham it's only natural; you can change split pants.

3. 5:48 AM

    C: @lenadunham Especially when people have already retweeted it...

4. 5:48 AM

    D: @lenadunham if i see you at shows this fw i promise to say hi and not just tweet you embarrassed about my shyness. this is my current goal

5. 5:49 AM

    E: @lenadunham Just saying, hypothetically, where might one get a spiffy see through mesh clubbin' shirt if one was asking for a friend?

6. 5:50 AM

    F: @lenadunham There is no greater shame than having a grammatically incorrect witticism retweeted. *flashbacks, nightmares, convulses*

7. 5:50 AM

    G: @lenadunham You think you could get me casted on girls as a date rapist who prematurely ejaculates? #notypo

8. 5:50 AM

    H: @lenadunham EW interviewed you. How about a novelist interviewing you?

9. 5:51 AM

    I: @lenadunham one letter makes ill the difference

10. 5:52 AM

    J: @lenadunham I *literally* split my seam and had my skirt fall off in peak hour in the city centre. You're right, a typo IS more shaming.

11. 5:53 AM

     J: @lenadunham (I documented my butt-showing shame by tweeting and recording my bare-assed antics. /Youtube link/). Because, y'know... ?

12. 5:55 AM

     K: @lenadunham Grow up.

13. 6:00 AM

     L: @K Hey, why you picking on @lenadunham?

14. 6:01 AM

     M: @C @lenadunham If you delete the tweet, it deletes all the retweets! Unless the person retweets the copy/paste way.

15. 6:02 AM

     C: @M @lenadunham I know, but I feel like I earned those retweets and I WANT THEM BACK!

16. 6:03 AM

     N: @lenadunham My tuxedo pants split as I walked on the Folger Library stage at a PEN/Faulkner reading. That was WAY WORSE than a tweet typo.

17. 6:19 AM

     O: @lenadunham I fell down a flight of stairs at the White House Correspondents Dinner in front of 100s of people once. It was worse.

18. 6:35 AM

     P: @lenadunham and how

19. 7:37 AM

     Q: @O fell down a flight of stairs during the People's Choice Awards, knocked down part of ET's platform, took Tom Hanks down with me.

20. 7:39 AM

     O: @Q LOLLL. OK, you win, although I did accidentally flash Tiki Barner once while at TCA. He had to turn his back to I could button up

21. 7:44 AM

     Q: @O now YOU win.

22. 2:53 PM

     R: @lenadunham ...story of my life

23. 8:08 PM

     S: @lenadunham A typo in a tweet consumes w/the kind of shame 1 has upon being caught eating food out of the trash. (I totes never do that.)

Though some of these responses (4, 5, 7, 8) are unrelated to the 'typo' theme, the majority engage with the tweet directly. Examining the ways in which this is done is interesting for what it tells us about the negotiation of a particular kind of social relationship (one which has argu-ably become more culturally salient since the advent of digital social media): the relationship between a celebrity and those who follow him or her. This is a distinctive kind of relationship, in that the online exchanges which sustain it are informal and may appear to be quite personal, but the parties are essentially total strangers, and their positions are not symmetrical (Lena Dunham's followers respond to her, and sometimes to one another, but in this thread she does not respond to any of them). The vast majority of Dunham's million-plus followers do not know her personally, offline; they know only her media persona. How do they use Twitter to construct their relationship with her?

Most respondents in this thread seem to be trying to construct an affiliative relationship with Lena Dunham, and they mark affiliation not only by expressing agreement with or approval of her original tweet, but also by using some of the same communicative strategies in their own tweets—for instance, meta-comments on the medium (e.g. B, C and F's remarks on the impos-sibility of correcting typos on Twitter), witticisms (e.g. the deliberate use of typos/gibberish by A and I), and hyperbole/self-deprecation (e.g. F, J and S all claim to be even more ashamed of their typos than Dunham, while N, O and Q compete to recount more and more embarrassing personal experiences). These strategies suggest that Dunham's followers identify with, and want to emulate, the kind of persona she projects on Twitter. Arguably, what they are constructing in their tweets is not only a relationship to Lena Dunham, but also an identity for themselves as 'the kind of person who likes (or is like) Lena Dunham'.

Here we have considered only those tweets that were written as direct responses to the initial message: as we said earlier, that message was retweeted and marked as a favourite by many more people, giving it a longer and more varied 'afterlife' which could also be traced and analysed. But what we have tried to show in this small-scale analysis is how computer-mediated literacy practices, and the strategies people use to construct identities and relationships online, may be illuminated by looking closely at even such tiny textual snippets as a tweet.

ACTIVITY

Below we reproduce some more of Lena Dunham's tweets (they are numbered from top to bot-tom, but listed as they would be on Twitter, in reverse chronological order, i.e. 20 is the earliest and 1 the latest.)

1 My personal criteria for engaging twitter debate: I wait until something just sits so wrong in my belly & bones that I must finally speak.
2 Imma be the first bitch to get a motion activated paper towel dispenser in my at-home bathroom
3 "This is a story of two girls, each of whom suspected the other of a more passionate con-nection with life." --Eleanor Bergstein
4 Approx. 78 people a day tweet me "I've seen your boobs more than I've seen my own." That CAN'T be true, says the literalist.
5 You just did! #onit RT @RyanKelling Someone tell @lenadunham to pair up Adam and Ray more often.

(Continued)

(Continued)

6 I hereby nominate my building to be the site of the 3rd installment in the If These Walls Could Talk franchise

7 Oh wow @DCpierson is rapping for everyone who pre-orders his book at http://crapkingdom.com/ . DC has a real cute video store guy vibe!

8 I know I'm tired because some girl from college's acoustic EP came on my shuffle and I just listened & listened

9 Let's start a trend where every time we do something awkward we pause then say "brought to you by the Helena Rubinstein Foundation" #PBS

10 Going through a phase where I straight up eat baguette in public like a Frenchman on the go

11 Tune in if you love, in no particular order, John Cameron Mitchell, Staten Island, dogs, vomit, Booth Jonathan, Adam, Yoko Ono, attitude

12 Tonight's episode of Girls was directed by Claudia Weill, who is a living legend, and written by Murray Miller, who is a human garbage can.

13 It's only the teensiest bits of trash in crevices, but the twitter response will end it! RT @ overwhitmanated You had me until the littering.

14 Other top vices include lateness and littering, aka things that do not directly cause cancer but do directly cause fights

15 I hardly drink, don't do drugs. My major vice is reading the "personal life" section of Wikipedia entries til' I'm doused in despair.

16 I need to retire the bit where I tell wine-savvy waiters "I'd like a red that tastes like juice"

17 Nothing says "I don't really want to chat" like sitting alone in a restaurant with your laptop open next to your personal pan pizza

18 Emotional nudity is way scarier than the physical kind to me. Every time you relate it feels like another miracle, a gem in a troll's belly.

19 Thank you for all the lovely supportive words re: the last ep of Girls. CC: @patrickwilson73 @SaltyShep @campsucks @JuddApatow

20 Twitter is a place to complain about food, but it's also a place full of people who make me excited about the world my children will live in

Analyse these texts by looking at their structure and content. What does Lena Dunham tweet about? How does she address her audience? On the basis of this slightly larger sample of her Twitter output, what can you say about her linguistic choices (e.g. vocabulary, grammar, spelling, punctuation) and how would you describe her rhetorical style?

If you prefer, you can do this activity using 20 consecutive tweets from another Twitter account of your choice.

SUMMARY

While no single analytic approach can cover all the diverse manifestations of CMD, in this chapter we have suggested some principles which may be generally applicable. One is to start by unpacking the technological and social influences on the discourse being analysed, since this helps you to see what analytic approach, or combination of approaches, will be most illuminating in a particular case (e.g. multimodal, corpus-based, ethnographic). Another principle is that communication in virtual settings should not be studied in isolation from the wider, 'real-world' context: though CMD is produced online, it has offline ramifications. A third principle is to avoid technological determinism and focus on what users *do* with technology. Rather than being seen as the end-product of a set of rules and norms which people auto-matically apply under certain technologically-mediated conditions, CMD is increasingly understood and studied as the product of social and cultural practices, in which people make creative and strategic use of the resources technology offers.

In the last chapter of Part II, we will see how a somewhat similar approach, focusing on the use writers make of the linguistic resources available to them, can be applied to multilingual writing, and used to analyse discourse in which different codes and scripts are mixed.

FURTHER READING

CMC is a fast-moving area of research, and it is now producing an increasing number of textbooks aimed at students. Recent examples include David Crystal's *Internet Linguistics* (2011), which concentrates on the descriptive linguistic analysis of internet-based texts, and David Barton and Carmen Lee's *Language Online* (2013), which approaches CMD from the perspective of the new literacy studies, showing how digital writing can be studied as a social practice. *Digital Discourse* (Thurlow and Mroczek 2011) is a research-based collection cover-ing a range of topics, methods and theoretical approaches. Articles on language use in digital media also feature regularly in the open-access electronic journal *Language@Internet* (www.languageatinternet.org/).

NOTES

1   SMS/texting is also usually included in the category of CMC, though before the smartphone era it was less ostensibly 'computer-mediated'.
2   According to Herring (2007), 'these are presented in an unordered, non-hierarchical relationship, on the further assumption that one cannot be assigned theoretical precedence over the other for CMD as a whole; rather, the relative strength of social and technical influences must be discovered for different contexts of CMD through empirical analysis'.
3   Textnovel, launched in 2008, is the first English-language mobile phone novel site and social networking service for authors and their readers (www.textnovel.com).
4   It can be argued that compared to an alphabetically written language like English, Japanese (which uses logographic and syllabic writing), allows more content to be delivered in a single instalment consisting of a limited number of characters. However, the popularity of *keitai* probably has more to do with cultural factors (e.g. the existence of large numbers of commuters equipped with mobile phones, which they use to pass the time spent travelling to/from work).
5   The original can be accessed at http://en.wikipedia.org/wiki/Wikipedia.
6   A point about ethics (discussed further in Chapter 12): these responses have been anonymized by substituting A, B, C, etc., for the name used by the tweeter. People who use Twitter cannot expect privacy, since it is a public platform (anyone can follow anyone), but they may expect their tweets to be ephemeral, in public circulation only for a limited time. For the purposes of our discussion, Lena Dunham's identity is relevant/important, but the identities of her individual followers are not. So even if we are not ethically obliged to do so, there is no reason for us not to protect their privacy by anonymizing them.

10 Multilingual discourse analysis

This chapter focuses on analysing written texts which are made up of more than one language, dialect or script. Like discourse that mixes writing with other modes, writing that mixes linguistic codes is not a new phenomenon,[1] but in contemporary conditions it does appear to be becoming more widespread and more visible. Here we look at some approaches to multilingual written discourse, and analyse some examples in which codes and scripts are mixed. Our examples are taken from various parts of the world, and from three different contexts where multilingual writing is commonly encountered: as part of the urban landscape, on paper and online.

CODE-SWITCHING IN SPEECH AND WRITING

Code-switching (CS) means alternating between two or more distinct linguistic varieties (languages or dialects) in a single stretch of discourse. The title of an article by the linguist Shana Poplack (1980) quotes a memorable example from the author's data: 'Sometimes I'll start a sentence in English *y termino en español*' ['and finish in Spanish']. Poplack, like many linguists, is interested in describing the structural linguistic factors which influence CS. Discourse analysts, however, are more interested in the social and communicative purposes CS serves. What motivates people to mix languages and dialects, and what effects does this produce?

A number of approaches have been used to study the social motivations and communicative functions of CS in speech. Carol Myers-Scotton (2006) gives an overview of the main ones, pointing out that they all build on the work of the interactional sociolinguist John Gumperz (1982). Gumperz developed the concept of a *contextualization cue*—a 'pointer' embedded in discourse which helps listeners to understand not just the meaning of the words a speaker utters, but how they relate to the previous exchange and the overall context. Prosodic and paralinguistic cues, such as pausing, laughter, a change in pitch, loudness or tone of voice, may be used to convey to the listener that 'this next bit is really important', or 'this is personal/sensitive information', or 'now I'm joking', or 'now I'm changing the subject'. For **bilingual** speakers, CS can also function as a contextualization cue. If a group of bilingual workers are chatting in Punjabi and then switch to English when an English monolingual colleague enters the room, the switch marks a change in the context, in this case triggered by the advent of a new participant (this is sometimes called *situational* CS). If a group of bilingual workers and their bilingual boss are chatting in Punjabi, and the boss switches to English, the switch itself redefines the context: even though the setting and participants have not changed, the boss's use of CS has shifted the frame from 'play' to 'work' and her own role in the group from 'peer' to 'person in authority' (this is sometimes called *metaphorical* CS).[2] The idea that CS responds to or creates a change in the contextual framing of an interaction has been elaborated in different ways by different theorists. One model draws on *accommodation theory*, which posits that communicators 'accommodate to' one another in discourse: most often they modify their linguistic behaviour to be more similar to their interlocutors, and so decrease social distance (this is called *convergence*), or—more unusually—they may do the opposite, increase social distance by making their behaviour less like their interlocutor's (*divergence*). CS can be understood as an accommodation strategy: a common motivation for switching is to accommodate an interlocutor's choice of code, as with the bilingual workers in our workplace example, who switch to English when they are joined by a non-Punjabi-speaking colleague.

A second model, the *markedness model* developed by Carol Myers-Scotton, suggests that participants in every communicative exchange recognize a set of rights and obligations (an 'RO set') which goes along with certain expectations about code-choice. The *unmarked* code-choice is the one that is considered 'normal' and socially appropriate for participants in that kind of exchange. In our imaginary workplace situation, for instance, English is the unmarked choice for work-related talk, while Punjabi is unmarked for casual exchanges among bilingual peers. Someone who made a *marked* choice (e.g. used Punjabi rather than English in a work-related interaction with the boss) would be signalling a rejection of, and desire to renegotiate, the usual RO set. Exactly what is conveyed by a marked code-choice depends on the details of the context, but in this case, the marked use of Punjabi could hypothetically signal the worker's desire to redefine the interaction as personal rather than professional, or to challenge the boss's authority, or to ingratiate himself with her by emphasizing their shared ethnic identity.

A third framework draws on *Conversation Analysis* (CA), an approach to spoken interaction which emphasizes its sequential (turn-by-turn) organization. Advocates of CA (e.g. Auer 1999) challenge the view that code-choices have the fixed meanings implied by statements like 'English is the unmarked choice for work-related talk'. They argue that the same code-choice may mean different things in different cases; understanding what CS accomplishes in a specific case requires the analyst to pay close attention to the preceding and following turns.

These approaches come from the study of *spoken* language, and it might be asked how useful they are for analysing multilingual *written* texts. The answer is, it depends on the kind of writing you want to analyse. Where writing is used for interaction (e.g. in online chat, or an exchange of comments on Facebook or YouTube), it is possible, and may well be fruitful, to ask how contributions are sequentially organized, whether participants accommodate to one another, whether their code-choices are marked or unmarked and what rights and obligations they aim to negotiate. At the end of this chapter we consider an example which lends itself well to this kind of analysis. But many multilingual texts are more difficult to analyse using frameworks developed for spoken CS, and the reasons take us back to one of the basic speech-writing differences discussed in Chapter 2: speech is organized temporally, whereas writing is organized spatially. Any instance of spoken CS will occur at an identifiable moment in time—we will hear *first* language A *and then* language B. In writing, by contrast, there need not be any 'first... and then'. Different languages may be juxtaposed within a single visual field, so that the reader encounters them simultaneously. Figure 10.1 is an example.

This text is bilingual and biscriptal (it combines English written in Roman script and Urdu written in Arabic script), but there is no predetermined order in which its constituent elements must be processed. A monolingual reader might glance at the whole text, register the presence of a language s/he cannot understand, and then concentrate exclusively on the part of the text

Figure 10.1

s/he can decode; a bilingual reader who is able to decode all of it can still follow a number of different reading paths. From the perspective of the reader/viewer, there is no 'moment' at which this text could be said to 'switch' from one code to another. Where a text is multilingual but contains no identifiable 'switch', we will refer from now on to code or language *mixing* rather than code-switching.

Written language mixing has been less studied than spoken CS, and both have arguably suffered from what Mark Sebba (2012: 1) calls 'a monolingual bias in most industrialised societies—the regulatory tendency which validates only "pure" language and regards language mixing ... as illegitimate. . . .'. Because of this bias, many people do not realize that multilingualism has been the norm rather than the exception in most communities and societies throughout human history (Evans 2013). It is also an increasingly visible aspect of today's industrialized societies, whose populations, particularly in large urban centres, are characteristically multi-ethnic and cosmopolitan. The proliferation of codes and scripts seen on signs, billboards, shop-fronts and graffiti turn the streets of our cities into multilingual texts.

LINGUISTIC LANDSCAPES: MULTILINGUAL DISCOURSE ON THE STREET

The photograph in Figure 10.2 was taken at the central bus station in Oxford, UK. It shows a sign located by the bay reserved for the 'hop-on-hop-off' city sightseeing bus. This sign indicates the 'passenger exit' in ten different languages. Each translation is placed between the flag of the country where the language is spoken and the drawings of a running man and an arrow

Figure 10.2

pointing toward the exit. Informationally, the sign is redundant: for one thing, the visual representation of a running man and the arrow would communicate the same message without any accompanying text; for another, a tourist who is in the right place to read the text will already be able to see the exit, which is right next to the sign. Ironically, the only message a stranger might need help understanding—'no passengers permitted to rear of bus'—is not translated.

According to Sebba (2012: 14), there are 'two different ways in which languages can alternate within the same textual composition (such as a sign, advertisement, or magazine article), reflecting degrees of integration or separation of the languages': they are labelled *parallelism* and *complementarity*. A text exhibits parallelism if the same content is repeated in two or more languages: the ten versions of 'passenger exit' on the bus station sign are an example. Parallel texts are commonly observed at airports and tourist sites, in instruction manuals for appliances and information leaflets accompanying medicines. In countries with more than one official language, there is often a legal requirement to provide parallel texts so that all citizens can read the content in their own first language.

By contrast, a text exhibits complementarity if—in Sebba's words—'two or more textual units with *different* content are juxtaposed within the framework of a textual composition' (2012: 15). Whereas parallel texts do not presume that the recipient can read more than one language, complementary texts 'seem to assume a reader who is *bi-* or *multiliterate* or who at least has sufficient reading competence in both languages' (Sebba 2012: 15). In our signage example, 'no passengers permitted to rear of bus', which only appears in English, is an example of complementarity.

If the information on the 'passenger exit' sign is, in context, redundant, it might be asked what purpose it serves to repeat it in ten different languages. Our answer would be that the purpose is largely promotional. Oxford is a popular tourist destination: this sign, located at one of the two main entry-points for foreign visitors (the other being the railway station), is welcoming new arrivals to the city and advertising the sightseeing bus which leaves from the same bay. But this is an isolated gesture: there are no other multilingual signs at the bus station to assist visitors who do not know English. The multilingual exit marks their entry into a monolingual English city.

Objects like the sign are part of the city's *linguistic landscape*, defined by Landry and Bourhis (1997: 25) as a combination of 'the language of public road signs, advertising billboards, street names, place names, commercial shop signs, and public signs on government buildings'. Studying 'linguistic landscape' means studying *publicly visible* language. Since cities are sites of potential language contact, this can shed light on issues of language management, policy, planning, ideologies and attitudes.

The point can be illustrated using examples from a city—Jerusalem, in Israel—which has been the subject of several studies linking linguistic landscapes to larger ideological and political conflicts (e.g. Spolsky and Cooper 1991). Israel has two official languages, Hebrew and Arabic, and their nominally co-official status would suggest that they, and their speakers, enjoy equality. But the (West) Jerusalem street sign shown in Figure 10.3 suggests otherwise.

The name of the street is apparently written in three languages, Hebrew, Arabic and English, but while the English part (King David St.) is indeed a *translation* of the Hebrew phrase (written on top), the Arabic part (in the middle), is only partly Arabic. It is partly a translation, and partly a *transliteration* of the Hebrew phrase. The first word (شارع) is the Arabic for 'street' (note that both Arabic and Hebrew are read from right to left); what follows is a rendering (in Arabic script) of how 'King David' is pronounced in Hebrew. Had it been written in Arabic, it would have read الملك داود (not دافيد هميلخ). The sign is thus a complementary text (Arabic + Hebrew-in-Arabic-script) rather than a parallel text written entirely in Arabic. The implication of the sign is that Arabic speakers should use the Hebrew word for 'king' and the Hebrew pronunciation of the name 'David'. The same expectation does not apply to English speakers, for whom everything is translated into English.

Another example of the unequal treatment of Arabic in the linguistic landscape of Jerusalem is shown on the sign in Figure 10.4, where the Arabic text is conspicuously smaller than the text written in Hebrew or Roman script.

Both of these examples tell us something about the way official language policy is implemented in Israel, and thus about the state's relationship to its Arab citizens (and to the many

Figure 10.3   **Figure 10.4**

Palestinian non-citizens who work in the city). Street signs can be read in this way because of their 'official' status: they are examples of what analysts call *top-down* linguistic landscaping—signs and notices produced by state or local authorities—rather than *bottom-up* linguistic land-scaping, which is produced by the public writing of ordinary citizens (Backhaus 2007: 12–53). As the examples from Jerusalem illustrate, top-down linguistic landscaping in multilingual settings is not always neutral and unbiased; the way state institutions deal with and display different languages is directly related to issues of power and inequality.

To explore the workings of 'bottom-up' linguistic landscaping, we will return to the streets of Oxford—this time moving away from the quintessentially English city which tourists come to see, and into the neighbourhood of East Oxford, where the population is ethnically diverse, and languages other than English (such as Arabic, Chinese, Greek, Persian, Polish, Russian and Urdu) are displayed prominently on shops, cafés and restaurants.

In Figure 10.5 we reproduce a photograph of a Polish food store ('Polski sklep') called 'Polski smak' (Polish taste) that welcomes customers in both Polish ('zapraszamy') and English ('welcome').

The shop window contains writing in two languages, but it is a case where—for the reasons discussed above—it would not make sense to talk about 'switching' between English and Polish. Readers of English, of Polish and of both languages will be able (or indeed obliged) to make sense of the text displayed to them in different ways. For instance, the phrase 'opening hours' is written in Polish only ('godziny otwarcia'), while the actual information on opening hours (e.g. 'Mon–Sat 9–20') appears only in English. This is complementarity rather than parallelism, since different information is given in each language, but it should still be possible for anyone who knows either

Figure 10.5

language (and is familiar with the concept of shopping hours) to work out when the shop is open. The door does feature a parallel text ('shop/zamów online'), drawing attention to the possibility of placing orders via the internet. Each text introduces a link to a website in the relevant language (Eng. 'shop online: www.polishtaste.eu' *vs.* Pol. 'zamów online: www.jedzenie.co.uk'). It turns out, however, that both links lead to a webpage exclusively in Polish. The lack of full parallelism and the predominance of Polish suggest that the shop is mainly targeting Poles who live in Oxford. But there is no indication that it wants to exclude or discourage non-Polish customers.

The example shown in Figure 10.6, however, sends a different, more exclusionary message. This sign, located in the same street as the Polish shop, is written in Arabic and advertises an establishment called 'King Tours'. The text reads: 'King Tours for tourism and general services. Ticket reservation, domestic and international trips, shipping services, general translation, letting of houses, flats and rooms'. The word 'King' is an Arabic transcription of the English word 'king' (کنغ) rather than the equivalent Arabic word (ملك). Nevertheless, the services offered are clearly being advertised exclusively to readers of Arabic: the sign provides no parallel or complementary text in English.

Our last example, Figure 10.7, was photographed on a visit to a Persian restaurant in East Oxford. Next to a large menu mounted on the wall, on which the names of Persian dishes were written in Roman script and accompanied by explanations in English (e.g. 'chello kebab koobideh' – 'two skewers of minced lamb seasoned with herbs'), there was a smaller blackboard with a complementary text which announced 'today's special' in English, followed by a list of dishes in Persian.

Asked to explain this text, the manager's first response was: 'I know, it should be in both English and Persian, but as you can see, this board is too small.' Then he said, 'We have a lot of customers who know Persian, and we have those who don't speak Persian, but know Persian

Figure 10.6

food. So, they can ask and we'll tell them what we have.' Finally, he offered: 'You know what, we don't know English that well to write those dishes in English.'

Translating a menu is not easy, regardless of how well you know the language: names of foreign dishes often remain untranslated (when we encounter 'spaghetti bolognese' on a menu we don't ask 'what's that in English?'). The real problem for the Persian restaurant manager is probably not so much how to translate the names of dishes as how to describe them for English-speaking diners. One of the three specials listed on the blackboard is 'ghormeh sabzi': a direct English translation would be 'herb stew', which is not very informative to someone unfamiliar with the dish. But unlike the large menu on the wall, the small blackboard does not have enough space for a fuller description. Creating a complementary bilingual text allows the linguistic and

Figure 10.7

spatial challenges to be reconciled in a way that does not exclude anyone: those who read Persian will know what 'today's special' is, while those who don't read Persian but do read English will know there is a 'special', so they can ask what it is.

We said earlier that analysing 'top-down' linguistic landscaping can tell us something about the workings of institutional power. Paying attention to 'bottom-up' linguistic landscaping in multi-ethnic urban settings can tell us something about the ways in which members of different communities mark the territory they inhabit, using a variety of literacy practices to inscribe their identities on public space, and to construct relationships of inclusion or exclusion with others who inhabit that space.

ACTIVITY

Identify a location in/around the area where you live or study, whose linguistic landscape is not monolingual. Within that location, and depending on its size and linguistic diversity, delineate a section to explore in more detail (it could be one street or city block, an entire shopping mall or a single building). Make a record of all the inscriptions visible in the section under scrutiny. If possible, take photos. Then consider the following questions:

1   How many different languages can you identify, and do you know/can you guess what all of
    them are? What are their relationships to one another? Did you observe examples of parallel
    and complementary texts? What was the balance between 'top-down' and 'bottom-up' lin-
    guistic landscaping?
2   Who would you say are the target readers of these texts? To what extent do they include or
    exclude others?
3   What purposes do you think are served by the language choices made in the texts you
    examined? Are their functions purely communicative/informational?

Compare your notes, photos and findings with those of others who did this activity.

SELLING MULTILINGUALISM

In many of the examples given so far, the motivation for the use of more than one language was
at least partly commercial—you maximize the market for a product or service by putting information about it in whatever languages your potential customers understand. But while working
on the activity, you may also have noticed examples of multilingualism (or occasionally,
pseudo-multilingualism) being used to promote a product, service or brand in a different, more
'symbolic' way. As well as being used for the communicative purpose of disseminating information about a product to as many potential customers as possible, foreign languages may be used
emblematically, to symbolize qualities and trigger cultural associations that are designed to
influence attitudes to the product.

If you find yourself in Singapore, for example, you may decide to have a cup of coffee at
tcc – The Connoisseur Concerto, described on its website as 'the leading chain of art boutique
caffès boasting a comprehensive selection of gourmet food and creative beverages'.[3] The name
of this chain combines the nouns *connoisseur* (an old French borrowing into English) and
concerto (an Italian musical term), creating a phrase that simultaneously evokes both Italy and
France, two countries that stand for refined taste, sophistication, 'gourmet' food and coffee,
fashion, etc. Words of French or Italian origin are also found in the 'about' section of the
chain's website quoted above (e.g. *boutique*, *caffè*, *gourmet*). The company's motto reads: 'Enjoy
d'Life'. Here, the *d'* which can occur before a noun in French and Italian (though normally only
if the noun begins with a vowel) is inserted into the English sentence 'enjoy life', where it has
no meaning or grammatical function. Its purpose is to create a 'fake' French/Italian, something
that visually resembles and will call up associations with France and/or Italy.

This emblematic use of languages, which relies on the intended reader recognizing, but not
necessarily understanding, the language in which a text is written, is also discussed by Jan
Blommaert (2010: 29–32), who gives the example of an expensive chocolate shop in Tokyo named
'Nina's Derrière' (the second word is French, but its meaning, 'behind/bottom', makes it an unfor-
tunate choice in this context). For Blommaert, such examples illustrate the linguistic effects of
globalization, which produces a continuous 'flow' of people, commodities, ideas and cultural
symbols (including linguistic ones) from one part of the world to another. To describe these new
conditions and their sociolinguistic consequences, Blommaert and others (e.g. Blommaert and
Rampton 2011) have adopted the term **superdiversity**, introduced by Vertovec (2007) to mean 'a
level and kind of complexity surpassing anything previously experienced in a particular society'.

Some commentators, however, have questioned whether contemporary linguistic diversity really is qualitatively different from anything that preceded it. Piller (2013), for instance, mentions a ninth-century graffito written in Viking runes, which was found in the Hagia Sophia in Istanbul: this reminds us that over a thousand years ago, major cities like Constantinople (as Istanbul used to be known) were extremely diverse in their social, ethnic and linguistic composition. What we observe today may be more a 'scaling up' of the language diversity that existed in the past than a fundamental change in the nature and complexity of multilingualism.

There is, however, one contemporary development that might be described as transformative: the advent of technologies which enable images and texts to travel from one part of the world to another at unprecedented speed. This kind of movement can influence writing practices in interesting ways, as was illustrated in Chapter 4 by looking at the trajectory of the Turkish word *çapulcu* during the 2013 protests in Turkey. In the next section we will look at the creative multilingual practices employed in another set of protests that drew global attention.

THE MULTILINGUAL ART OF PROTEST

In Egypt, an uprising against the regime of President Hosni Mubarak started on 25 January 2011; on 11 February, Mubarak resigned. During those first eighteen days, demonstrators verbalized their revolt on signs, placards and banners, many of which incorporated drawings and cartoons. While most of the writing was in Arabic, some messages included foreign languages, such as English, Chinese, Spanish, German and Russian (Figure 10.8, shows a selection of photographs taken during the protests.) In some cases, the foreign languages may have been intended for the international audience watching events in Egypt on TV, but in many others, the way they were combined with Arabic pointed to a different motivation. Rather than addressing foreigners, the protestors were sending a metaphorical message to their own president, who was perceived as being deaf to their demands. That message could be glossed as: 'if you can't understand us/Arabic, maybe you'll understand this'. One popular chant, which also found its way onto written signs, communicated the message explicitly: it said, in Arabic, 'Talk to him in Hebrew, he doesn't understand Arabic' (kallimū bil-ʿibri, mabyifham-shi ʿarabi[4])—a strong and offensive metaphor given the history of Arab–Israeli conflict. Other signs made the same point by actually using other languages, on their own or mixed with Arabic.

In Figure 10.8 we can see, at the top left, a monolingual, English-only sign; in the middle, a parallel, English–Arabic bilingual sign; at the top right, a monolingual sign in unidiomatic Spanish ('fuera bastante', where the 'correct' form would read 'Fuera, basta' – 'Out, enough'); and at the bottom, an Arabic–Chinese bilingual sign. The Arabic text on the top line reads: 'If you don't understand Arabic', while the bottom line in Arabic reads 'get lost, Mubarak in Chinese'— although, according to a native Chinese speaker we consulted, the expression used in the Chinese part is stronger and more abusive than 'get lost'. Though none appears in this photograph, there were also occasional messages that included ancient Egyptian hieroglyphics. Few readers, in Egypt or elsewhere, would have had any idea if these messages were 'correct', or even meaningful, but their emblematic significance was clear. They metaphorically equated the hated dictator with the ancient Egyptian pharaohs, and also sent the same 'since you obviously don't understand Arabic ...' message as the 'talk to him in Hebrew' chant.

Figure 10.8

In November 2012, tens of thousands of protesters congregated outside the Presidential pal-ace to demonstrate against Mohamed Morsy, the first democratically-elected president in post-Mubarak Egypt, after he issued a decree granting himself virtually unlimited powers. Among the many signs the demonstrators carried was a large banner reiterating the message that had been directed to Mubarak in the early days of the revolution. It creatively combined Arabic and English in a rhymed, bilingual, biscriptal couplet:

إرحل يعني إمشي يللي مبتفهمشي

إرحل يعني GO فاهم و لا NO؟

It is easier for non-Arabic speakers to understand the structure of this text if it is rewritten in the Romanized Arabic known in Egypt as 'Franco', which uses the Roman alphabet plus num-bers (here, 7 and 3) to represent sounds that there are no Roman letters for. An English gloss for each line is given in italics—the translation is a liberal one, preserving the rhyme which is an important feature of the original:

1) er7al ya3ny emshy, yally mabtefhamshy

you're the one who doesn't know, but 'leave' means you have to go

2) er7al ya3ny GO, fahem wala NO?

'irhal' means GO, got it or NO(t)?

The first line reproduces a chant that was popular in the early days of the uprising. It addresses the president as 'oh you, who don't understand' (*yally mabtefhamshy*), and wittily offers him a 'translation' from one kind of Arabic into another ('*er7al* means *emshy*'). The contrast here is between the more formal Arabic إرحل ('leave, depart') and the more colloquial إمشي ('go, go away…'). Both forms are perfectly understandable to native speakers. The second line further emphasizes the idea that the president does not understand Arabic by translating إرحل into English, GO.

In demonstrations, the signs and banners carried by protestors create temporary linguistic landscapes. Somewhere between these and the more permanent landscapes created by public signage, we find graffiti, a form of street art that has flourished in Cairo and other Egyptian cities since the revolution. Like signs and banners, graffiti may make use of different languages and scripts. The examples in Figure 10.9 were photographed in January 2013, on the eve of the revolution's second anniversary. As well as expressing resentment towards the police (visually through the use of the Nazi swastika, and verbally through the acronym ACAB ('all cops are bastards')), these graffiti also reflect the tensions between secularists and Islamists that were growing at the time.

In Figure 10.9 we see a monolingual and biscriptal text at the top left. The giant: 'I'm an *ikhwani* (a member of the Muslim Brotherhood)!' – the kid: 'Screw you! I'm the Revolution!' At the top right there is a bilingual, monoscriptal text reading: 'ACAB – All Cops Are *welad wes5a* ['bastards'], #No 5rfan' [5rfan = *kherfan*, 'sheep', a derogatory term for the Islamists which implies they are brainless/brainwashed].[5] At the bottom is a multilingual, multiscriptal text. The Arabic on top reads: 'We learned (how to bring about) a revolution from the Prophet'. The Prophet's name is given in both Arabic and English in the English part, above the multilingual 'I'm a Muslim' section. On the left side there is a portrait of 'Atef El Gohary, the martyr of the Abbasseya massacre, 2 May 2012'.

Some of the examples presented in this section contain instances of code-switching in the sense explained at the beginning of this chapter (e.g. 'all cops are *welad wes5a*'). But they could not easily be analysed using the approaches to spoken CS which we summarized earlier. In Sebba's terminology (2012: 6), conversational CS is *spoken, interactive, synchronous* and *sequential*. Our examples are none of these things. Neither the protestors holding the banner, nor the graffiti artist(s) who composed the message on the wall, could be said to have been accommodating to their interlocutors, renegotiating their rights and obligations in the course of an exchange, or exploiting the sequential structure of conversational turn-taking. But the idea of a contextualization cue can usefully be applied to these cases. Making use of foreign languages and/or engaging in code-switching can be understood as *discourse strategies* (another term used by Gumperz (1982)): linguistic resources are deployed both to articulate

Figure 10.9

the protestors' message of dissent and to make clear how that message is meant to be taken—for instance, as serious or humorous, witty, ironic or insulting.

MULTILINGUAL DISCOURSE ON PAPER

So far we have taken our examples mainly from the streets, but language mixing is also found in more 'traditional' forms of writing, such as personal letters, diaries, newspapers, magazines and books. Herbert Schendl has analysed the mixing of English, Latin and French in early English written texts: he concludes that 'written code-switching was a widely used and accepted discourse strategy in many different text types and was not even stigmatised in more formal texts' (2012: 40). This testifies to the multilingual character of mediaeval Britain, but we should not assume that the majority of the population at the time was multilingual or multiliterate. On the contrary, multilingualism—and literacy of any kind—was reserved for a privileged few.

Work like Schendl's shows how the study of multilingual literacy practices can shed light on various aspects of social history. Another illuminating example is a corpus-based study of language-mixing in personal letters written by women between 1400 and 1800. This research, carried out by Arja Nurmi and Päivi Pahta (2012), focused on the practice of mixing English with other languages (e.g. French, Italian, Latin). They found this was related to the identity of the addressee, and to the social aspirations of the writer, but it was also affected by the writer's gender. Women used language mixing less frequently in letters than men had been found to do in previous research, and their language mixing followed particular conventions: addresses tended to be written in French (often regardless of where the letter was sent to or from); occasionally, opening and/or closing formulae were written in a foreign language, as were quotations, proverbs and fixed phrases, specialist terminology and euphemisms. Few women displayed the ability to compose freely in a foreign language, without resorting to pre-existing formulas. These findings can be related to the limited educational opportunities available to women during the period: most had not had the opportunity to become function-ally bilingual.

Today, literary and other creative writers may choose to mix two or more languages for aesthetic/stylistic purposes, to lend credibility to the dialogue when representing bilingual characters, or to explore and comment on issues of identity, diversity, racism, etc. A striking example is the work of the Swedish novelist and playwright Jonas Hassen Khemiri, born in 1978 in Stockholm to a Swedish mother and a Tunisian father: Khemiri mixes standard Swedish, 'broken' (immigrant) Swedish, Arabic, French and English in order to explore the second-generation immigrant experience, alienation and the quest for identity. In the USA, Spanish/English language mixing is employed by Latino/a writers like Gloria Anzaldúa and Junot Díaz to elaborate the nuances of 'hyphenated' cultural identities (Montes-Alcalá 2012); in Britain, the mixing of standard English with local and non-standard varieties (e.g. Scots, London Jamaican) features in the work of novelists and poets such as James Kelman and Linton Kwesi Johnson.[6] As Shahrzad Mahootian (2005) observes, these literary uses of lan-guage mixing have given the practice more mainstream visibility and cultural legitimacy. Mahootian herself has analysed examples of intentional language mixing in a range of texts (both literary and non-literary), taking a 'repertoire and resources' approach in which bi- or multilingual writers are seen as creatively exploiting the linguistic resources available to them. She concludes that language mixing in print media 'serves to delineate territory, socially and politically, and to turn the tables with respect to the imbalance of powers' (2012: 208).

By making particular language choices, multilingual writers may tell us something not only about their own identities, but also about those of their target readers. Angermeyer (2005: 517–18) gives the example of a personal ad that appeared in *Russian Bazaar* (Русскй базар), a Russian language newspaper published in New York. The text in Russian (and Cyrillic script) reads: 'nice woman, 50/162/115 [age/height/weight], of Jewish ethnicity, with employment, apartment, and citizenship, but without a man, in search of a man, age 52 to 58'—and here the advertiser shifts to English and the Roman alphabet—'with similar qualities. Brooklyn resident, please'. By employing CS in this way, the writer identifies both herself and her prospective part-ner ('with similar qualities') as bilinguals comfortable with language mixing. A different kind of exclusion through language choice is illustrated by Zeinab Ibrahim (2006), who reports that, since 2000, job advertisements written exclusively in English have started to appear in a major Arabic-only Egyptian daily newspaper (*Al-Ahram*). The message is clear: 'the selection process starts from the moment of the ad's publication, and those who cannot read and understand this ad, need not apply'.

MULTILINGUAL DISCOURSE ONLINE

In the early days of the internet, many scholars predicted that new technology would reinforce the global dominance of English. It subsequently became clear, however, that both as a technology and as a (virtual) space, the net would be multilingual (Danet and Herring 2007). Nowadays, with the advent of Web 2.0, which enables social networking, content sharing, and the creation of new content by web-users (often working collaboratively, as we noted in Chapter 9), the internet is a major site of language contact and mixing.

It is also a site that presents multilingual users with complex choices. One important influence on code-choice has always been audience—the writer's understanding of who s/he is writing for. But for a twenty-first-century bi- or multilingual writer composing online—for instance, posting a status update on Facebook—the question of audience is more complicated than it was for someone writing a letter 500 years ago. The potential audience for the message is much larger, and is likely to include both multilingual and monolingual readers. Choosing to post in language A means that anyone who does not understand A will be excluded. On the other hand, the writer's decision to use a particular language does not guarantee that all subsequent contributions will be made in that language. Another user, having understood the post in language A, may decide to comment in language B, if B is a language that both users share (Figure 10.10). So, depending on who participates and what choices they make, a thread that began with a status update in a single language may evolve into a highly multilingual text.

The same principle applies in other cases where online writers do not know all the people with whom they are communicating. In their study of the photo-sharing platform Flickr, Barton and Lee (2013) examined the literacy practices of users writing profile pages, captions, tags and comments. Focusing on Flickr users for whom English was not a first language, and combining ethnographic methods with multimodal discourse analysis, the authors found that decisions about whether or not to mix languages were affected not only by informants' own linguistic resources, but also by the content of the images they uploaded, their imagined audience, and the purposes for which they used Flickr. An image depicting an element of the local culture was likely to be described in the local language, but if users wanted to attract more viewers or project a 'glocal' (both local and global) identity, they were more likely to opt for English. Barton and Lee also found that Flickr users responding to others' comments tended to use the same language as the commentator—an example of what is labelled 'convergence' in accommodation theory. This brings us back to our earlier discussion of approaches to spoken CS, where we suggested that these approaches are most useful for analysing written data where the writing being analysed is interactive. Comments posted on sites like Flickr are one example of interactive writing, and we will end this chapter by considering another in some detail.

Below we reproduce a short exchange between Mona and Gamal, two Egyptian Twitter-users in their twenties. Though both are bilingual, an examination of their previous Twitter output reveals that Mona usually tweets in English, while Gamal usually tweets in Arabic. Our analysis will concentrate on the choices they make in this particular interaction; we will suggest that all three of the approaches to (spoken) CS that we outlined earlier have some explanatory value in

Figure 10.10

this regard. The exchange took place in February 2011 during the anti-Mubarak uprising, and it begins with Mona tweeting her reaction to something she saw on TV. The subject of the tweet, Ahmed Shafiq, was a senior military officer whom Mubarak, in one of his last attempts to hold on to power, had just appointed as prime minister. Omar Soliman, referred to later in the exchange, was another of the president's military supporters who had been made vice-president— a position that had been vacant for years.

Mona (tweets in English with a tag in Romanised Arabic – 'ya ragal', 'oh man, oh boy'):

Ahmed Shafik ya ragal is speaking on Al Arabiya, I love your sweater !!

Gamal (comments on Mona's tweet, but shifts to Arabic – divergence):

@Mona الراجل دا عنده شوية بلوفرات حلوه احنا مقبلين على مرحلة بلوفرات

[@Mona That man has a few nice sweaters, we're entering a sweater phase]

Mona (accommodates and responds in Arabic – convergence):

والاجندات كمان حضرتك رجل الاجندات عمر سليمان @Gamal

[*@Gamal And agendas too, Sir, the man of agendas is Omar Soliman*]

Gamal (sums up in Arabic – the conversation then ends):

مصر مقبلة على مرحلة البلوفرات مع شفيق ولاجيندات مع سليمان هنضحك ضوحك

[*Egypt is entering the sweater phase with Shafiq and the agenda phase with Soliman. We'll be laughing big time*]

Shafiq's sweaters were to become the object of widespread ridicule among the revolutionaries. What they objected to was not so much his style (or lack of it) as his attempt to make himself appear more likeable by wearing casual clothing. Ultimately, the sweater jokes were aimed at Mubarak: they were an expression of dissatisfaction with his decision not to step down. The 'agenda' jokes (alluded to by Mona in her second contribution) were a reaction to the official media campaign that portrayed demonstrators as 'agents with (foreign) agendas'.

It is possible that one factor motivating Gamal to diverge from Mona's original language choice was the 'local' character of her initial comment, which displayed her close engagement with the day-to-day or even minute-to-minute course of political events in Egypt. If Gamal saw English as an incongruous (or 'marked') code in which to comment on those events, his response might have been intended to communicate something like 'we are Egyptians discussing Egyptian politics, so the appropriate ('unmarked') code is Arabic, not English'. In Myers-Scotton's terms, this would be an attempt to negotiate a different set of rights and obligations. By accommodating (converging) to Gamal's code-choice, Mona signalled her willingness to accept his proposal.

We pointed out earlier that different approaches to CS need not be seen as mutually exclusive: in our analysis, we have used both accommodation theory and the markedness model. Could we also draw on the Conversation Analysis approach? Practitioners of CA reject general assertions like 'Arabic is the unmarked choice for discussing local topics': they would be more inclined to analyse Gamal's switch as a response to something in the previous 'turn', i.e. Mona's opening tweet. Is there something about that text that might prompt a response in Arabic? We think the answer is yes: though her tweet is predominantly in English, Mona does insert (in Roman script) the Arabic affective tag 'ya ragal'. That suggests that the audience she has in mind is bilingual, able to read Arabic as well as English—in which case Gamal might well reason that it is legitimate for him to respond in Arabic. Mona's next tweet, also in Arabic, confirms that she accepts his move as legitimate, or at least that she is not challenging its legitimacy.

Though a purist might disagree, we do not feel we have to choose between the markedness and the CA-based interpretation of what motivates Gamal's switch: his behaviour could have been influenced *both* by his understanding of the topic as 'local' (and thus more appropriately discussed in Arabic) *and* by his awareness of the implications of the Arabic tag Mona used in her initial tweet. In reality, people often base their choices on several considerations rather than just one. In this case, however, another contextual factor that might need to be considered is the public, rather than private, nature of communication via Twitter. Though the @ character can be used to pick out a specific addressee (as it is in some of the tweets above), users' tweets will normally also be seen by everyone else who follows them. Mona, a prolific tweeter, has many followers, some of whom may not read

Arabic (which is not the language she normally tweets in). What would a non-Arabic speaking follower make of her exchange with Gamal? The shift to Arabic (initiated by Gamal but not resisted by Mona) excludes non-Arabic speakers; if they do not want to be excluded, what they are left with is what current machine translation software can offer. Testing one machine translation programme on Gamal's first tweet (2) produced this:

> Da guy has a sweet little pullovers we verge on stage for pullovers.

It is not a good translation, but it is more than a non-Arabic speaker would have been able to make of the same sentence ten years ago. As technology continues to develop, we should expect further reconfigurations in online multilingual literacy practices.

SUMMARY

In this chapter we defined code-switching and outlined some approaches to its social motivations in speech. Multilingual written discourse, however, raises different questions: we illustrated a range of these by looking at language mixing in linguistic landscapes, the emblematic use of languages for commercial purposes, and the creative verbalization of political revolt in multilingual/scriptal protest signs and graffiti. Finally, we referred to some recent studies of print and online writing that treat languages, and by extension language mixing, as resources writers draw on to say something about themselves, their imagined readers, or the larger context in which they write.

FURTHER READING

Myers-Scotton (2006) is a clear introduction to bilingualism; in Chapter 6 the author provides a good overview of social approaches to (spoken) CS. Backhaus (2007) gives an informative overview of previous research on linguistic landscapes before proceeding with his own analysis of the linguistic landscape of Tokyo. Sebba, Mahootian and Johnson (2012) is an edited collection dealing specifically with mixed-language written discourse.

NOTES

1   In fact it is very old: on multilingual and multiscriptal writing in the ancient world, see Adams, Janse and Swain (2002).
2   The distinction between situational and metaphorical code-switching was made in a pioneering article by Blom and Gumperz (1972).
3   www.theconnoisseurconcerto.com/about/about-tcc.html
4   A 'liberal' English translation that gives the flavour of the rhymed original is: 'to him Hebrew should be spoken/his Arabic is all broken'.
5   In this example, the hashtag character # used on Twitter and the English-language acronym 'ACAB' ('all cops are bastards') are global rather than local symbols; used in a mixed Arabic/English text, they

produce an overall effect that could be called 'glocal' (a fusion of global and local): the writer positions himself as an Egyptian, but an Egyptian in touch with a transnational culture of protest that uses shared, non-local slogans and media.

6   These examples could be multiplied: language and dialect mixing are employed for literary/artistic purposes by writers from Ireland to India and Singapore to South Africa. The study of literary uses of multiple codes and scripts, informed by insights from both literary and linguistic scholarship, is a developing field: there is published work on specific texts, authors, places and language combinations, but at present we do not know of any accessible source which offers a geographically and linguistically wide-ranging survey of contemporary multilingual/multiscriptal literary production.

III Applications

Working with written
discourse in social
research

In Chapter 1 we noted that many research projects which are not specifically about language or discourse nevertheless involve collecting and analysing data in the form of speech or writing. Often, social researchers process these data using some form of content analysis; but we suggested that paying attention to the *form* of discourse—the linguistic choices people make when they communicate their attitudes, beliefs and experiences—can sometimes produce additional insights. In this chapter, we return to the uses of discourse analysis in social research, and discuss some examples in more detail.

USING WRITING AS DATA

In the earlier text *Working with Spoken Discourse* (Cameron 2001), the chapter dealing with this topic focused on the kinds of talk which are produced specifically for research purposes, such as interviews and focus group discussions. Face-to-face interviewing remains a much-used method, but today it has also become common for interactions between researchers and research subjects to be conducted using new digital media—in which case they may make use of writing rather than speech.

Analysing written texts which are generated for research purposes raises some of the same issues as analysing face-to-face interview talk. The principle that all discourse is shaped by its context applies in both cases: it needs to be borne in mind that when people are being interviewed by a researcher, they will generally answer questions in a way that reflects their understanding of 'research' as an activity and the interview itself as a communicative event. With written responses, however, it is also important to consider the affordances of different media. If you conduct research using an asynchronous form of CMC (e.g. email, posts to an online discussion forum or a dedicated page on a site like Facebook), participants will be able to plan and edit their responses in ways that would be impossible in face-to-face speech or synchronous chat. Depending on the nature of the research, a medium that permits planning and editing may be either an advantage (because it allows people to craft more considered responses to questions) or a disadvantage (because it makes it easier for people to conceal their opinions and control the researcher's impression of them). The choice of one medium over others will often be made primarily for practical reasons (e.g. that participants are scattered across several different time-zones), but if you do have more than one option, it is worth considering what different media may offer apart from practical convenience.

Issues of the kind just raised may become more salient for social researchers in future. At present, though, most studies which use written discourse as data do not generate it specifically for research purposes, but rather take it from a pre-existing source. For example, researchers with an interest in popular culture, or the construction of public opinion on social and political issues, very often turn to mass media discourse as a source of information and insight. Researchers in history, politics or sociology who study work, the professions, knowledge and politics may draw on relevant examples of expert discourse (e.g. scientific, medical, legal and educational), and the written texts produced by institutions such as governments, businesses or political parties. Researchers in a range of disciplines are also paying increasing attention to the output of digital social media. For instance, texts that appeared on Facebook and Twitter have been used by analysts of recent protest movements like the Occupy movement and the 'Arab spring', where social media played an important role in organizing and publicizing political events.

One recent trend in research involves what is known as '**Big Data**'—using the power of computing technology to capture and analyse vast quantities of information. The information may relate to the workings of the natural world (as with the hundreds of particle collisions which are recorded every second at the Large Hadron Collider), or to some aspect of human social behaviour. For social scientists who want to amass data on this scale, one obvious place to look is online, where millions of interactions take place every hour. In Chapter 7, for instance, we mentioned a study of writing on Twitter (Bamman et al. 2012) which analysed more than nine million tweets. By the standards of Big Data, this is not a very large sample, but it is clearly much too large to be subjected to the in-depth scrutiny that is the hallmark of qualitative discourse analysis.[1] Some researchers have suggested that as we develop more sophisticated quantitative tools for analysing larger samples, smaller-scale qualitative approaches will become less useful, or maybe even obsolete.

But others have argued that purely quantitative approaches have inherent limitations. The problems that can arise are exemplified by the story of a study (Back, Küfner and Egloff 2010) which set out to analyse all the messages sent to more than 85,000 pagers in the USA on a single day. The day in question was 11 September 2001, when terrorists attacked the World Trade Center and other US targets; the researchers wanted to track Americans' emotional responses to these events. They used an automated text analysis tool, Linguistic Inquiry and Word Count, to quantify the frequency of words that expressed particular emotions. The results appeared to show a steady rise in the anger expressed by message-senders during the day. But when another researcher (Pury 2011) reanalysed the same data by looking at the messages line by line, she saw that there was a problem with the earlier analysis. A single message, automatically generated by a computer and sent repeatedly to the same pager, accounted for over a third of the 'anger' words that had been counted in the original study. This particular message was clearly irrelevant for the researchers' purposes: it was not sent by a human, nor was it a comment on the events of 9/11 (it was a warning that a computer system urgently needed to be rebooted). Once it was discounted, the level of anger expressed in the sample fell dramatically.

While this particular problem could have been avoided by excluding computer-generated messages from the sample, the 9/11 study raises a general issue which has been pointed out by web ethnographer danah boyd (2010). Statistical analysis is good for identifying patterns in a sample, but on its own it does not tell you what those patterns mean. If your data are human interactions, whose meaning is context-dependent, interpreting statistical patterns in isolation may lead to inaccurate or simplistic conclusions. For instance, Big Data research on people's social networks has often assumed that you can measure the *strength* of a connection between two individuals in a network by quantifying the *frequency* with which they communicate. As boyd points out, though, the frequency of communication between A and B may have nothing to do with how close or significant their relationship is: 'I may spend a lot more time with my collaborators than my mother but that doesn't mean that my mother is less important'. If you want to make claims about the meaning and significance of people's interactions, you need more than just content- and context-free statistics about how often they interact: it will be more revealing to examine the messages they exchange.

Approaching written data as discourse means not only considering questions of meaning and context, but also paying some attention to the linguistic form—the way language is used in the texts you are examining. That does not necessarily mean that your analysis must be highly technical, using linguists' specialist terminology or paying attention to every detail of spelling or syntax. Outside the study of language itself, those details are only of interest if they affect the interpretation of the data in ways which are consequential for your conclusions. But there are aspects of language which it may be important or interesting to look at, even though language itself is not the focus of your investigation. In the rest of this chapter we want to illustrate the point in relation to a social phenomenon which interests researchers in a number of academic disciplines for a variety of reasons: sex.

We have chosen to focus on sex for two reasons. One is the diversity of the research that is done on the subject. In one recent issue of the interdisciplinary journal *Sexualities* (16: 3–4, 2013), the topics addressed by contributors included the performances of sex workers in a Nevada brothel, attitudes to same-sex marriage among evangelical Christians in New York City, young heterosexuals' views on the use of condoms, the effects of ageing on gay men's sexual experiences, the involvement of elite male sports teams in sexual assault, and the online behaviour of visitors to a gay club in the virtual world Second Life. The second reason, however, relates to something that the majority of these articles have in common, despite the diversity of their subject-matter. For obvious reasons, few studies of sex are based on direct observation of people's sexual behaviour. Most depend on evidence drawn from discourse, what is said and written *about* sex. In the journal just referred to, for instance, ten out of twelve articles make use of discourse data. Much of this material comes from inter-views or focus group discussions conducted by the researchers, but some of it is taken from textual sources such as websites and newspapers. Other kinds of writing that have been or could be used by researchers interested in some aspect of sex include policy documents, legal judgments, medical and scientific texts, written materials produced for sex education or therapy, magazine articles offering information/advice on sexual health, sexual relation-ships or sexual performance, romance fiction, erotic narratives, captions and subtitles accompanying pornographic images and films, instruction manuals for telephone sex work-ers, personal ads, dating profiles and online sex chat.[2]

In the discussion that follows we will ask how the analytic approaches presented in this book might help social researchers to make productive use of evidence from sources like these. The three examples we will discuss in detail come from different genres, media and cultural settings, but in all of them, evidence from/about writing is used to shed light on a similar set of questions: how desire is communicated, and how individual expressions of desire can be related to wider social discourses—not only on sex itself, but also on gender, power, identity and morality.

STUDYING DESIRE THROUGH LITERACY PRACTICES

'During the 1990s', writes the anthropologist Laura Ahearn (2003: 107), 'the residents of [the village of] Junigau, Nepal, dramatically redefined the emotion of romantic love. In a departure from previous cultural norms and practices, *desire itself came to be seen as desirable*' (emphasis in original). Central to this redefinition was the emergence of a new literacy practice, the exchange of love letters between unmarried men and women. In the past, this kind of correspondence had not been possible because very few women were able to read and write. Letter-writing itself was a familiar practice, but it was almost exclusively used by men to keep in touch with male relatives while away from home. In the 1980s and 1990s, however, the village became involved in a number of economic development projects. This resulted, among other things, in more girls going to school and more adult women attending literacy classes. The textbooks from which they learned to read and write were, as Ahearn puts it (2003: 109), 'saturated with "development discourse"' emphasizing individual agency and its connection to social progress. One expression of this new ideology was a shift away from the tradition of arranged marriage, in which young adults accepted the partners selected for them by their families and assumed or hoped that love would follow, towards the idea of marrying a partner of your own choice, someone you already loved, and who reciprocated your feelings. However, cultural norms still prohibited unmarried men and women from conducting romantic relationships openly. Instead they pursued their courtships by exchanging the love letters which both sexes were now capable of writing.

Ahearn's research focused mainly on the practice of love-letter writing, what it meant to those engaged in it and how it affected the wider community. Her methods were ethnographic: she spent an extended period of time living in the village, participating in its activities, and talking to the villagers whose literacy practices she was studying. But where possible, she also analysed the love letters themselves: as she points out, these texts were a valuable source of evidence, because their writers used them not only to express their feelings for the intended recipient, but also, more generally, 'to talk about what love meant to them, what they desired from a love relationship and what kinds of people they wanted to become' (Ahearn 2003: 109).

In a sample of over 200 letters which villagers shared with her, Ahearn detected two recurring, and seemingly rather contradictory, discourses on desire. On one hand, writers portrayed desire as an involuntary response to its object, something which cannot be controlled, and which is a source of pain as much as pleasure. An example is the following passage, written by Vajra to his beloved, Shila (Ahearn 2003: 113):[3]

> What on earth is this thing called love? Once one falls into its web, one is ready to do anything at the invitation of one's beloved. Why, oh why, is it that what you say, memories of you, and affection for you are always tormenting me?

At the same time, the texts were full of allusions to the 'development discourse' which emphasized the agency of individuals. Even though the villagers represented themselves as having no agency in the sphere of love itself, their letters repeatedly expressed the belief that love would empower them in other spheres of life. In the letter quoted above, Vajra assures Shila that 'these days nothing is impossible in this world. A person can do anything'. Another young man, Bir Bahadur, tells his future wife Sarita in a letter that 'the "main" meaning of love is "life success"'. Later in their correspondence he writes: 'When love and affection become steady, one will certainly be able to obtain the things one has thought and worried about' (Ahearn 2003: 113).

Ahearn relates this apparent contradiction to younger villagers' understanding of the discourse which they had encountered in their schoolbooks and through the media they had access to (e.g. Nepali national radio and popular Hindi films). Whereas older villagers regarded romantic love as embarrassing and socially disruptive, younger ones associated the ability to experience it with a 'modern' or 'developed' form of personhood. Traditionally, it was family obligations that had exerted the strongest influence on important life-decisions, but younger villagers were starting to embrace an alternative view which gave more weight to the individual's own wishes. As Sarita explained to Ahearn in a conversation about whether she should elope with Bir Bahadur: 'You should wear the flower you like, you know. You should wear the flower that *you yourself* like' (2003: 120, emphasis in original). What villagers expressed in their love letters was not only their desire for a particular person, but also a desire for desire itself, and the associated values of personal freedom and 'life success'.

The analysis outlined so far does not depend on a very fine-grained analysis of the language used in the letters: it is not difficult to spot the key words and phrases that point to the presence in these texts of two recognizably different discourses, one which uses a language of unwilled emotion (e.g. love as source of 'torment', or a 'web' into which the individual 'falls'), and another which appropriates the language of development (e.g. 'life success', 'nothing is impossible'). But considerations of linguistic form become more significant when Ahearn considers the impact of new ideas and new literacy practices on the traditional relations between the sexes in Junigau. As she points out, both the practice of letter-writing and the elopements to which it could lead were objectively more risky for women than for men. A woman who was discovered conducting a pre-marital relationship stood to lose her reputation; if that particular relationship did not work out, she might find that no one else was willing to marry her. And even if the correspondence did lead to marriage, by choosing to elope rather than accept a union arranged by her parents, a woman might forfeit the support of her natal family. That would be a serious loss if the marriage turned out to be unhappy, or if her husband's mother, in whose household she would be living, treated her badly. Ahearn found that this difference in the social situations of women and men was reflected in the way their letters were written.

Villagers of both sexes used ellipsis, omitting names and other compromising information in case their letters were intercepted: 'still, if you're going to beg forgiveness then ...... you'll have no other choice but to.......' (Ahearn 2003: 114). Women, however, used more ellipses than men, which suggested an even higher degree of caution on their part. They also made more references to the importance of trust in romantic relationships. This reflected another female concern, about what would happen if a man's protestations of undying love turned out to be insincere. Men, on the other hand, made more use of the development discourse, and sometimes inserted bits of English (symbolically, the language of development and modernity) into their texts. This reflected both the more extensive schooling most men had received, and their greater freedom to pursue—or at least imagine pursuing—their individual ambitions for 'life success'.

The detailed picture Ahearn presents of social change in Junigau is not based only on her reading of villagers' letters: it also draws extensively on the cultural knowledge she acquired, and the personal relationships she developed, during an extended period of participant observation. (The relationships were also crucial for gaining access to the letters, since the villagers would not have shared them with someone they did not know and trust.) But the letters were clearly important: by paying attention to their form as well as their content (to features like the use of ellipsis or the insertion of English phrases and terms drawn from the specialized vocabulary of development), Ahearn was able to gain a deeper insight into many of the questions that were central to her study.

STUDYING DESIRE THROUGH PERSONAL ADVERTISEMENTS

Laura Ahearn studied expressions of desire which were exchanged in private and in secret. Our second example concerns a category of written texts which project individuals' private desires into the public domain: personal advertisements. These texts are usually anonymous or pseudonymous (thus protecting the writer's privacy by concealing her/his true identity), but they are composed to be read by an audience of strangers, and circulated, sometimes globally, via printed or digital media.

The use of the media as a forum for personal advertising goes back as far as the eighteenth century, when 'matrimonial columns' first appeared in English newspapers. Until the end of the twentieth century, advertisements soliciting the interest of potential partners were printed alongside other 'classified' advertisements promoting anything from used cars to home hair-dressing services. More recently, however, a large proportion of personal advertising has migrated online, to specialist dating websites. The affordances of new digital media make them well suited to this purpose: websites impose fewer limitations than print media on the length and the number of ads, they can include photos and links to other websites, they are easily searchable and they allow immediate posting or updating of their content.

What users may be looking for on dating websites (in western societies, at least) spans a broader range today than it did 300 or even 50 years ago. It is possible to advertise for same-sex as well as other-sex partners, and while some advertisers still hope to find a spouse or enter into a long-term committed relationship, others are more interested in casual recreational sex. Not surprisingly, researchers interested in the forms of desire which are typical of a particular (sub) culture have often turned to personal advertisements as an abundant, convenient and revealing source of data.

The traditional personal ad is highly condensed and formulaic. Justine Coupland (1996) describes its prototypical structure as follows:

> 1. advertiser   2. seeks   3. target   4. goals   5. [optional comment]   6. reference

Celia Shalom (1997: 190) reproduces an example which follows this template:

> 1. female graduate, 35, fit and fairly attractive 2. seeks 3. intelligent, professional male, 35+, 4. for friendship, fun and maybe more. 5. photo appreciated. 6. box 906.

Many studies have used the information that appears in slots (1) and (3) as a basis for drawing conclusions about what attributes are perceived as desirable by members of a particular society, and how these vary in relation to gender and sexual preference. In the case of gender, numerous studies have found that heterosexual men and women specify different attributes when describing the kind of person they desire: men tend to foreground women's physical appearance, whereas women focus more on men's economic and social status. In her study of ads placed in the London weekly magazine *Time Out* over a four-month period in 1995, Celia Shalom (1997) found that the single most common term used about women by straight men was 'attractive' ('slim' was also in the top five), whereas in ads placed by women seeking men the most popular descriptor was 'professional' ('intelligent' and 'tall' also featured in the top five). The example reproduced above conforms to this pattern. In ads placed by gay men and lesbians, by contrast, Shalom found that the commonest term used to describe the desired other was 'similar'. 'Similar' also featured among the top five terms in ads placed by heterosexuals, of both sexes; but it was significantly more common in ads for same-sex partners, and especially in those placed by lesbians.

The texts which made up Shalom's sample were in most cases brief and predictable, following the same structural template and using the same keywords (e.g. *attractive, professional*) and abbreviations (e.g. *GSOH*, 'good sense of humour') repeatedly. But the shift to online dating sites, where users can post longer and more detailed personal profiles, has produced more linguistically elaborate texts. To illustrate what social researchers can learn by paying attention to the use of language in online dating profiles, we will consider a study conducted by Ksenija Bogetić for her Master's dissertation, analysing profiles from dating websites used by men seeking men in Serbia.

The aspect of the profiles which particularly interested Ksenija was the use some writers made of two languages, Serbian and English. In her sample of 200 profiles taken from two popular websites, almost all were written mainly in Serbian, and some were written exclusively in that language. However, a high proportion (54%) also contained some English, raising the question of what purposes the mixing of languages served. It was clear that writers were not using English for the practical purpose of making their profiles accessible to readers who could not understand Serbian. With very few exceptions, the key information (e.g. describing the advertiser and the target in terms of age, appearance, tastes, etc.) was given only in Serbian, making the profile useless to anyone who could not decode the Serbian text. This suggested that English was being used for symbolic rather than purely functional purposes. What, though, did it symbolize in this context?

There is a body of research on gay or 'queer' language use outside the anglophone world (a range of examples are collected in Leap and Boellstorff 2004) which suggests that it is common for English to be appropriated as a symbolic marker of in-group identity. The uses to which it is put are diverse and locally varied, however. Sometimes English words and expressions are borrowed to name concepts or practices for which the local language does not have terms, or has only negative terms. Sometimes, mixing English with a local language may symbolize identification not only with a local subculture, but also with a global gay culture. In some contexts, the use of English may signify a speaker's orientation to what are locally conceptualized as non-traditional, 'modern' or 'western' values. For members of sexual minority groups this may be one way to express an oppositional political stance, asserting the desire for equality and freedom. In Serbia, a post-communist European country where sex between men has only recently been decriminalized, and homosexuality continues to attract strong social and religious disapproval, some profile-writers do seem to use English in this way. One profile in the sample begins: 'Young in body and soul. mature mind. take me. To a place where gay men are treated equally'. There are also profiles which contain quotations from English-language texts that are shared cultural references for members of the community, such as songs which are popular in gay clubs. However, the most striking pattern of alternation between Serbian and English in this set of profiles appears to serve a more complicated purpose: it is a resource some writers use to negotiate what they evidently perceive as the problematic relationship between their masculine gender identities and their desire for intimacy with other men.

The first two examples reproduced below are from profiles written entirely in Serbian. They exemplify what was found to be a common tendency in the sample, for writers to construct a stereotypically 'masculine' persona. They identify themselves as gay in the sense of having a sexual preference for other men, but they also insist that both they and the partners they desire are 'normal' representatives of their gender, that is, masculine rather than 'effeminate'.

1. ok sam lik.[4] Ne volim feminizirane retarde. Bitna mi je diskrecija, a uzitak je zagarantnvan.
   I am an ok guy. I don't like effeminate retards. Discretion matters to me, pleasure guaranteed.

2. Trebas da budes iz Novog Sada ili okoline, da imas preko 20 godina i da volis mladje momke, da budes normalan strejt gej
   You should be from Novi Sad or the surrounding area, aged over 20 and you should like younger guys, be a normal straight gay

The emphasis placed on masculinity in these texts is obvious in the content ('effeminate retards'; 'a normal straight gay'), but it is also apparent in the *style* writers use, which contains numerous features popularly associated with men's language. Each text consists of a series of direct statements which specify the writer's preferences in uncompromising terms ('I don't like...'; 'you should be...'). No attempt is made to create rapport with the reader, or even to address him politely. Text (1) makes some reference to the reader's desires in the phrase 'pleasure guaranteed', but this is also a self-aggrandizing move on the writer's part, an assertion of his own sexual prowess. Text (2), with its list of the criteria a respondent must meet, reads more like a job specification than a personal advertisement.

Where profile-writers employ English, however, they often depart from this 'hypermasculine' mode of address. The English passages foreground the interpersonal function of language, and construct a different kind of persona for the writer (in the examples below, English is shown in bold type):

3. Normalan i diskretan, tražim sličnog. Bez smaranja na četu. odgovaram samo ozbiljnima. Fem stop matorci stop. **Kiss & love ;)**
   Normal and discreet, looking for similar. Don't bug me on chat. I respond only to serious ones. Fem stop old guys stop. **Kiss & love ;)**

4. Samo za ozbiljnu vezu, VA i okolina. Imam 20 godina, ali to ne znaci da sam naivan, matorci i sakupljaci slika odjebite!! Pozitivan sam lik, pričljiv, obrazovan, normalan. **Let me be your cutie pie** :)
   Only for a serious relationship, [name of town] and surrounding areas. I am 20, but that doesn't mean I am naïve, old guys and picture collectors fuck off!! I am a positive character, talkative, educated, normal. **Let me be your cutie pie** :)

5. Upoznaj me pa ces videti, ne volim da pricam o sebi. **Sweet teddy for hugs and more**. Skype### !!
   Meet me and you'll see, I don't like talking about myself. **Sweet teddy for hugs and more**. Skype### !!

The Serbian parts of these texts have the same stereotypically masculine qualities that we noted in texts (1) and (2). The writers' self-descriptions are brief and basic: in (5) the writer declines to give a description because 'I don't like talking about myself', while the other two emphasize that they are 'normal'. They are direct about what they do and (especially) do not want ('don't bug me on chat', 'only for a serious relationship'), and sometimes they are markedly impolite ('old guys and picture collectors fuck off!!').[5] In the English parts, by contrast, the language is more intimate, empathetic and playful, using affectionate formulas, diminutives ('cutie pie') and smiley faces. There are other examples where writers use English to represent themselves as small and vulnerable: for instance, 'I'm a little bear, I like your company, write to meeee!' and 'I'm just a little kid and someone should take care of me'.

In these examples it appears that mixing Serbian with English allows writers to present them-selves in two contrasting ways within the same text: the main part of the profile establishes their credentials as appropriately 'masculine', while additions made in English perform a less rigidly normative gender identity, and hint at desires which are not made explicit in the Serbian part of the text (e.g. to be loved and taken care of). Because these alternative identities and desires are expressed in a foreign language, however—often briefly and formulaically, and usually as a postscript to the main text—it is not clear how seriously the writers intend to claim them. In some cases, it seems possible that the writer's English is limited, and that he may not be aware of all the nuances of meaning that will be picked up by a reader who knows English well. In other cases, however, it appears that the writer is being consciously ironic: the writer of example (6), for instance, adds a final comment in Serbian which distances him from the 'romantic' attitudes evoked in the preceding English segment:

6. Pisi pa ces saznati. **All you need is love**... ali da ne preterujemo.
    Write and you'll find out. **All you need is love**... *but let's not exaggerate.*

Research on written discourse in which people advertise themselves to potential partners shows that even short and highly conventionalized texts may communicate complex meanings, and that a full understanding of what they communicate may require attention to their linguistic form as well as their content. Writers may convey meaning not only through the propositions they encode in words, but also by choosing to alternate between different languages, or to use formal features which have stereotypical associations with certain qualities or categories of people (e.g. the association between obscenity and masculinity, or diminutives/smileys and femininity).

While Ksenija Bogetić's study was designed to investigate a linguistic phenomenon (the use of English in texts composed by and for Serbs), her analysis also sheds light on the larger cultural discourses of gender and sexuality which writers of dating profiles must negotiate. Our third example looks more closely at how competing discourses can be identified in texts. Since we are dealing here with the notion of discourse which is associated with Foucault and his concept of 'power/knowledge', we will focus on a text which purports to offer expert advice on sex.

STUDYING DESIRE THROUGH ADVICE TEXTS

The text we will analyse in detail in this section appeared in the men's lifestyle magazine *Men's Health* (*MH*), in a column called 'The Sexual Adventurer' (*MH*, January/February 2013: 61–2, see Figures 11.1 and 11.2). Its author is the magazine's newly-hired sex columnist, Nichi Hodgson (described as a 'dominatrix turned sex educator'), and its topic is *polyamory* (the practice of openly maintaining sexual relationships with more than one partner at a time).

Before we turn to the *MH* text, let us consider how *polyamory* is defined in the *Oxford English Dictionary*, whose entry for the word was added in 2006:[6]

CORE SEX

NEW!
THE SEXUAL
ADVENTURER   BY NICHI HODGSON

CANNED HEAT

Is there such a thing as the guilt-free affair? *MH*'s new sex columnist says yes. Welcome to the world of polyamory

Here's the thing: one person cannot give you everything. No matter how happy you are with your partner, few people could deny occasionally fantasising about having more. More sex with more women, without sacrificing the intimacy (or the sex) you have with the woman you love. Here's the other thing: that fantasy can be a reality. It's called polyamory. It's adult, it's evolved and it's very, very satisfying.

Let's say your primary partner (as the jargon goes) isn't into your space princess kidnap fantasy. In a polyamorous set-up, secondary and tertiary partners can be brought into the fold to share those pleasures with you. If you can juggle it, polyamory lets you have sex with as many women as your schedule allows, without lies or sneaking around.

Right now, for instance, I'm juggling the following: one guy who likes to tie me up, the odd slave who likes to be tied up, a couple of guy-friends for hot, hard vanilla sex and the occasional hook-up with a female friend. It's a lot, perhaps, but from this set-up, I get care, affection, friendship and all the kinds of sex I crave. And so can you. *If* you can sell the idea.

THE BARE TRUTH
You have to be both up-front and subtle. Suggest that after one too many break-ups you've come to question whether monogamy can really work. Say, "I'm looking for a different kind of arrangement this time around." Not, "How do you feel about being the girl who gives me messy head once a month?" You must be open: one former partner of mine wanted a poly arrangement, only he

neglected to mention it until six months in, when he declared that he "wasn't monogamous". If he'd informed me at the outset I would still have wanted to date him. But by the time I found out, I had already fallen in love in a monogamous way, and didn't want to share him.

LEVEL PLAYING FIELD
Your proposal shouldn't come as a surprise, either. Most successful poly couples (or triads, or quadrangles) are on the same page to begin with. If your partner is more reluctant – agreeing to it only because she fears losing you – that's a recipe for untold stress, resentment, and heartache. If your girl can't stand you passing comment on attractive women, she will take serious persuading.

Try working hypothetical extras into your fantasies first. I got a reluctant ex, for example, to imagine me having sex with another woman and worked it into our dirty talk. Then I asked him if I could carry out the fantasy for real.

Dating multiple people at once does, of course, make the concept of fidelity redundant. Instead, loyalty comes to the fore. During the build-up (and, in fact, at all times during the relationship), you have to assert your loyalty to your primary partner – even when you're arranging dates and sex with other women. This could mean not discussing your finances with a new girlfriend, or asking your primary partner before you arrange a date with your secondary.

Similarly, whether it's sofa-cuddling or deep-throating, be sure to always keep some activities that are just for your

Get away with several partners? Yes we can!

NICHI HODGSON'S BOOK 'BOUND TO YOU' (HODDER) IS OUT NOW

◢ @MENSHEALTHUK

Figure 11.1

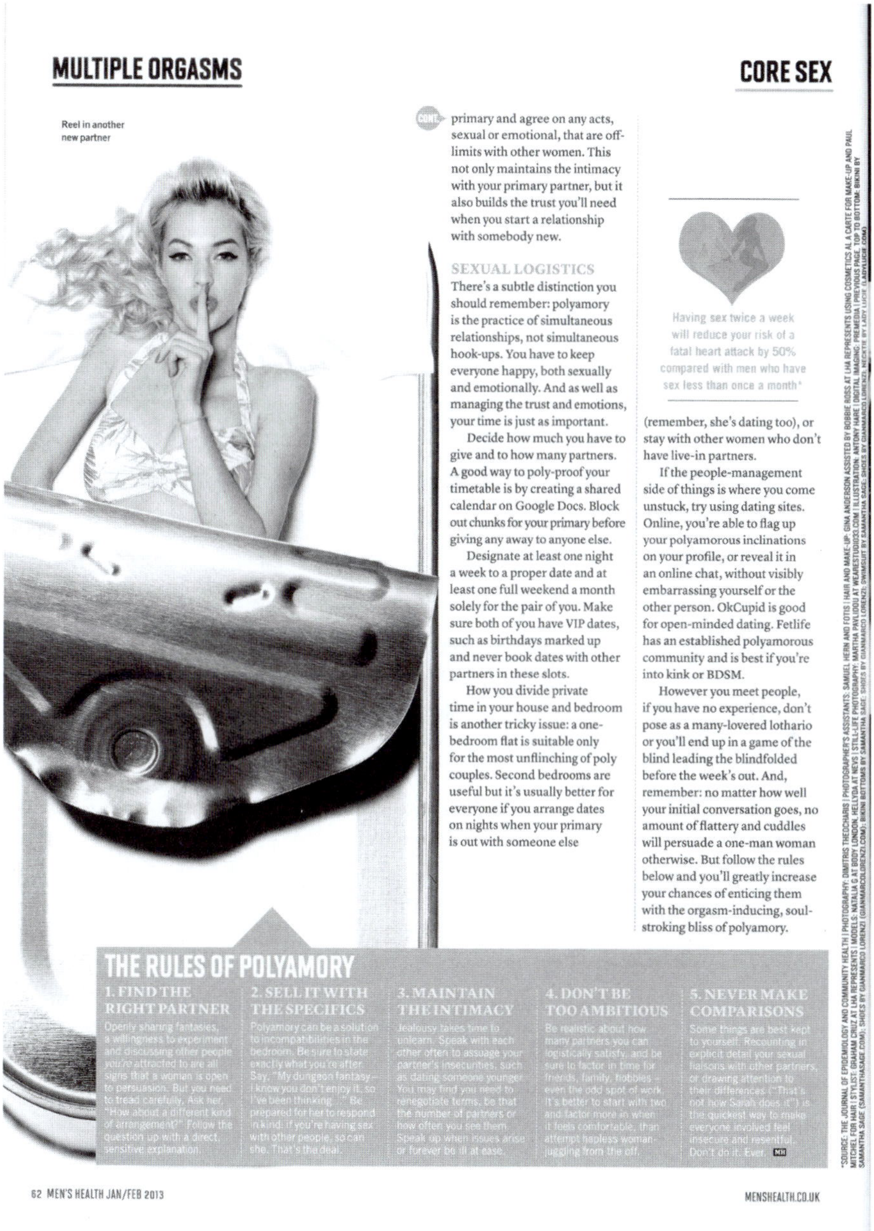

MULTIPLE ORGASMS

CORE SEX

Reel in another new partner

primary and agree on any acts, sexual or emotional, that are off-limits with other women. This not only maintains the intimacy with your primary partner, but it also builds the trust you'll need when you start a relationship with somebody new.

SEXUAL LOGISTICS

There's a subtle distinction you should remember: polyamory is the practice of simultaneous relationships, not simultaneous hook-ups. You have to keep everyone happy, both sexually and emotionally. And as well as managing the trust and emotions, your time is just as important.

Decide how much you have to give and to how many partners. A good way to poly-proof your timetable is by creating a shared calendar on Google Docs. Block out chunks for your primary before giving any away to anyone else.

Designate at least one night a week to a proper date and at least one full weekend a month solely for the pair of you. Make sure both of you have VIP dates, such as birthdays marked up and never book dates with other partners in these slots.

How you divide private time in your house and bedroom is another tricky issue: a one-bedroom flat is suitable only for the most unflinching of poly couples. Second bedrooms are useful but it's usually better for everyone if you arrange dates on nights when your primary is out with someone else

Having sex twice a week will reduce your risk of a fatal heart attack by 50% compared with men who have sex less than once a month*

(remember, she's dating too), or stay with other women who don't have live-in partners.

If the people-management side of things is where you come unstuck, try using dating sites. Online, you're able to flag up your polyamorous inclinations on your profile, or reveal it in an online chat, without visibly embarrassing yourself or the other person. OkCupid is good for open-minded dating. Fetlife has an established polyamorous community and is best if you're into kink or BDSM.

However you meet people, if you have no experience, don't pose as a many-lovered lothario or you'll end up in a game of the blind leading the blindfolded before the week's out. And, remember: no matter how well your initial conversation goes, no amount of flattery and cuddles will persuade a one-man woman otherwise. But follow the rules below and you'll greatly increase your chances of enticing them with the orgasm-inducing, soul-stroking bliss of polyamory.

THE RULES OF POLYAMORY

1. FIND THE RIGHT PARTNER

Openly sharing fantasies, a willingness to experiment and discussing other people you're attracted to are all signs that a woman is open to persuasion. But you need to tread carefully. Ask her, "How about a different kind of arrangement?" Follow the question up with a direct, sensitive explanation.

2. SELL IT WITH THE SPECIFICS

Polyamory can be a solution to incompatibilities in the bedroom. Be sure to state exactly what you're after. Say, "My dungeon fantasy – I know you don't enjoy it, so I've been thinking ..." Be prepared for her to respond in kind: if you're having sex with other people, so can she. That's the deal.

3. MAINTAIN THE INTIMACY

Jealousy takes time to unlearn. Speak with each other often to assuage your partner's insecurities, such as dating someone younger. You may find you need to renegotiate terms, be that the number of partners or how often you see them. Speak up when issues arise or forever be ill at ease.

4. DON'T BE TOO AMBITIOUS

Be realistic about how many partners you can logistically satisfy, and be sure to factor in time for friends, family, hobbies – even the odd spot of work. It's better to start with two and factor more in when it feels comfortable, than attempt hapless woman-juggling from the off.

5. NEVER MAKE COMPARISONS

Some things are best kept to yourself. Recounting in explicit detail your sexual liaisons with other partners, or drawing attention to their differences ("That's not how Sarah does it") is the quickest way to make everyone involved feel insecure and resentful. Don't do it. Ever. MH

*SOURCE: THE JOURNAL OF EPIDEMIOLOGY AND COMMUNITY HEALTH

62 MEN'S HEALTH JAN/FEB 2013

MENSHEALTH.CO.UK

Figure 11.2

polyamory, *n*. [...] The fact of having simultaneous close emotional relationships with two or more other individuals, viewed as an alternative to monogamy, esp. in regard to matters of sexual fidelity; the custom or practice of engaging in multiple sexual relationships with the knowledge and consent of all partners concerned.

1992 J. L. Wesp *Proposal for alt.poly-amory* in *alt.config* (Usenet newsgroup) 21 May,

I propose to form the group alt.poly-amory. It would be a place for people who have multiple lovers to talk about the various problems unique to us.

1992 *Re: Reasons not to be Monogamous* in *soc.singles* (Usenet newsgroup) 28 May,

Serial monogamy is often more risky than long term polyamory.

1998 *Guardian* 21 July ii. 2/3

The burgeoning polyamory community in the US—with its offshoot organisation in Britain—is supporting and promoting all kinds of polygamous relationships.

2005 *Seattle Weekly* (Nexis) 2 Mar. 75

[He] began preaching meditation, polyamory, and disco dancing as ways of unmooring oneself from earthly ties.

Entries in dictionaries like the *OED*, which illustrates the history and usage of words with dated quotations from authentic sources, can sometimes offer insights into the formation of new discourses. In this case, for instance, it is interesting that although the practice referred to in the definition goes back further than the last decade of the twentieth century, the earliest written uses of the word quoted in the entry are from 1992,[7] and both come from Usenet, an online source. This suggests that CMC was probably important for the emergence of a discourse on polyamory: by enabling practitioners to locate and interact with one another, it helped to disseminate a term which was not previously in wide circulation.

Introducing the term *discourse* in Chapter 1, we said that one of its meanings—the one associated with Foucault—refers to historically and culturally constructed stories that circulate in society and resonate so powerfully as to shape our social reality. One very powerful story about sexual relationships is the one we may call the *happily-ever-after* or *till-death-us-do-part* story. This is about the union of a *couple*, *two* people (traditionally a man and a woman, though several countries have recently given legal recognition to same-sex unions) whose relationship is supposed to be *monogamous*. Having additional sexual relationships is often labelled 'cheating' (though how this is talked and written about may depend on the gender of the 'cheater'). Advocates of polyamory, however, want their practice to be—as the *OED* entry puts it—'viewed as an alternative to monogamy': they have constructed a 'competing discourse' which challenges the dominant one, presenting polyamorous relationships as no less legitimate or satisfying than conventional monogamous ones. Here we will ask how polyamory is constructed in *MH*'s discourse, and how far this construction challenges dominant discourses about sexual relationships.

The *MH* text belongs to the category of 'expert advice', which is a staple ingredient of both men's and women's magazines. Other pieces in this issue of the magazine offer advice on playing golf, playing tennis, body-building, 'gym-fuel' food, curing a hangover and earning some extra cash. As this list suggests, a large proportion of the advice given concerns sport and exercise: for regular readers, the heading 'Core Sex' at the top of the sex column will recall the idea of strengthening one's *core* stability, which belongs to the domain of fitness (as well as the term *hardcore*, most often applied to pornography). The implication is that sex is like going to the gym, something an expert can tell you how to make the most of. It is unusual, however, for *MH* to present its readers with a *female* expert. The magazine's editorial team is predominantly male, and in this issue all the other experts are men. However, in this case, the writer's gender adds an extra dimension to her expertise: as a woman she is assumed to have 'inside knowledge' that her male readers lack. In addition, sex advice delivered by a woman to men has the advantage of appearing 'objective' and deflecting potential accusations of sexism.

In the text itself, the writer uses several strategies to establish her authority. One is referring to her personal experience of polyamory, first by enumerating her current relationships ('Right now, for instance, I'm juggling the following: …', which, she admits, is 'a lot, perhaps, but from this set-up, I get care, affection, friendship and all the kinds of sex I crave'), and later when advising readers to 'be open', unlike one of her former partners, who asked for 'a poly arrange-ment' six months into their relationship, when she had 'already fallen in love in a monogamous way, and didn't want to share him'. In the first case, she speaks as someone readers can identify with ('if I can do it, *you* can do it'). In the second case, by contrast, she speaks for the reader's female partner—she is a woman who, if approached sensitively and at the right moment, could be talked into a polyamorous relationship ('if I can do it, *she* can do it').

As well as the authority of personal experience, the text appeals to common-sense wisdom about sex and relationships. An example is the opening paragraph, which makes the important discursive move of suggesting that the desire for multiple partners is natural and inevitable:

> Here's the thing: one person cannot give you everything. No matter how happy you are with your partner, few people could deny occasionally fantasising about having more. More sex with more women, without sacrificing the intimacy (or the sex) with the woman you love.

Another 'common-sense' feature of this passage is its assumption that the 'people' being referred to and addressed are not only male, but also *heterosexual* (they are said to desire 'more sex with more women'). Although the author later tells us that her own current arrangement includes 'the occasional hook-up with a female friend', nowhere in the article do we find any indication that the word 'partner', used in relation to the male reader, might refer to another man (cf. 'If your partner is more reluctant – agreeing to it only because *she* fears losing you…', 'If your *girl* can't stand you passing comment on attractive *women*,…', '… you have to assert your loyalty to your primary partner – even when you're arranging dates and sex with other *women*'). This reading is supported by the visual illustrations that accompany the text (one shows a stack of three sardine cans with a woman lying in each; another shows two women facing in opposite directions, enclosed in a stylized heart). *Men's Health* means 'Straight Men's Health': bisexual and gay men are excluded even from a text about the unconventional sexual practice of polyamory.

Once established as inevitable, polyamory is discursively constructed as *healthy*. Here the authority invoked is not experience or common sense, but science: a quotation (or paraphrase) from the *Journal of Epidemiology and Community Health*, which claims that 'having sex twice a week will reduce your risk of a fatal heart attack by 50% compared with men who have sex less than once a month'. The implication is that only a man with multiple partners can be sure of having sex often enough to avoid doubling his risk of a fatal heart attack.

Jennifer Wesp, whose 1992 proposal to establish a polyamory usenet newsgroup provides one of the earliest quotations used in the *OED*, is a woman. So is Nichi Hodgson, the author of this column. And so is Morning Glory Zell-Ravenheart, mentioned in several texts on the internet as having used the word *polyamorist* in her essay 'A Bouquet of Lovers' even before Wesp's proposal. Nevertheless, the *MH* text reads as if polyamory were a 'male thing', something 'He' is ready to start practising as soon as he can talk 'Her' into it. This is apparently not an easy task: 'no matter how well your initial conversation goes, no amount of flattery and cuddles will persuade a one-man woman otherwise'. To address this problem, the main part of the article, along with a sidebar headed 'The rules of polyamory', offers guidelines for creating a perfect 'sales pitch' ('*If* you can sell the idea'; 'Sell it with the specifics'). The author several times advises men on what they should say when trying to 'sell' polyamory to women: 'Ask her, "How about a different kind of arrangement?" Follow the question up with a direct, sensitive explanation.' Although readers are reminded that their female partners are also free to have sex with others, the space devoted to teaching 'Him' how to convince 'Her' suggests an underlying assumption that the female partner is the one who will have to come to terms with the arrangement. A scenario in which 'He' would have to deal with 'Her' proposal to 'go poly' is not envisioned.

It is also instructive to look at some of the phrases used about polyamorous relationships in headings and other editorial additions to the main text:

> Is there such a thing as *the guilt-free affair*? *MH*'s new sex columnist says yes.

> *Get away with* several partners? Yes we can!

> *Reel in* another new partner

Though the article, like the *OED*, defines polyamory as open and consensual non-monogamy, these formulas recast it in terms of the traditional opposition between monogamy and adultery, and more specifically as a licence for men to 'cheat'. Polyamorous relationships are likened to extramarital 'affairs' (i.e. illicit relationships conducted without a spouse's knowledge/consent), described as something men can 'get away with', and presented as a licence to 'reel in' a new 'catch'. The metaphor of sex as fishing is repeated in the visual illustration, showing women in sardine cans—an image which also references the idea of promiscuous men compartmentalizing their relationships with different women. Represented in this way, polyamory becomes part of a *patriarchal* discourse that reproduces the man's position of dominance over women.

This article presents itself as a contribution to a new discourse on sexual relationships which supposedly rejects the traditional, patriarchal and heteronormative assumptions of the dominant 'monogamy discourse'. But examining the text more closely suggests that the challenge is more apparent than real: the same assumptions which pervade traditional discourse are recycled in this discussion of polyamory.

ACTIVITY

Online you can read another article on polyamory ('When two just won't do'), which was published in the *Guardian* newspaper in 2003 (go to http://goo.gl/N4p4M). How is this text similar and how is it different from the *MH* column discussed above? Putting the two texts together, what 'competing discourses' on polyamory and/or monogamy can you identify?

SUMMARY

This chapter has discussed the potential uses of written discourse analysis in research which aims to shed light on social rather than specifically linguistic phenomena. We have pointed out that many social research projects make use of discourse data, and we have focused on a topic—sex—where the difficulty of directly observing people's behaviour makes researchers particularly reliant on this kind of evidence. In fact, researchers are not just interested in discourse about sex because ethical considerations prevent them from watching the 'real thing'. Most social scientific research on sex is less concerned with describing physical sexual acts than with understanding what those acts, and the associated relationships and desires, mean to the human actors engaged in them. For that purpose, discourse on sex is of interest in its own right. The examples given in this chapter show how discourse analytic methods, which involve paying close attention not only to what is written but to the way it is written—to questions of medium, genre, text structure, code-choice, terminology, metaphors, the construction of stance and voice, the relation of text to visual images, etc.—can enhance researchers' understanding of the texts they examine, and thus of the social practices they are studying.

FURTHER READING

The topic of sex (sexual identities, desires and practices) is approached from a broadly discourse analytic perspective in a number of books which are written by linguists but accessible to non-linguists, including Paul Baker's *Sexed Texts* (2008) and Deborah Cameron and Don Kulick's *Language and Sexuality* (2003). A wide-ranging interdisciplinary collection is *The Language and Sexuality Reader* (Cameron and Kulick 2006). William Leap and Tom Boellstorff's *Speaking in Queer Tongues* (2004) deals with gay and other sexual minority language-use around the world. The linguistic/discursive construction of romantic love and erotic desire is the subject of an older collection, Keith Harvey and Celia Shalom's *Language and Desire* (1997), which includes chapters on literary and fictional texts as well as personal advertisements.

NOTES

1   Many writers suggest that 'Big Data' is not defined by the absolute size of the sample or the sheer quantity of information collected, but rather by the use made of technology to share, aggregate (add together) and cross-reference multiple data sources. boyd and Crawford (2012), who make this argument, also argue that aggregating and cross-referencing increase the risk that information will be misinterpreted because it has been taken out of context (see further below).

2   Some studies of personal/dating ads are referenced later in this chapter. For the other genres listed here, a classic discussion of medical/scientific discourse on sex is Martin (1991); discourse on gender/sexuality in men's, women's and teenage girls' magazines is examined in Benwell (2003), Farvid and Braun (2006) and Jackson (1996); romance fiction and erotic narratives are analysed by Talbot (1997) and Hoey (1997); Hall (1995) describes instruction manuals for telephone sex workers; Jones (2008) deals with televideo cybersex.

3   All quotations in this section are Ahearn's translations from the original Nepali.

4   We should clarify that the inclusion of the (originally English) word 'OK' does not make this sentence an example of writing in English: the word has been 'nativized' (i.e. incorporated into the Serbian language), and in this case the word order shows that the sentence in which it appears is Serbian (in other cases, like *retarde*, 'retards', in the same example, there is evidence of nativization in the word ending—the -e is a Serbian rather than an English inflection).

5   It should not be thought that the emphasis placed on what one does *not* want, and the negative or hostile tone in which this is often conveyed, is a unique feature of Serbian dating profiles. Negative attitudes to 'effeminacy' are also attested in studies of English-language advertisements (Baker 2003), and the more general issue of negative/hostile language is debated within the Anglo-American gay community www.fabmagazine.com/story/not-just-a-preference).

6   http://goo.gl/DpTWy. We have omitted details of the word's pronunciation and etymology.

7   This does not mean that the word polyamory was only coined in 1992; the OED requires evidence from 'public' written sources to authenticate new terms, but most will have been used earlier in speech and/or 'private' writing. In addition, the first use of a term cited in the OED is simply the earliest example lexicographers were able to find when the entry was compiled: it is not uncommon for earlier examples to be discovered subsequently. In the case of polyamory, there is evidence of its being used before 1992; for a discussion of the origins and history of the term, see http://goo.gl/qtyFl.

12 Designing your own projects

This chapter is intended to help you think about planning and conducting your own small-scale research project.[1] Our discussion is organized around the key decisions every researcher has to make: what question to investigate, what kind of data to collect, how to analyse the data and how to structure a written account of the research. To illustrate it concretely, we will refer to projects carried out by three of our own students, Ksenija Bogetić, Tamar Holoshitz and Beth McCarthy.[2]

The idea of 'doing research' can seem daunting, but anxiety often stems from unrealistic ideas about what is expected. At PhD level, research has to make a substantial and original contribution to knowledge in a particular academic discipline. Below that level, however, its purpose is educational: to develop your knowledge and practical skills by exploring a question that interests you in depth. It is not unknown for a student project to produce insights worth sharing in a scholarly publication.[3] But when that happens, it is a bonus: it is not a requirement for student projects in general.

ASKING QUESTIONS

The starting point for planning any project is defining a research question to investigate. To make a good project, the question needs to be:

1. Well defined and specific—not vague, and not too general.
2. Related to your own interests, but also related in some way to previous research and discussion on the subject.
3. Manageable—you need a question that can realistically be investigated with the resources at your disposal.

You might be thinking: why do I have to have a question? Can't I just choose a kind of discourse I'm interested in, like 'recipes' or 'comic books', put a collection of examples together, and analyse them? A lot of student projects do begin from an interest in a particular kind of discourse—often one the student is knowledgeable about because it is part of their life outside their studies. This is not a bad starting point: research projects take time and effort, so it helps if you find the material you're working on interesting, and if you already know something about it from experience. But 'I'd like to look at recipes' is only a starting point, not a concrete research plan. Even if you define what you're going to do as 'analysing the language used in recipes', that is still too vague to be helpful. What aspects or features of the language are you going to look at? What kinds of recipes are you going to sample? What is your argument or angle going to be?

Here it is useful to consider the second part of point (2), relating your project to previous research and discussion. Reading some published studies in the area that interests you is an important part of your planning: as you read, you will get a sense of what research has already been done on the kind of discourse you want to look at, and you can ask yourself how your own work might be able to build on existing knowledge. In the 'recipes' case, for instance, one of us once had a student who compared recent bestselling recipe books with older ones: the question was whether the discourse of recipe books had become less formal and more personal in the era of the TV 'celebrity chef'. Rey's (2001) study of *Star Trek* scripts (see Chapter 2) is another study investigating historical change. '[How] have the conventions changed over time?' is a question that will work for many written discourse genres.

Another possibility is to take a question that has been studied in relation to one language/culture and ask it about a different language/culture. In many areas of discourse analysis there has been more research on English than on anything else, so students may be able to build on existing knowledge by looking at data from another language they know. In the age of global media, it is sometimes possible to make a direct comparison between two or more linguistically and/or culturally distinct versions of the same discourse 'product': for instance, Machin and van Leeuwen (2005) analyse different national editions of *Cosmopolitan* magazine, Kelly-Holmes (2010) discusses the marketing of McDonald's in different territories and languages, while Theo van Leeuwen and Usama Suleiman (2010) compare two different versions of the Egyptian superhero comic *Zein*, one produced in Arabic for a local audience, the other in English for international circulation.

A third way to build on existing knowledge is exemplified by Tamar Holoshitz's study of the reporting of sexual violence in conflict situations, discussed in Chapter 7. Tamar had read a number of published studies dealing with the reporting of sexual violence in western 'domestic' contexts, which had found a tendency to blame victims while downplaying the responsibility of perpetrators. Her question was whether the same tendency would be evident in the reporting of sexual violence when the setting was a foreign conflict zone. To investigate this question, she based her approach on that of earlier research: for instance, she examined many of the same linguistic features that were discussed in previous studies. But by analysing data from a context which had not been studied in detail before, she was able to make a new contribution to the discussion.

Beth McCarthy also took earlier work as a model—specifically, the kind of critical discourse analytic work which looks for biases in news reporting by comparing the treatment of a particular issue or event in sources which differ in their political allegiances or the social composition of their audiences. At the time she was planning her project, one of the biggest news stories in Britain concerned the conduct of the news media themselves. One Sunday newspaper, the *News of the World* (*NoTW*), had been closed following a scandal about its engagement in the illegal practice of 'phone hacking' (covertly accessing people's mobile phones to get personal information for use in stories). Public outrage about this had erupted in 2011, after it was revealed that the *NoTW* had targeted not only the phones of celebrities and public figures, but also those of crime victims, including a young girl who had been abducted and murdered. Many readers and advertisers expressed their disgust by boycotting the newspaper, and its proprietor, Rupert Murdoch, decided to take the drastic step of closing it altogether. The closure was covered extensively by the British media, and Beth decided to look at differences in the way different media outlets presented it. But the nature of the issue gave her an idea for making her study slightly different from previous ones. The company that owned the *NoTW*, Rupert Murdoch's News International, also owned several other British newspapers, including the *Times* (a 'quality' daily newspaper) and the *Sun* (a popular tabloid). Rather than asking the 'classic' CDA question—how newspapers' treatment of the story reflected their political allegiances or the social profile of their readers—Beth asked whether their coverage was influenced by the variable of *ownership*—whether newspapers owned by News International reported the *NoTW* closure more sympathetically than newspapers owned by commercial rivals. (We will come back to what she found later on.)

Sometimes, a question may be prompted by debates going on in other academic fields. In Chapter 7, for instance, we discussed a study of hedging in biomedical research articles (Gross and Chesley 2012), which found that the frequency of hedging was lower in articles reporting commercially funded research. Although the study addressed a question about language, it was clearly inspired by concerns about commercial sponsorship that had already been raised in science and medicine. Other studies have been designed to test the validity of popular beliefs or assertions made in the media. For example, research has been carried out to investigate the common perception that young people's use of SMS is undermining their ability to write correctly in other contexts (we mentioned one Swiss study in Chapter 9; Crystal (2008) also discusses the issue).

With some questions, like the one about whether young people's spelling is being affected by the conventions of SMS, the answer is of interest whatever it turns out to be. In other cases, however, not all answers to a question are equally interesting, and some would render it pointless to pursue the question at all. For instance, if van Leeuwen and Suleiman had found that the English version of *Zein* was just a direct translation of the Arabic version, their question—how the comic was adapted for different (local and global) audiences—would have become irrelevant. In fact, though, it is unlikely they embarked on their research without already knowing that there were differences between the two versions. Many research projects begin with the researcher noticing something like this informally, and then designing a study to investigate it systematically. In other cases, a researcher may decide to test whether an idea is worth pursuing by carrying out a pilot study with a small amount of data. The results will show whether there is anything of interest to say about the material you are considering; beyond that, a pilot study can help to identify the patterns that would be worth exploring in a larger sample.

Even the most interesting question is no good to you, however, unless it is one you have the resources to investigate. Partly, this is about scale: if you are working on your own and your time is fairly short, you will only be able to analyse a limited amount of data, and your question needs to be framed with that in mind. But you also need to be sure you can get hold of the kind of data you need. In some cases, this may raise ethical issues, which need to be considered at the planning stage.

RESEARCH ETHICS

Most universities now have ethical guidelines governing all research on 'human subjects' undertaken by any of their members, including students. Often you cannot begin a research project that involves human subjects without first seeking approval from a university ethics committee or review board. Most discourse analysis projects will not fall into the category of high-risk studies needing very close scrutiny: you won't, for instance, be giving people an experimental drug or a series of electric shocks. But a discourse analytic project could involve working with a 'vulnerable' group (e.g. young children or people with learning disabilities), or collecting texts containing sensitive personal information. Even if neither of those considerations apply, any project for which the data are provided by living individuals must meet the basic standards for ethical research.

The most basic ethical requirement is obtaining participants' *informed consent*. 'Consent' means that the people who provide data for a project must be asked to participate, and must voluntarily agree to do so (in most situations, ethics committees will want you to obtain a signed consent form from each participant). 'Informed' means that participants must understand what they are consenting to. Researchers must give them clear information about the nature and purpose of the research, what data they are being asked to provide, and what the researcher is going to do with the data. This doesn't mean explaining every detail of a project—most people won't be interested in the nuances of the research question and the analytic approach—but anything which might directly affect participants should be discussed with them. For instance, a researcher who intends to publish material containing extracts from participants' discourse should make sure they have no objection. They should also be told how their privacy will be protected if they agree. It is standard procedure to disguise participants' real identities by using pseudonyms, and by altering any personal details that might make them recognizable, in any text that is going to be seen by people other than the researcher (that includes student projects and dissertations as well as published books and articles). Another standard procedure is to tell participants that they can withdraw their consent at any time, without needing to give a reason.

You may be wondering how relevant these points are to research projects dealing with *written* discourse. The answer is that it is relevant in some cases, but not all: it depends on the kind of writing you want to analyse and the sources you take your data from. If you use data from a pre-existing corpus, for instance, you can assume that the corpus compilers have already obtained consent from any individuals whose 'private' discourse—e.g. personal letters or academic essays—is included in the sample. And if your data come from sources which are published or fully public (e.g. newspapers, books, journals, open access websites, billboards, street signs, graffiti), they are already in the public domain and there is no issue of consent.[4]

There are, however, some kinds of written discourse which can only be used as data with the author's permission. We have already given two examples: personal letters and academic essays. These texts were originally produced for a specific purpose and a known addressee (the recipient of the letter or the teacher who marked the essay): if you want to use them for a different purpose and reproduce bits of them for a different audience, you must obtain the author's consent. The same applies to other kinds of informal 'everyday writing'—diaries, postcards, shopping lists, notes passed in class—and to private communications in other media, such as text messages, emails and most items circulated via social media. We say 'most' because some social media platforms are public, with no restrictions on who can access messages: on Twitter, for instance, most tweets are at least temporarily available to be read and reproduced (retweeted) by anyone. On sites like Facebook, by contrast, the owner of an account has more control: most users do not make everything they post public, but restrict its circulation to their friends. This means the material must be regarded as private, and consent will be needed to use it for research purposes.

The increasing interest of discourse researchers in using data collected online has raised new ethical questions. For instance, *whose* consent do you need to take data from Facebook? Social media are about interaction and sharing: typically, the owner of a Facebook account will not be the only person whose words appear on their page. If you want to analyse a portion of a timeline, is it enough to seek permission from the individual whose timeline it is, or do you need to get consent from everyone whose presence is represented by a comment or a piece of shared content? On this question there is still some variation in researchers' views and their practices (the ethical issues raised by social media research are discussed in detail by D'Arcy and Young (2012)). Most would agree, however, that one practice students often consider using for convenience— compiling a data-sample from the private emails, text messages, instant messages or social media communications sent to them by their own friends—is not ethical unless the friends in question have given permission. It is potentially a breach of trust to share messages which were sent to you privately with a larger audience (even if it is only the teachers who will mark your work). If you want to use your friends as a source of data, you must ask. Our experience suggests that few will refuse—they just appreciate being given a choice.

We make this point about the importance of treating friends ethically because students collecting data for small-scale projects often look close to home. But as increasing numbers turn to global digital media as a source of data, it is also necessary to be aware of your ethical responsibility to strangers. On the internet it is easy to collect large amounts of discourse produced by people you do not know and will never meet. As Penelope Eckert observes, though, the apparent anonymity of these sources can be deceptive: the internet also provides tools which can be used by anyone who reads your data to search for the original text and identify its source. Eckert says: 'it is up to researchers to be sure that they are not gathering and publishing data that the speakers intend to be private, or that can be traced to their origins if they in any way pose a threat to the originators' (2013: 17).

On the internet, it is not always easy to know what users intend, or assume, to be 'private'. Consider, for instance, the case of websites which serve as forums for discussion and content-sharing among people with a common interest. Many of these sites require users to register and provide some personal information before they can gain access; but while anyone can register (making the site effectively 'public'), the fact that registration is required may foster a belief among users that their interactions are quasi-private exchanges among people who are all there for the same reason. Researchers can take advantage of this to study groups or subcultures which would not be easy for an outsider to access offline. They can register as site-users and use the material this gives them access to as data for their research. This strategy was used by Ksenija Bogetić in her study of Serbian gay men's online dating profiles (see Chapter 11). On many dating sites, including one of the two that Ksenija took data from, you can only access other people's profiles if you yourself have a profile which they can look at. Ksenija therefore created a (very minimal) profile for herself.

Once again, there are differing views on whether this is an ethical way of collecting data. It could be argued that a researcher who creates a personal profile on a site s/he is investigating is posing as something s/he (probably) is not, and that this is a form of unethical deception. Some people argue that even just 'lurking' on a site without explicitly identifying yourself as a researcher is unethical, since other site-users will have no idea that any research is going on. Others, however, find this attitude over-scrupulous, pointing out that on the internet, everyone understands that people may not be telling each other everything about themselves. Researchers are not the only people who are economical with the truth on dating sites. It might also be asked why the internet should be treated in a different way from the print media. Before online dating, as we saw in Chapter 11, printed personal ads were sampled and reproduced in many published studies: this did not prompt ethical objections, since if someone had placed an ad in a national newspaper, it seemed reasonable to assume that they did not regard it as a private communication. Another view might be that minor deceptions (like not telling users of the site you are lurking on that you are actually a researcher) are only unethical if they put others at risk of harm. If no one will be harmed, then perhaps a researcher's failure to be completely transparent can be justified by the contribution her or his research makes to knowledge.

ACTIVITY

In the light of the points made in this section, consider the questions below. If you are reading this book for a class, discuss the questions in a small group and compare your own responses with those of other group members.

1   Do you think researchers who gain access to a website for research purposes but do not disclose their purposes to other users are acting unethically? Why or why not?
2   Does the use of data obtained in this way pose any risk of harm to the users of the site? If yes, what risks might it pose, and what can researchers do to prevent or minimize harm?

While some ethical requirements are enforced by institutions, many decisions are finally a matter for the researcher's individual judgment. If you think something is unethical, then you do not have to do it: even if your university's guidelines allow it and other researchers have done it, you should make your own judgment and follow your own conscience.

COLLECTING DATA: WHAT KIND AND HOW MUCH?

When you choose a question to investigate, that will usually determine what kind of data you need, and point you towards the most useful sources. For instance, Ksenija Bogetić's question was how a certain group of people—Serbian gay men—use language to advertise themselves to potential sexual partners; she therefore chose to take her data from the two dating websites which are used most extensively by gay men in Serbia. Beth McCarthy's question was about the influence of media ownership on the reporting of an event involving a particular media company, News International: this meant her data sample had to consist of reports dealing specifically with that event, and it had to include items taken from both News International-owned sources and sources which were not owned by News International. In the former category there were only two newspapers she could have used, the *Times* and the *Sun*; she therefore chose to sample two non-News International titles which compete with the *Times* and the *Sun* for readers: the *Guardian* (which, like the *Times*, is a 'quality' newspaper addressed to educated middle-class readers), and the *Mirror* (which, like the *Sun*, is a popular tabloid with a mainly working-class readership).[5]

Tamar Holoshitz's project on the reporting of sexual violence in conflict settings presented her with more choices about the composition of her sample. What she chose to do was examine reports on two different settings (the Democratic Republic of Congo and Abu Ghraib prison in

Iraq) in one newspaper, the *New York Times*. In principle, she could have chosen to look at a larger range of news sources, but since this was a small-scale project, concentrating on a single source made it more manageable and more focused. Her choice of the Abu Ghraib scandal as a case-study was partly motivated by an interest in how the western media reported sexual violence perpetrated by their own military forces overseas, and whether that differed from their reporting of the acts of foreign soldiers, such as the armed militias of the DRC. Therefore, her source needed to be a US news outlet. It also needed to be one that devoted significant resources to international news coverage (though most large US newspapers had covered the Abu Ghraib scandal extensively, many would not have provided enough material on the DRC). Ideally, she also needed a source which maintained a publicly accessible and easily searchable online archive from which text could be extracted in electronic form (this was especially relevant because she wanted to do some of the analysis using concordancing software). The *New York Times* was one of the sources that met these specifications.

One of the commonest questions students ask concerns the size of their data sample: 'how many texts/words do I need?' In fact, there is no standard answer to that question. How large a sample needs to be depends on a number of considerations: some of these are practical, relating to the issue of manageability, while others are more theoretical, relating to the nature of your research question and the kind of analysis you want to do. Most approaches to discourse involve qualitative analysis, and that places limits on the amount of data it is possible to deal with—not only because of the time it takes to analyse a set of texts in fine detail, but also because of the space required to present the analysis in writing. Student projects generally have a word-limit as well as a deadline: if you have more to discuss than you can deal with in the number of words allowed, there is a risk that your analysis will look thin and superficial. The 'right' amount of data for a project is enough to give your analysis substance and make it convincing, but not too much to allow you to do a thorough analysis and present it fully. In a small-scale project, therefore, keeping the sample-size manageable is as much of an issue as finding enough data to make the sample meaningful. The question you have to consider is how to limit your sample in a principled way, one which does not depend on arbitrary or purely subjective decisions about what to include and what to leave out.

This question loomed largest for Beth McCarthy, whose undergraduate project had to be done in a few weeks and written up in no more than 6,000 words. The event whose representation she had decided to study had generated an enormous amount of discourse in the media: even after she had selected a subset of sources to focus on, there was still more material than she could deal with in the time and space available. How could she select a small fraction of it without inviting the criticism that she was 'cherry picking' her data, using only texts which supported her hypotheses? Her solution was to impose a time-frame: she would analyse everything published in all of her chosen sources on a single day—the day after the closure of the *News of the World* was announced, when reactions to the announcement dominated the output of the British news media. This gave her a sample of 75 items, comprising 55,842 words in all.

Tamar Holoshitz, writing a Master's dissertation (for which she had a few months' research time and more than three times as many words as Beth), was able to handle a larger quantity of data, but she still needed to select it in a principled way. She began by searching the *New York Times* archive for reports on the setting which had received less coverage, the DRC. She used the search term 'rape Congo' to identify the items whose content was relevant, and she limited the search to items tagged 'world news' to ensure all items would be news reports rather than features and opinion pieces. This gave her 111 items. When she read through them to check that they were relevant, some of them proved to be mainly about other conflicts (e.g. in Rwanda and Sudan), with only incidental references to the DRC. These were discarded, leaving a sample of 89 items comprising 62,050 words. Tamar then set out to construct a comparable sample for the other setting, Abu Ghraib, on which she knew the amount of material available would be larger, because the US media took a greater interest in a story that directly involved the US military. Once again, she limited the search to 'world news', but this time she also limited it to a single year, 2004 (the year when the abuse of prisoners at Abu Ghraib was first exposed and officially investigated). Her search yielded 224 items, which she reduced to 89 using the archive's capacity to sort and order items by relevance. Selecting the 89 most relevant items gave her a sample which matched the number of items in the DRC sample, though it was still larger in terms of the number of words (95,455).

It was not only in word-length that Tamar's two samples were not exactly matched: whereas the DRC corpus was a more or less complete collection of all the *Times'* reporting on the issue over a period of 15 years, the Abu Ghraib corpus contained only a subset of the reports that had appeared in a single year. But when you are investigating real-world data (rather than designing a laboratory experiment), it is not always possible to control all the variables. As a student, you will generally get credit for showing awareness of this when you present your research in writing. The 'methods' section of your report or dissertation is a place not only to describe what you did, but also to draw attention to any problems you encountered, explain the decisions you made and acknowledge imperfections in the design of your study. When Tamar came to write up her dissertation, she could point out that the much greater volume of reporting on Abu Ghraib made it impossible to match the two samples exactly, and explain what she had done to get the best match and the most relevant data possible without 'cherry picking' her examples.

Another thing you can do to show your understanding of the inevitable limitations of small-scale research projects is be suitably cautious about the claims you make. If you have carried out your analysis competently, your findings will be valid for the data you have examined, but you should be careful about generalizing beyond that sample. What is true about the *New York Times'* reporting on sexual violence in the DRC, for instance, might or might not be true for other US newspapers, other western English-language newspapers, non-anglophone western newspapers, non-western reporting (e.g. journalism produced by Arabs for an Arab audience), or the output of other media (e.g. TV news channels).

CHOOSING AND USING ANALYTIC APPROACHES

For each of the activities in the 'Approaches' chapters of this book, we selected an example and asked questions about it to give you practice in applying a particular approach to data. When you design your own project, your procedure should be the opposite. Rather than starting with an approach, you should start with your question and the data you want to analyse, and choose an approach (or a combination of approaches) which fits with that question and those data. Your project will be assessed not only on how well you executed the kind of analysis you decided to do, but also on whether you chose an analytic approach which was appropriate for your study.

This is another area in which you can usefully relate your project to previous research. If your project is modelled directly on an earlier study, asking the same question but applying it to data from a different language, culture, time-period or context, you will probably want to use the same analytic approach that was used in the study you are taking as a model. But even if you do not have a specific model, you can ask yourself what approaches have been used in studies asking similar questions to yours, or using the same kind of data you want to use. You can also ask what frameworks already exist for analysing a particular linguistic phenomenon (e.g. register variation, epistemic stance-marking, code-switching). Of course, there might be more than one framework you could use. In that case, the judgment you have to make is which one will work best for your question or your data. But knowing what earlier researchers did will at least narrow down the options.

That said, you do not have to follow earlier models slavishly: you can vary the approach used in previous research if you think there is a good reason to do so. Tamar Holoshitz, for instance, chose a research topic (the representation of sexual violence in news reports) where most previous researchers had used some variant of CDA. Tamar took many insights from previous research: her decisions about what linguistic features to look at were influenced by earlier CDA studies of both news discourse and the representation of sexual violence. However, rather than using the CDA approach exclusively, she chose to combine it with corpus analysis. Partly this was because she wanted to ensure her analysis did not just reflect her own intuitions about the data (an argument for using corpus methods which we discussed in Chapter 7). But in addition, she wanted to ask questions about the frequency and distribution of certain features in a relatively large data sample. Corpus methods are designed to address those questions, whereas CDA is not.

The difference between CDA and corpus analysis is one instance of the more general difference between qualitative and quantitative methods. Which type you use—and if you use both, what the balance between them should be—depends on your question and the claims you want to be able to make. If your claim is that a certain linguistic pattern (e.g. the use of agent-deleted passives) has a particular, ideologically non-neutral effect, the evidence you need to present will be qualitative: showing how the pattern works in a detailed, contextualized analysis of one or more specific examples. But if you want to claim that the pattern occurs consistently in a sample of texts, or that its frequency is significantly higher than the frequency of some alternative pattern, or that it is more common in one subset of texts than in another, then the evidence you need to present will be statistical, dependent on numbers. Tamar wanted to be able to make both kinds of claims, and therefore she used both qualitative and quantitative analysis. Beth McCarthy's project also combined qualitative and quantitative approaches. To investigate whether News International-owned papers reported the closure of the *News of the World* in a more sympathetic/ less critical way than papers owned by its commercial rivals, she investigated a number of features suggested by earlier CDA studies of bias in news reporting. Some of these did not lend themselves to quantification, but others required it if the argument was to be convincing.

It is generally acknowledged in CDA that main headlines are a highly salient feature of newspaper discourse, but since there is only one in each story, a small sample like Beth's may not contain enough of them to make statistical analysis meaningful. In addition, what is interesting about headlines may not be captured by that kind of analysis. The point can be illustrated using the following examples from reports on the closure of the *NoTW*:

1. World's End: Paper Axed After 168 Years (*Sun*)
2. Hacked to death: After 168 years, News of the World is shut down as scandal claims its biggest scalp (*Times*)
3. Shrewdest of surrenders; by sacrificing the News of the World, Murdoch's son and the dynasty live to fight another day (*Guardian*)

It cannot be claimed that these headlines exemplify a pattern seen consistently throughout the sample, but that does not mean there is nothing to say about them. The interesting thing about them is that they all use the same overarching metaphorical schema, likening the closure of the *NoTW* to a killing (*axed, hacked, scalp, sacrifice*); but there is a difference in the way they approach the question of who or what should be held responsible. The first two examples, both from NI-owned titles, avoid the issue of blame by using agentless passive verbs. In (1), no agent or cause is identified at all; in (2), the added final clause puts *scandal* in the subject/agent slot, which might suggest that responsibility is being attributed to the 'scandalmongers' in the non-NI-owned press. In example (3), by contrast, taken from a non-NI-owned title, responsibility is clearly attributed to Murdoch and his 'dynasty'. The closure is presented in quasi-military terms as a strategic 'sacrifice' made to protect his larger commercial interests.

With some features, however, Beth did want to use counting to demonstrate that there was a consistent pattern of ownership-related difference. For instance, her analysis showed that the News International titles devoted a higher proportion of words to direct quotations from named sources. Quotation is a device which allows a newspaper to avoid overtly 'taking sides', since what is reported is explicitly presented as the opinion of the source being quoted. However, the newspaper's own position may be manifested covertly in its choice of sources. As well as using more reported speech overall, the two NI titles used significantly more quotations from company representatives; non-NI titles, by contrast, quoted more statements made by critics of NI. Another pattern Beth investigated related to epistemic stance-taking, as reflected in the use of a small set of words referring to the proposition that the *NoTW* had systematically broken the law. One of these words, *revelation*, treats the proposition as an established fact to which the writer is fully committed; two other words, *allegation* and *claim*, present the proposition as unproven and the writer as either neutral or sceptical about it. Beth found that *revelation* was used most frequently—and more frequently than either of the other words—in the *Guardian* (a rival of NI and also the newspaper which broke the phone-hacking story). Conversely, it was the least common of the three in both the NI-owned titles. The tabloid *Sun* showed an overwhelming preference for *claim*, while the 'quality' *Times* favoured *allegation* (the latter was also the commonest term used in broadcast sources, which are required to maintain impartiality).

Both Beth and Tamar had data samples large enough to make quantification meaningful for at least some of the variables they examined. But many projects are done with much smaller samples and use only qualitative analysis. There is nothing wrong with that, so long as the analysis presented supports the claims being made. The analyses we have presented in earlier chapters, often of single texts or a small number of related texts, show that a limited quantity of material can serve as the basis for a meaningful discussion of a larger issue, whether linguistic (e.g. how code-switching works in multilingual written discourse) or social (e.g. how the problem of 'obesity' is discursively constructed).

Another thing you may need to consider when choosing an analytic approach is whether your question is purely about language, or whether it also requires attention to other modes of communication. As we pointed out in Chapter 8, it can be argued that all discourse is multimodal to a greater or lesser extent: how far you should focus on non-linguistic modes in a project on written discourse depends not only on the nature of the data you plan to analyse, but also on what aspects of the data are most relevant to your research question. In their study of *Zein*, for instance, van Leeuwen and Suleiman were dealing with a discourse genre, the comic book, which combines visual and verbal resources. Their question—how the Arabic and

English versions of the comic differed—was in principle a question about both language and visual images. In practice, however, they found that the differences were mainly linguistic, not visual. Whereas the narrative and dialogue diverged significantly in the Arabic and English texts, the drawings were the same in both, and the use of typography was similar. So, while they did make some use of Kress and van Leeuwen's framework for analysing multimodal texts, this was not as central to their study as they might have assumed before they began to analyse the data. A good analysis of any sample of data will focus on what turns out to be most interesting about it: your judgment of what is interesting should inform your decisions on what kind of analysis to do.

Decisions on whether to use quantitative methods or multimodal approaches are essentially decisions about how to analyse the texts that constitute your data. But as David Barton and Carmen Lee (2013) point out, some research questions may be about *practices* rather than—or as well as—texts. As we have seen elsewhere in this book, a focus on practice (on what people do with writing and how it fits into their everyday lives) is typical of the 'new literacy studies' (e.g. the work on everyday/vernacular literacies we mentioned in Chapter 2), of some research on CMD (e.g. Androutsopoulos's study discussed in Chapter 9) and of anthropological studies dealing with writing (e.g. Ahearn's work on love letters, described in Chapter 11). Research which has this focus does not just analyse texts, but also uses ethnographic methods, observing the relevant practice in context and talking to participants about it.

Even in a project which does focus primarily on texts, and uses some form of discourse analysis as its central method, it may be possible to use methods designed to investigate practice as a supplementary source of insight. In their study of *Zein*, for instance, van Leeuwen and Suleiman drew on interviews Suleiman conducted with comic book publishers, writers and artists in various parts of the Arab world. The information this provided about the practice of making comic books was helpful for the researchers' understanding of why certain conventions were used, and how conscious the producers were of the choices they made.

PUTTING IT IN WRITING

It is a common misconception that 'analysis' and 'writing up' are separate stages of a research project, and that the analysis has to be finished before the writing can begin. We think writing is better seen as an integral part of the analytic process: organizing your thoughts in written form helps to clarify what you have discovered, and what you think it means. You can start drafting your report or dissertation while you are still in the process of analysing your data; some parts of the text, such as the introduction and the discussion of previous research, can be drafted even earlier (this can help to clarify what your aims are and how your project relates to earlier discussions of the topic).

Another thing which is helpful at an early stage is to have at least a provisional structure for the piece of writing you will eventually produce. There is no single 'standard' structure, but many project reports and dissertations have some variant of the structure below:

1. A title and (if required by the regulations, as it often is in dissertations) an abstract—a brief summary of the whole project.
2. A table of contents listing the sections of the text and giving page numbers so that the reader can find them easily.

3. An introduction: this should tell the reader what general topic and what specific questions will be addressed by the researcher, and why they are of interest.
4. A literature review discussing the most important previous research that is relevant to your project.
5. A methods section explaining how you designed and carried out your project: what your data consist of, why you chose the sources you did, how you compiled the sample, what approach you took to analysing it and why, what problems you encountered and how you solved them (or why they couldn't be fully solved). If your research raised ethical issues, they should also be discussed in this section.
6. A section setting out the findings of your analysis and discussing their meaning and significance. It is also common for this part of a report or dissertation to be split into two separate 'findings' and 'discussion' sections, but this is something writers should decide on the basis of what suits their project best. If what you are going to present is a close qualitative analysis of one or more textual examples, it can be hard to separate analysis and interpretation/explanation; the division makes more sense if you are presenting the results of quantitative analysis.
7. A conclusion summarizing what the research has shown and how it answers the questions you began with, and drawing attention to any problems, limitations or issues to be explored in future research.
8. A bibliography listing all the published (and if relevant, unpublished) sources you have cited or quoted in your work.
9. Appendices containing material which could not be included in the text itself, but which the reader might need to consult. For instance, you might need to include copies of the texts you analysed—or if your sample contains a large number of them, a couple of indicative examples—to show what they looked like in their full and original form. If you used corpus methods, you might want to include tables of word frequencies, keyword lists or screenshots of KWIC concordances. (Any tables and graphs you have made to display the key findings of your research should normally go in the text, but if you want the reader to have access to 'rawer' data, you can put it in an appendix.) Finally, if you used methods like interviewing, or data from private sources, which require consent from participants, you should include a clean copy of the form you asked them to sign.

It is possible to deviate from this structure. There are things that need to be included in any report on a research project, but the way you organize the text should reflect the logic of its content. You might decide that there is no logical reason to separate the introduction and the literature review; conversely, it might make sense to split your findings/discussion section into more than two parts. Tamar Holoshitz, for instance, presented her findings on each of the two conflict settings in a separate chapter of her dissertation, and then discussed the differences and their implications in a further chapter.

When writing up a small-scale research project there are certain general principles which you should bear in mind. We have already mentioned one of these, being modest: acknowledge any problems in the design of your study and be cautious about the claims you make for its findings (e.g. avoid generalizing beyond the evidence you have been able to look at and discuss any exceptions to the patterns you describe). Another principle is to illustrate your points with examples. Rather than just telling the reader what is in your data, *show* the reader by choosing one or more extracts which demonstrate the point clearly. A third principle (one which requires particular care because the penalties for not observing it can be severe) is to be scrupulous about using other people's work and words. References to previous research—published or unpublished, accessed in print or online—should be full, clear and set out according to accepted scholarly conventions. We will not discuss those conventions in detail here because they vary across academic disciplines: you will probably be given guidelines on which referencing system to use by your department, teacher or supervisor. Whatever system you use, though, you need to give references for any material you quote, cite or discuss which is not your own. Readers need to know that it comes from another source, and they need to be given enough information on the source (who wrote it, when, where it was published) to go and check it for themselves if they want to.

Writing up should not be seen as just a chore that you perform in haste when the important work is finished and the deadline is looming. The report or dissertation which presents your project is its public face, and it is worth taking time to ensure you present it to its best advantage. However interesting your question, your data and your findings may be, if you don't present your research in a way that enables others to understand and appreciate its contribution, it will not have the impact it should, nor earn you the credit you deserve.

SUMMARY

In this chapter we have tried to address some of the questions students have about the process of planning and carrying out a small-scale research project. We have referred to three actual student projects, which show that even with limited resources, it is possible to do something interesting and worthwhile. We will conclude, though, by repeating the point we made at the beginning, that the main value of student projects lies in what students learn by doing them. We hope this chapter will help you to make the most of the opportunity a project offers to experience the challenges and enjoy the rewards of working with written discourse.

FURTHER READING

There are many general texts on designing research projects in particular disciplines (e.g. linguistics, sociology) or areas of inquiry (e.g. education, health, media); here we can only mention a small number which have a particular focus on discourse analysis. For linguists, Barbara Johnstone's *Qualitative Methods in Sociolinguistics* (2000) includes some examples of discourse-oriented projects, as well as discussions of general issues such as research ethics. Another useful resource (especially for more advanced students), with chapters giving detailed practical advice on ethics, interviewing, ethnography, corpus methods and discourse analytic approaches, is *Research Methods in Linguistics* (Podesva and Sharma 2013). Barton and Lee's *Language Online* (2013) contains a chapter on researching online texts and practices.

NOTES

1   By 'small-scale' here we mean, essentially, a project that is done as part of a larger course of study—for instance, an end-of-class assignment or an undergraduate or Master's dissertation. The main type of student project this definition excludes is the doctoral thesis, a larger-scale, freestanding piece of research which is done over a much longer period. Doctoral students may find parts of this chapter helpful, but they should bear in mind that they will be subject to a different set of requirements.
2   Ksenija and Tamar undertook the research described here for their Master's dissertations: we have already mentioned their projects in earlier chapters (7 and 11). Beth's project was done as part of her undergraduate degree course. We thank them all for allowing us to make use of their work.

3   One of the student projects discussed here, Tamar Holoshitz's, was subsequently turned into an article and accepted for publication by a journal (Holoshitz and Cameron 2014).

4   Reproducing published material may require permission from the original publisher to avoid breaching copyright law. However, most uses of published material in student projects, which serve a purely educational purpose and have a very limited circulation, would be unlikely to raise this problem.

5   Beth also examined the written reports that appeared on the websites of two major news broadcasters, the BBC (a public service organization funded by a licence fee paid by all TV owners in the UK), and Sky News (a commercial provider owned by BSkyB, a company in which Rupert Murdoch's News Corporation has a significant financial stake). This enabled her to compare explicitly partisan news sources (newspapers) with broadcast sources which are required (in the UK) to maintain impartiality or 'balance'.

Glossary

Affordances   The possibilities and constraints associated with a particular **mode**, **medium** or technology of communication.

Big Data   Refers to datasets of extremely large size, often compiled by aggregating data from many sources, and requiring a lot of computing power to collect, store and analyse.

Bilingual/multilingual   These terms may describe either an *individual* who uses two or more languages (though not necessarily for all the same purposes, e.g. a bi/multilingual speaker may only read and write in one of the languages they speak), or a *society* in which two (or more) languages are habitually used (though individual members of the society concerned may only know one of them). The analogous terms *biliterate* and *multiliterate* describe individuals/communities who engage in reading and writing in two or more languages.

Code-switching   Alternating between two different linguistic systems or 'codes' (e.g. languages or dialects) in the same stretch of discourse.

Cohesion   A property of **text**; *cohesive* devices indicate how the parts of a text relate to one another.

Collocation   A statistical pattern of co-occurrence between words/expressions, often investigated using corpus methods. The analyst takes a word and investigates which other words or expressions it most frequently collocates with, that is, appears in close proximity to; this can tell us something about the way the word is used in practice (e.g. what it is used to talk/write about, and whether its connotations tend to be positive or negative).

Communicative competence   Language users' knowledge of what will count as linguistically and socially appropriate in a particular communicative context. (The reason you rarely find spellings like 'gr8' in PhD theses, or sequences like 'whereas it is argued by X that...' in text messages.)

Context   Information that contributes to the meaning/interpretation of a piece of text, but is not actually contained in it. Includes both *linguistic* context (the surrounding, and especially preceding, discourse) and *situational/social* context (relevant aspects of the world beyond the text, e.g. medium, setting, topic, relationships between producer and recipient, etc.).

Corpus (pl. *corpora*)   A sample of authentic language compiled to be used as data for the empirical study of the language(s) concerned. Today it usually means a sample which is large in size, stored in computer-readable form and encoded so that it can be searched and analysed using computer software.

Deictic (adj., noun *deixis*)   Describes items in discourse which 'point to' features of the context, so that interpreting their meaning in a given case depends on contextual information: they include words relating to spatial and temporal location (e.g. *here, there, then, now*) and pronouns referring to people or objects (e.g. *you, us, it*).

Diacritic   Mark attached to a written character, usually to signify that it represents a different sound from the same character without the diacritic, e.g. <u> and <ü> in German, <c> and <ç> in Turkish.

Digraphia   The written representation of one language system in two different graphic forms, i.e. **scripts**: e.g. Serbian is commonly written in both the Cyrillic and the Roman alphabets.

Ellipsis   The omission of linguistic material, sometimes conventionally marked with (...) in written discourse. Typically, constituents which are linguistically or contextually predictable are omitted to reduce a message's length or the effort required to compose it (e.g. 'coming to the lecture?' rather than 'are you coming to the lecture?').

Ethnography   An approach developed by anthropologists for studying unfamiliar cultures in which the central technique is participant observation (living among your subjects, observing and taking part in their everyday activities). In other fields of social science, the term is often used more loosely to describe methods that involve direct interaction between researcher and research subjects, e.g. interviewing people about their writing practices as well as analysing the output of those practices.

Eye-dialect   A way of writing that is meant to convey to the reader visually that the variety being represented is a non-standard dialect rather than the standard variety of the language.

Genre   A text-type that is socially recognized: members of the relevant linguistic community can identify examples of it, and (usually) have one or more category labels for it. Examples of written genres include letter, article, personal ad, graffito, email, text message.

Grapheme   The smallest meaningful unit of written language, typically a character of whatever **script** a language is written in. Graphemes may consist of more than one character, if the combination functions as a single unit. Examples in English include <ch>, <sh> and <th>.

Hedge   A linguistic device that weakens the force of a proposition and signals that the speaker or writer is not fully committed to it. Hedging devices in English include modal auxiliary verbs (e.g. it *might/may/could* be that...), verbs relating to the status of knowledge (e.g. *seem, appear*), adverbs and adjectives (e.g. *possibly*/it is *possible* that...). Devices that do the opposite, strengthening the force of a proposition and signalling a higher level of commitment to it, are called *boosters*.

Hypotactic (adj., noun *hypotaxis*)   A style of discourse that organizes information hierarchically, distinguishing higher-level (main) clauses from **subordinate clauses** which are grammatically dependent on a main clause (e.g. 'I don't eat burgers [main] because I'm a vegetarian' [dependent/subordinate]). This contrasts with a *paratactic* style (noun *parataxis*) where the organization is additive: a series of main clauses are simply juxtaposed (e.g. 'I don't eat burgers. I'm a vegetarian') or linked by coordinating (rather than subordinating) conjunctions like *and* (e.g. 'I'm a vegetarian and I don't eat burgers.') Hypotaxis is associated with formal and highly planned discourse, especially expository writing.

Intertextuality   The phenomenon of texts invoking or alluding to other texts, whether directly, by quoting them, more indirectly, by incorporating bits of their content or features of their form, or by being part of a series of related texts which readers are assumed to have followed.

Lingua franca   A language of wider communication used among people who do not share a first language. In contemporary conditions, English is the world's most widely-used lingua franca.

Literacy practices   Things people in a particular culture/community do with written language.

Medium (plural *media*)   A communication channel through which messages are transmitted/ disseminated, e.g. print, radio, the internet. *Mass media* are channels which disseminate the same message to a very large number of recipients (e.g. national newspapers); the term *social media* refers to digital platforms designed for social networking and/or content sharing (e.g. Facebook, Twitter, Flickr).

Modality   Refers to the use of devices which present some state of affairs as more or less real/unreal, credible/incredible, certain, probable, possible, unlikely, impossible, etc.

Mode   A **semiotic** (meaning-making) resource used in communication, e.g. spoken language, written language, film, music.

Multimodal(ity)   Using two or more modes/semiotic resources in a single communication.

Nominal/noun phrase   A phrase referring to an entity (person, object, concept) in which the key or 'head' word is a noun (a noun phrase may consist of a noun on its own, as in 'squirrels are grey', but it may also consist of a noun plus other material, e.g. 'the squirrels in your garden are grey', 'the squirrels you see in your garden are grey', 'grey squirrels are everywhere'.

Orality   Term used by some theorists to describe the cultural practices and ways of thinking found in non-literate societies/communities.

Orthography   The rules governing the use of a writing system for a particular language. Though often used to mean just spelling, orthography in principle includes other writing-specific features, such as the use of punctuation marks and capitalization (which can vary across languages).

Paralinguistic (adj., noun *paralanguage*)   Applied to features like laughter, whispering and shouting, which are not linguistic (i.e. part of the language system itself), but which contribute to the meanings communicated via speech.

Paratactic   See **hypotactic**

Parts of speech   Traditional term for 'word classes', categories of words which behave in a similar way grammatically, such as 'noun', 'pronoun', 'verb', 'adjective', 'adverb', 'preposition', 'determiner'.

Passive   'Active' and 'passive' are terms used to describe (a) verb forms and (b) sentences constructed with those verb forms. 'Shakespeare wrote *Hamlet*' is active: it contains the active verb 'wrote'. '*Hamlet* was written by Shakespeare' is passive: it contains the passive form of the verb, 'was written', made by using the appropriate form of the auxiliary verb *be* ('was') and the participle form of the main verb *write*, 'written'. In an active sentence the grammatical subject is usually the doer of the action denoted by the verb (e.g. Shakespeare is the person who wrote the play *Hamlet*). In a passive sentence, the target/recipient/outcome of the action becomes the grammatical subject (e.g. in '*Hamlet* was written by Shakespeare' the subject is the play rather than the writer).

Phoneme   A unit within the sound system of a language: the smallest unit of sound that can make a difference to meaning in that language. For instance, *rent* and *lent* are different words in English, therefore

/r/ and /l/ are phonemes in English. (In Japanese, substituting one for the other would not produce a different word, so in the Japanese sound system they are not separate phonemes.)

Postmodification   Postmodifiers are constituents of a **noun phrase** that come after the 'head' noun (whereas constituents that come before the noun are *premodifiers*). In 'the grey squirrels in your garden', the head noun is *squirrels*, the adjective *grey* is a premodifier and 'in your garden' is an example of postmodification.

Pragmatics   The study of meaning in context and, particularly, of how messages are interpreted in context by their recipients using real-world knowledge and inference as well as their knowledge of the linguistic code.

Prepositional phrase   A grammatical constituent which combines a preposition with a noun phrase (e.g. 'in your garden', 'on your bike', 'for a change'). Prepositional phrases can be used as **postmodifiers** within **noun phrases**.

Prosodic (adj., noun *prosody*)   In linguistics, prosody refers to the rhythms, stress patterns and pitch contours of spoken language. The term is also used in literary studies to talk about metre in poetry. Some corpus linguists use the label *semantic* or *discourse* prosody to describe the tendency of words to acquire positive or negative meanings through their regular **collocations**.

Register   A variety of language whose use is associated with, and whose characteristics reflect, contextual factors such as the setting, purpose, subject matter and genre (e.g. tabloid journalism, sports commentary, expository writing).

Relative clause   A kind of **subordinate clause** which is contained inside a noun phrase and **postmodifies** a noun, e.g. 'the squirrels [*(that) you see*] in your garden'.

Script   An inventory of written characters plus conventions for their use in texts (e.g. whether they are written/read from left to right or right to left, if/how they are joined up). Some scripts were designed for a single language (e.g. Hangul for Korean), but many are used to write a number of different languages, albeit with some variation in the precise character-set used for each (e.g. many European languages are written in Roman script; Arabic script is used to write Arabic, Persian and Urdu). A single language may be written in more than one script: written Japanese, for instance, makes use of three.

Semiology/semiotics   The study of sign-systems. Both terms derive from the work of early twentieth-century thinkers: *semiology* comes from the writings of the Swiss linguist Ferdinand de Saussure, while *semiotics* was the term used by the US philosopher C. S. Peirce. Today they are often not distinguished. Used as an adjective, *semiotic* means 'relating to signification/the making of meaning'.

Stance   The position taken by a speaker/writer on the matter under discussion and/or towards the addressee. *Affective* stance relates to the expression of the speaker/writer's feelings, while *epistemic* stance is the position taken by a speaker/writer in relation to knowledge-claims—how committed s/he is to the factuality or truth of a given proposition. **Hedges** and boosters are markers of epistemic stance, along with other devices indicating **modality**.

Standardization   The process of making and codifying (writing down) rules for the use of a language or linguistic variety. The main goal of standardization is to reduce variation in usage and promote uniformity—everyone using the same words and grammatical forms, the same spellings of words, etc. The rules are disseminated via reference works like dictionaries and grammar books, the teaching of the language in educational institutions, and the output of the mass media, especially the publishing industry, whose products are typically edited to make them conform to standard language norms.

Subordinate clause   A clause which is grammatically dependent on another clause in the same sentence (e.g. in 'I don't eat burgers because I'm a vegetarian', 'because I'm a vegetarian' is subordinate to/dependent on 'I don't eat burgers'. The reverse isn't true—'I don't eat burgers' is a complete sentence without the 'because' part). Subordinate clauses may be introduced by subordinating conjunctions like *because*, *whereas*, *although*, which show how they are connected to the main clause (e.g. *because* signals that the relationship is causal). See also **hypotactic**.

Superdiversity   A term used to describe the highly complex forms of ethnic, cultural and linguistic diversity that globalization has produced in many places today.

Synchronous   'Occurring at the same time'; the term is used to describe forms of digital communication like chat and IM (instant messaging) where participants have to be online simultaneously. Other kinds of online exchange (e.g. contributing to a thread of comments on a website) do not require participants to be co-present in real time, and are described as *asynchronous*.

Text   A piece of discourse, spoken or written, which is internally coherent and functions in context as a unit. A text can be a unit of any size, from one word (e.g. a traffic sign saying STOP) to many thousands of words (e.g. a book like this one).

Transcription   A written representation of speech.

Transliteration   A rewriting of a text written in one script using a different script.

Vernacular   Originally the term denoted a language used in everyday speech, as opposed to a learned, 'superordinate' language (like Latin in early modern Europe) used for specialized purposes, and mainly in writing. On this definition, 'vernacular literacy' means reading and writing in a language you speak. In current usage, however, *vernacular* is often used to mean the most casual and unregulated forms of language used in everyday life. 'Vernacular writing/literacy' can thus refer to informal writing, writing produced outside an institutional (e.g. academic, business, professional) context.

Writing system   A system for representing language graphically. The main types of writing system are distinguished by whether the basic units represented are words ('logographic writing'), syllables ('syllabic writing') or individual sounds ('alphabetic writing'). Within each category there are multiple **scripts**: the Arabic, English, Greek, Hebrew and Russian languages all have alphabetic writing systems, but each makes use of a different script (respectively, Arabic, Roman, Greek, Hebrew and Cyrillic).

Bibliography

Adams, J. N., Janse, Mark and Swain, Simon (eds) (2002) *Bilingualism in Ancient Society: Language Contact and the Written Text*. Oxford: Oxford University Press.

Ahearn, Laura (2001) *Invitations to Love: Literacy, Love Letters and Social Change in Nepal*. Ann Arbor, MI: University of Michigan Press.

Ahearn, Laura (2003) 'Writing desire in Nepali love letters', *Language and Communication* 23(2): 107–22.

Ahmad, Rizwan (2011) 'Urdu in Devanagari: Shifting orthographic practices and Muslim identity in Delhi', *Language in Society* 40(3): 259–84.

Allington, Daniel (2011) 'Material English', in Daniel Allington and Barbara Mayor (eds), *Communicating in English: Talk, Text, Technology*. Abingdon: Routledge. pp. 267–92.

Androutsopoulos, Jannis (2006) 'Introduction: Sociolinguistics and computer-mediated communication', *Journal of Sociolinguistics* 10(4): 419–38.

Androutsopoulos, Jannis (2008) 'Discourse-centred online ethnography', in Jannis Androutsopoulos and Michael Beißwenger (eds), *Data and Methods in Computer-Mediated Discourse Analysis*. Special Issue, *Language@Internet* 5. [www.languageatinternet.de]

Androutsopoulos, Jannis (2011) 'Language change and digital media: A review of conceptions and evidence', in Tore Kristiansen and Nikolas Coupland (eds), *Standard Languages and Language Standards in a Changing Europe*. Oslo: Novus. pp. 145–61.

Angermeyer, Philipp Sebastian (2005) 'Spelling bilingualism: Script choice in Russian American classified ads and signage', *Language in Society* 34(4): 493–531.

Argamon, Shlomo, Koppel, Moshe, Fine, Jonathan and Shimoni, Arat Rachel (2003) 'Gender, genre and writing style in formal written texts', *Text* 24: 321–46.

Auer, Peter (1999) *Code-switching in Conversation: Language, Interaction and Identity*. London: Routledge.

Back, M. D., Küfner, A. C. P. and Egloff, B. (2010) 'The emotional timeline of September 11, 2001', *Psychological Science* 21: 1417–19.

Backhaus, Peter (2007) *Linguistic Landscapes: A Comparative Study of Urban Multilingualism in Tokyo*. Clevedon, UK, Buffalo, NY, and Toronto: Multilingual Matters.

Baker, Paul (2003) 'No effeminates please: A corpus-based analysis of masculinity via personal adverts in *Gay News/Times* 1973–2000', in Bethan Benwell (ed.), *Masculinity and Men's Lifestyle Magazines*. Oxford: Blackwell. pp. 243–61.

Baker, Paul (2006) *Using Corpora in Discourse Analysis*. London: Continuum.

Baker, Paul (2008) *Sexed Texts: Language, Gender and Sexuality*. London: Equinox.

Baker, Paul, Gabrielatos, Costas and McEnery, Tony (2013) *Discourse and Media Attitudes: The Representation of Islam in the British Press*. Cambridge: Cambridge University Press.

Bamman, David, Eisenstein, Jacob and Schnoebelen, Tyler (2012) 'Gender in Twitter: Styles, stances and social networks'. Paper presented at NWAV 41, Bloomington, Indiana.

Baron, Dennis (2009) *A Better Pencil: Readers, Writers and the Digital Revolution*. Oxford: Oxford University Press.

Baron, Naomi (2000) *Alphabet to Email: How Written English Evolved and Where It's Heading*. London: Routledge.

Baron, Naomi (2008) *Always On: Language in an Online and Mobile World*. Oxford and New York: Oxford University Press.

Barthes, Roland (1977) *Image—Music—Text*. Trans. Stephen Heath. London: Fontana.

Barton, David (2007) *Literacy: An Introduction to the Ecology of Written Language* (2nd edn). Malden, MA: Blackwell.

Barton, David and Lee, Carmen (2013) *Language Online*. Abingdon: Routledge.

Barton, David and Papen, Uta (eds) (2010) *The Anthropology of Writing: Understanding Textually Mediated Worlds*. London: Continuum.

Beaugrande, Robert de (2004) 'Critical discourse analysis from the perspective of ecologism', *Critical Discourse Studies* 1: 113–41.

Bell, Allan (1991) *The Language of News Media*. Oxford: Blackwell.

Bennett, Sue, Maton, Karl and Kervin, Lisa (2008) 'The "digital natives" debate: A critical review of the evidence', *British Journal of Educational Technology* 39(5): 775–86.

Benwell, Bethan (ed.) (2003) *Masculinity and Men's Lifestyle Magazines*. Oxford: Blackwell.

Besnier, Niko (1995) *Literacy, Emotion and Authority: Reading and Writing on a Polynesian Atoll*. Cambridge: Cambridge University Press.

Biber, Douglas (1988) *Variation across Speech and Writing*. Cambridge: Cambridge University Press.

Biber, Douglas and Conrad, Susan (2001) 'Register variation: A corpus approach', in Deborah Schiffrin, Deborah Tannen and Heidi Hamilton (eds), *The Handbook of Discourse Analysis*. Malden, MA: Blackwell. pp. 175–96.

Blom, Jan-Petter and Gumperz, John (1972) 'Social meaning in linguistic structures: Code-switching in Norway', in John J. Gumperz and Dell Hymes (eds), *Directions in Sociolinguistics: The Ethnography of Communication*. New York: Holt, Rinehart, and Winston. pp. 407–34.

Blommaert, Jan (2010) *The Sociolinguistics of Globalization*. Cambridge: Cambridge University Press.

Blommaert, Jan and Rampton, Ben (2011) 'Language and superdiversity', *Diversities* 13(2): 1–21. UNESCO [www.unesco.org/shs/diversities/vol13/issue2/art1]

Bloor, Meriel and Bloor, Thomas (2007) *The Practice of Critical Discourse Analysis*. London: Hodder Arnold.

Bloor, Thomas and Bloor, Meriel (2013) *The Functional Analysis of English* (3rd edn). Abingdon: Routledge.

boyd, danah (2010) 'Privacy and publicity in the context of Big Data', *WWW*. Raleigh, NC, 29 April. [www.danah.org/papers/talks/2010/WWW2010.html]

boyd, danah and Crawford, Kate (2012) 'Critical questions for Big Data: Provocations for a cultural, technological and scholarly phenomenon', *Information, Communication & Society* 15(5): 662–79.

Brewer, John (1997) *The Pleasures of the Imagination: English Culture in the Eighteenth Century*. Chicago, IL: University of Chicago Press.

Cameron, Deborah (2001) *Working with Spoken Discourse*. London: Sage.

Cameron, Deborah (2006a) 'Verbal hygiene for women: Linguistics misapplied?', in *On Language and Sexual Politics*. Abingdon: Routledge. pp. 95–111.

Cameron, Deborah (2006b) 'Language, gender and advertising standards', in *On Language and Sexual Politics*. Abingdon: Routledge. pp. 27–42.

Cameron, Deborah (2007) 'Dreaming of Genie: Language, gender difference and identity on the web', in Sally Johnson and Astrid Ensslin (eds), *Language in the Media*. London: Continuum. pp. 234–49.

Cameron, Deborah and Kulick, Don (2003) *Language and Sexuality*. Cambridge: Cambridge University Press.

Cameron, Deborah and Kulick, Don (eds) (2006) *The Language and Sexuality Reader*. Abingdon: Routledge.

Canagarajah, Suresh (1999) *Resisting Imperialism in English Language Teaching*. Oxford: Oxford University Press.

Chandler, Daniel (1994) *Semiotics for Beginners* [WWW document] [www.aber.ac.uk/media/ Documents/S4B/]

Chari, Tendai (2010) 'Representation or misrepresentation? The *New York Times*'s framing of the 1994 Rwanda Genocide', *African Identities* 8(4): 333–49.

Chilton, Paul (1985) *Language and the Nuclear Arms Debate: Nukespeak Today*. London: Frances Pinter.

Clark, Kate (1998) 'The linguistics of blame: Representations of women in the *Sun*'s reporting of crimes of sexual violence', in Deborah Cameron (ed.), *The Feminist Critique of Language*. London: Routledge. pp. 183–97.

Cook, Guy (2006) *The Discourse of Advertising* (2nd edn). London: Routledge.

Cotter, Colleen (2003) 'Discourse analysis and the media', in Deborah Schiffrin, Deborah Tannen and Heidi Hamilton (eds), *The Handbook of Discourse Analysis*. Malden, MA: Blackwell. pp. 416–36.

Cotter, Colleen (2010) *News Talk: Investigating the Language of Journalism*. Cambridge: Cambridge University Press.

Coulmas, Florian (2003) *Writing Systems: An Introduction to their Linguistic Analysis*. Cambridge: Cambridge University Press.

Coulmas, Florian (2013) *Writing and Society: An Introduction*. Cambridge: Cambridge University Press.

Coupland, Justine (1996) 'Dating advertisements: Discourses of the commodified self', *Discourse & Society* 7(2): 187–207.

Crystal, David (2001) *Language and the Internet*. Cambridge: Cambridge University Press.

Crystal, David (2008) *Txtng: The Gr8 Deb8*. Oxford: Oxford University Press.

Crystal, David (2011) *Internet Linguistics: A Student Guide*. London and New York: Routledge.

Crystal, David (2012) *Spell It Out: The Singular Story of English Spelling*. London: Profile.

Danet, Brenda and Herring, Susan C. (2007) *The Multilingual Internet: Language, Culture, and Communication Online*. New York: Oxford University Press.

D'Arcy, Alexandra and Young, Taylor Marie (2012) 'Ethics and social media: Implications for sociolinguistics in the networked public', *Journal of Sociolinguistics* 16(4): 532–46.

Deumert, Ana and Masinyana, Sibabalwe Oscar (2008) 'The use of English and isiXhosa in text messages: Evidence from a bilingual South African sample', *English World Wide* 29(2): 117–47.

Dijk, Teun van (1991) *Racism and the Press*. London: Routledge.

Dijk, Teun van (2003) 'Critical discourse analysis', in Deborah Schiffrin, Deborah Tannen and Heidi Hamilton (eds), *The Handbook of Discourse Analysis*. Malden, MA: Blackwell. pp. 352–71.

Eckert, Penelope (2013) 'Ethics in linguistic research', in Robert Podesva and Devyani Sharma (eds), *Research Methods in Linguistics*. Cambridge: Cambridge University Press. pp. 7–20.

Eliot, Simon (2007) 'From few and expensive to many and cheap: The British book market 1800–1890', in Simon Eliot and Jonathan Rose (eds), *A Companion to the History of the Book*. Oxford: Blackwell. pp. 291–302.

Emigh, William and Herring, Susan C. (2005) 'Collaborative authoring on the Web: A genre analysis of online encyclopedias', in *Proceedings of the Thirty-Eighth Hawai'i International Conference on System Sciences (HICSS-38)*. Los Alamitos: IEEE Press.

Evans, Nicholas (2013) 'Multilingualism as the primal human condition: What we have to learn from small-scale speech communities'. Keynote lecture, Ninth International Symposium on Bilingualism, Singapore, 12 June 2013. [http://goo.gl/5EZeP]

Fairclough, Norman (1995) *Critical Discourse Analysis*. London: Longman.

Fairclough, Norman and Wodak, Ruth (1997) 'Critical discourse analysis', in Teun van Dijk (ed.), *Discourse as Social Interaction*. London: Sage. pp. 258–84.

Farvid, Pantea and Braun, Virginia (2006) '"Most of us guys are raring to go anytime, anyplace, anywhere": Male and female sexuality in *Cosmopolitan* and *Cleo*', *Sex Roles* 55(5–6): 295–310.

Ferrara, Kathleen, Brunner, Hans and Whittemore, Greg (1991) 'Interactive written discourse as an emergent register'. *Written Communication* (January) 8: 8–34.

Fishman, Joshua (2010) *European Vernacular Literacy: A Sociolinguistic and Historical Introduction.* Bristol: Multilingual Matters.

Foucault, Michel (1972) *The Archaeology of Knowledge and the Discourse on Language.* New York: Pantheon.

Fowler, Roger (1991) *Language in the News: Discourse and Ideology in the British Press.* London: Routledge.

Fowler, Roger (1996) *Linguistic Criticism.* New York: Oxford University Press.

Fowler, Roger, Hodge, Bob, Kress, Gunther and Trew, Tony (1979) *Language and Control.* London: Routledge.

Gillen, Julia and Hall, Nigel (2010) 'Edwardian postcards: Illuminating ordinary writing', in David Barton and Uta Papen (eds), *The Anthropology of Writing: Understanding Textually Mediated Worlds.* London: Continuum. pp. 169–79.

Glasgow Media Group (1980) *More Bad News.* London: Routledge.

Gray, Bethany and Biber, Douglas (2012) 'Current conceptions of stance', in Ken Hyland and Carmen Sancho Guinda (eds), *Stance and Voice in Written Academic Genres.* Basingstoke: Palgrave Macmillan. pp. 15–33.

Gries, Stefan and Newman, John (2013) 'Creating and using corpora', in Robert Podesva and Devyani Sharma (eds), *Research Methods in Linguistics.* Cambridge: Cambridge University Press. pp. 235–62.

Gross, Alan and Chesley, Paula (2012) 'Hedging, stance and voice in medical research articles', in Ken Hyland and Carmen Sancho Guinda (eds), *Stance and Voice in Written Academic Genres.* Basingstoke: Palgrave Macmillan. pp. 85–100.

Gumperz, John (1982) *Discourse Strategies.* Cambridge: Cambridge University Press.

Hall, Kira (1995) 'Lip service on the fantasy lines', in Kira Hall and Mary Bucholtz (eds), *Gender Articulated.* London: Routledge. pp. 183–216.

Halliday, M. A. K. (1971) 'Linguistic function and literary style: An enquiry into the language of William Golding's "The Inheritors"', in Seymour Chatman (ed.), *Literary Style: A Symposium.* New York: Oxford University Press. pp. 330–65.

Halliday, M. A. K. (1994) *Introduction to Functional Grammar* (2nd edn). London: Edward Arnold.

Halliday, M. A. K. and Matthiessen, Christian (2004) *An Introduction to Functional Grammar.* London: Hodder Education.

Hanley, J. Richard (2010) 'English is a difficult writing system for children to learn: Evidence from children learning to read in Wales', in Kathy Hall, Usha Goswami, Colin Harrison, Sue Ellis and Janet Soler (eds), *Interdisciplinary Perspectives on Learning to Read: Culture, Cognition and Pedagogy.* London and New York: Routledge. pp. 117–29.

Harris, Zellig (1952) 'Discourse analysis', *Language* 28: 1–30.

Harvey, Keith and Shalom, Celia (eds) (1997) *Language and Desire: Encoding Sex, Romance and Intimacy.* London: Routledge.

Heath, Shirley Brice (1983) *Ways with Words: Language, Life and Work in Communities.* Cambridge: Cambridge University Press.

Hellinga, Lotte (2007) 'The Gutenberg revolutions', in Simon Eliot and Jonathan Rose (eds), *A Companion to the History of the Book.* Oxford: Blackwell. pp. 207–19.

Herring, Susan C. (2001) 'Computer-mediated discourse', in Deborah Schiffrin, Deborah Tannen and Heidi Hamilton (eds), *The Handbook of Discourse Analysis.* Malden, MA: Blackwell. pp. 612–34.

Herring, Susan C. (2004) 'Computer-mediated discourse analysis: An approach to researching online behavior', in S. A. Barab, R. Kling and J. H. Gray (eds), *Designing for Virtual Communities in the Service of Learning.* New York: Cambridge University Press. pp. 338–76.

Herring, Susan C. (2007) 'A faceted classification scheme for computer-mediated discourse', *Language@ Internet.* [www.languageatinternet.org/articles/2007/761]

Herring, Susan C. and Paolillo, John (2006) 'Gender and genre variation in weblogs', *Journal of Sociolinguistics* 10(4): 439–59.

Hiatt, Mary (1977) *The Way Women Write.* New York: Teachers' Press.

Hoey, Michael (1997) 'The organization of narratives of desire: A study of first-person erotic fantasies', in Keith Harvey and Celia Shalom (eds), *Language and Desire: Encoding Sex, Romance and Intimacy*. London: Routledge. pp. 85–105.

Holoshitz, Tamar and Cameron, Deborah (forthcoming, 2014) 'The representation of sexual violence in conflict settings', *Gender and Language*.

Horobin, Simon (2013) *Does Spelling Matter?* Oxford: Oxford University Press.

Hunston, Susan (1994) 'Evaluation and organization in a sample of written academic discourse', in Malcolm Coulthard (ed.), *Advances in Written Text Analysis*. London: Routledge. pp. 191–218.

Hyland, Ken (2012) 'Undergraduate understandings: Stance and voice in final year reports', in Ken Hyland and Carmen Sancho Guinda (eds), *Stance and Voice in Written Academic Genres*. Basingstoke: Palgrave Macmillan. pp. 134–50.

Ibrahim, Zeinab (2006) 'Borrowing in Modern Standard Arabic', in Rudolf Muhr (ed.), *Innovation and Continuity in Language and Communication of Different Language Cultures 9*. Frankfurt: Peter Lang. pp. 235–60. [www.cmu.edu/dietrich/modlang/people/faculty/zeinab-ibrahim.html]

Jackson, Stevi (1996) 'Ignorance is bliss when you're just seventeen', *Trouble & Strife* 33: 50–60.

Jaffe, Alexandra (ed.) (2000) Non-standard orthography: special issue, *Journal of Sociolinguistics* 4(4).

Jaffe, Alexandra, Androutsopoulos, Jannis, Sebba, Mark and Johnson, Sally (eds) (2012) *Orthography as Social Action: Scripts, Spelling, Identity*. Berlin: de Gruyter.

Jaworski, Adam and Coupland, Nikolas (eds) (2006) *The Discourse Reader*. London: Routledge.

Jewitt, Carey (ed.) (2009) *The Routledge Handbook of Multimodal Analysis*. Abingdon: Routledge.

Johnstone, Barbara (2000) *Qualitative Methods in Sociolinguistics*. New York: Oxford University Press.

Jones, Rodney (2008) 'The role of text in televideo cybersex', *Text & Talk* 28(4): 453–73.

Kelly-Holmes, Helen (2010) 'Languages and global marketing', in Nikolas Coupland (ed.), *The Handbook of Language and Globalization*. Malden, MA: Blackwell. pp. 475–92.

Kohnen, Thomas and Mair, Christian (2012) 'Technologies of communication', in Terttu Nevalainen and Elizabeth Closs Traugott (eds), *The Oxford Handbook of the History of English*. Oxford: Oxford University Press. pp. 261–84.

Koller, Veronika and Mautner, Gerlinde (2004) 'Computer applications in critical discourse analysis', in Caroline Coffin, Ann Hewings and Kieran O'Halloran (eds), *Applying English Grammar: Functional and Corpus Approaches*. London: Hodder Arnold. pp. 216–28.

Kress, Gunther and van Leeuwen, Theo (1996) *Reading Images: The Grammar of Visual Design*. London: Routledge.

Lakoff, Robin (1975) *Language and Woman's Place*. New York: Harper & Row.

Landry, Rodrigue and Bourhis, Richard (1997) 'Linguistic landscape and ethnolinguistic vitality', *Journal of Language and Social Psychology* 16(1): 23–49.

Lazar, Michelle (2000) 'Gender, discourse and semiotics: The politics of parenthood representations', *Discourse & Society* 11: 373–400.

Lazar, Michelle (ed.) (2005) *Feminist Critical Discourse Analysis*. Basingstoke: Palgrave Macmillan.

Leap, William and Boellstorff, Tom (eds) (2004) *Speaking in Queer Tongues: Globalization and Gay Language*. Urbana, IL: University of Illinois Press.

Leeuwen, Theo van (1999) *Speech, Music, Sound*. London: Macmillan.

Leeuwen, Theo van (2004) 'Ten reasons why linguists should pay attention to visual communication', in Philip Le Vine and Ron Scollon (eds), *Discourse and Technology: Multimodal Discourse Analysis*. Washington, DC: Georgetown University Press. pp. 7–20.

Leeuwen, Theo van and Suleiman, Usama (2010) 'Globalizing the local: The case of an Egyptian superhero comic', in Nikolas Coupland (ed.), *The Handbook of Language and Globalization*. Malden, MA: Blackwell. pp. 232–54.

Lemke, Jay (1995) *Textual Politics: Discourse and Social Dynamics*. London: Taylor & Francis.

Lillis, Theresa (2013) *The Sociolinguistics of Writing*. Edinburgh: Edinburgh University Press.

Machin, David (2007) *An Introduction to Multimodal Analysis*. London: Bloomsbury Academic.

Machin, David and van Leeuwen, Theo (2005) 'Language style and lifestyle: The case of a global magazine', *Media, Culture and Society* 27(4): 577–600.

Machin, David and van Leeuwen, Theo (2010) 'Global media and the regime of lifestyle', in Nikolas Coupland (ed.), *The Handbook of Language and Globalization*. Malden, MA: Blackwell. pp. 625–43.

Mahootian, Shahrzad (2005) 'Linguistic change and social meaning: Codeswitching in the media', *International Journal of Bilingualism* 9(3–4): 361–76.

Mahootian, Shahrzad (2012) 'Repertoires and resources: Accounting for code-mixing in the media', in Mark Sebba, Shahrzad Mahootian and Carla Jonsson (eds), *Language Mixing and Code-Switching in Writing: Approaches to Mixed-language Written Discourse*. New York and London: Routledge. pp. 192–211.

Martin, Emily (1991) 'The egg and the sperm: How science has constructed a romance based on stereotypical male-female roles', *Signs* 16(3): 485–501.

McLuhan, Marshall (1962) *The Gutenberg Galaxy: The Making of Typographic Man*. Toronto: University of Toronto Press.

Meinhof, Ulrike H. and Richardson, Kay (1994) *Text, Discourse and Context: Representations of Poverty in Britain*. London: Longman.

Meyer, Charles (2002) *English Corpus Linguistics: An Introduction*. Cambridge: Cambridge University Press.

Mills, Sara (1997) *Discourse*. London: Routledge.

Milroy, James and Milroy, Lesley (2012) *Authority in Language: Investigating Standard English* (4th edn). Abingdon: Routledge.

Montes-Alcalá, Cecilia (2012) 'Code-switching in US Latino novels', in Mark Sebba, Shahrzad Mahootian and Carla Jonsson (eds), *Language Mixing and Code-Switching in Writing: Approaches to Mixed-language Written Discourse*. New York and London: Routledge. pp. 68–88.

Myers, Greg (1998) *Ad Land: Brands, Media, Audiences*. London: Arnold.

Myers-Scotton, Carol (2006) *Multiple Voices: An Introduction to Bilingualism*. Oxford: Blackwell.

Nishimura, Yukiko (2011) 'Japanese *Keitai* novels and ideologies of literacy', in Crispin Thurlow and Kristine Mroczek (eds), *Digital Discourse: Language in the New Media*. Oxford: Oxford University Press. pp. 86–109.

Nurmi, Arja and Pahta, Päivi (2012) 'Multilingual practices in women's English correspondence 1400–1800', in Mark Sebba, Shahrzad Mahootian and Carla Jonsson (eds), *Language Mixing and Code-Switching in Writing: Approaches to Mixed-language Written Discourse*. New York and London: Routledge. pp. 44–67.

Olson, David (1994) *The World on Paper: The Conceptual and Cognitive Implications of Writing and Reading*. Cambridge: Cambridge University Press.

Ong, Walter J. (1982) *Orality and Literacy: The Technologizing of the Word*. London: Methuen.

Piller, Ingrid (2013) 'Erasing diversity', *Language on the Move* (research blog) [http://goo.gl/jL0Ke] or [www.languageonthemove.com/language-globalization/erasing-diversity].

Podesva, Robert and Sharma, Devyani (eds) (2013) *Research Methods in Linguistics*. Cambridge: Cambridge University Press.

Poplack, Shana (1980) 'Sometimes I'll start a sentence in English Y TERMINO EN ESPAÑOL', *Linguistics* 18: 585–618.

Prensky, Marc (2001) 'Digital natives, digital immigrants', *On the Horizon*, MCB University Press 9(5). [http://bit.ly/1OVTicm].

Pury, Cynthia L. S. (2011) 'Automation can lead to confounds in text analysis: Back, Küfner, and Egloff (2010) and the not-so-angry Americans', *Psychological Science* 22: 835–6.

Rey, Jennifer M. (2001) 'Changing gender roles in popular culture: Dialogue in *Star Trek* episodes from 1966–1993', in Douglas Biber and Susan Conrad (eds), *Variation in English: Multi-dimensional Studies*. London: Longman. pp. 138–56.

Schendl, Herbert (2012) 'Literacy, multilingualism and code-switching in early English written texts', in Mark Sebba, Shahrzad Mahootian and Carla Jonsson (eds), *Language Mixing and Code-Switching in Writing: Approaches to Mixed-language Written Discourse*. New York and London: Routledge. pp. 27–43.

Schiffrin, Deborah, Tannen, Deborah and Hamilton, Heidi (eds) (2003) *The Handbook of Discourse Analysis*. Malden, MA: Blackwell.

Scribner, Sylvia and Cole, Michael (1981) *The Psychology of Literacy*. Cambridge, MA: Harvard University Press.

Sebba, Mark (2007) *Spelling and Society: The Culture and Politics of Orthography around the World*. Cambridge: Cambridge University Press.

Sebba, Mark (2012) 'Researching and theorising multilingual texts', in Mark Sebba, Shahrzad Mahootian and Carla Jonsson (eds), *Language Mixing and Code-Switching in Writing: Approaches to Mixed-language Written Discourse*. New York and London: Routledge. pp. 1–26.

Sebba, Mark, Mahootian, Shahrzad and Jonsson, Carla (eds) (2012) *Language Mixing and Code-Switching in Writing: Approaches to Mixed-language Written Discourse*. New York and London: Routledge.

Shalom, Celia (1997) 'That great supermarket of desire: Attributes of the desired other in personal advertisements', in Keith Harvey and Celia Shalom (eds), *Language and Desire: Encoding Sex, Romance and Intimacy*. London: Routledge. pp. 186–203.

Sperber, Dan and Wilson, Deirdre (1995) *Relevance: Communication and Cognition* (2nd edn). Oxford: Blackwell.

Spolsky, Bernard and Cooper, Robert L. (1991) *The Languages of Jerusalem*. Oxford: Clarendon Press.

Standage, Tom (1998) *The Victorian Internet: The Remarkable Story of the Telegraph and the Nineteenth Century's On-Line Pioneers*. London: Weidenfeld & Nicolson.

Street, Brian (1984) *Literacy in Theory and Practice*. Cambridge: Cambridge University Press.

Stubbs, Michael (1983) *Discourse Analysis: The Sociolinguistic Analysis of Natural Language*. Oxford: Blackwell.

Stubbs, Michael (2004) 'Human and inhuman geography: A comparative analysis of two long texts and a corpus', in Caroline Coffin, Ann Hewings and Kieran O'Halloran (eds), *Applying English Grammar: Functional and Corpus Approaches*. London: Hodder Arnold. pp. 247–74.

Swales, John (1990) *Genre Analysis: English in Academic and Research Settings*. Cambridge: Cambridge University Press.

Talbot, Mary (1997) '"An explosion deep inside her": Women's desire and popular romance fiction', in Keith Harvey and Celia Shalom (eds), *Language and Desire: Encoding Sex, Romance and Intimacy*. London: Routledge. pp. 106–22.

Tanaka, Keiko (1994) *Advertising Language: A Pragmatic Approach to Advertisements in Britain and Japan*. London: Routledge.

Thurlow, Crispin (2006) 'From statistical panic to moral panic: The metadiscursive construction and popular exaggeration of new media language in the print media', *Journal of Computer-Mediated Communication* 11(3). [http://jcmc.indiana.edu/vol11/issue3/thurlow.html].

Thurlow, Crispin and Mroczek, Kristine (eds) (2011) *Digital Discourse: Language in the New Media*. Oxford: Oxford University Press.

Toolan, Michael (1997) 'What is critical discourse analysis and why are people saying such terrible things about it?', *Language and Literature* 6: 83–103.

Turkle, Sherry (1995) *Life on the Screen: Identity in the Age of the Internet*. New York: Simon & Schuster.

Vaisman, Carmen (2011) 'Performing girlhood through typographic play in Hebrew blogs', in Crispin Thurlow and Kristine Mroczek (eds), *Digital Discourse: Language in the New Media*. Oxford: Oxford University Press. pp. 177–96.

Vertovec, Steven (2007) 'Super-diversity and its implications', *Ethnic and Racial Studies* 29(6): 1024–54.

Widdowson, Henry (1995) 'Discourse analysis: A critical view', *Language and Literature* 4: 157–72.

Williamson, Judith (2003) 'Retrosexism', *Eye Magazine* 48(summer): 44–5.

Yaghan, Mohammad Ali (2008) '"Arabizi": A contemporary style of Arabic slang', *Design Issues* 24(2): 39–52.

Index